Asking For It

ALSO BY KATE HARDING

The Book of Jezebel (*with Anna Holmes and Amanda Hess*)
Lessons from the Fat-o-Sphere: Quit Dieting and Declare a
    Truce with Your Body (*with Marianne Kirby*)

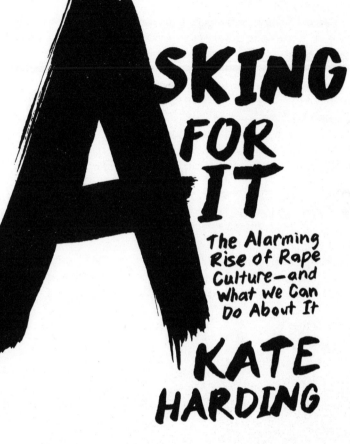

ASKING FOR IT

The Alarming
Rise of Rape
Culture—and
What We Can
Do About It

KATE HARDING

Da Capo

LIFE
LONG

A Member of the Perseus Books Group

Designed by Jack Lenzo
Set in 11-point Kennerly by the Perseus Books Group

Library of Congress Cataloging-in-Publication Data

Harding, Kate, 1975–
  Asking for it : the alarming rise of rape culture—and what we can do about it /
Kate Harding.
     pages cm
  Includes bibliographical references and index.
  ISBN 978-0-7382-1702-4 (paperback)—ISBN 978-0-7382-1703-1 (e-book)
1. Sexual harassment of women. 2. Rape. 3. Women—Crimes against. I. Title.

HV6556.H37 2015
364.15'32--dc23

2015012298

First Da Capo Press edition 2015
Published by Da Capo Press
A Member of the Perseus Books Group
www.dacapopress.com

Note: The names and identifying details of people associated with certain events described in this book have been changed. Any similarity to actual persons is coincidental.

Da Capo Press books are available at special discounts for bulk purchases in the U.S. by corporations, institutions, and other organizations. For more information, please contact the Special Markets Department at the Perseus Books Group, 2300 Chestnut Street, Suite 200, Philadelphia, PA, 19103, or call (800) 810-4145, ext. 5000, or e-mail special.markets@perseusbooks.com.

10 9 8 7 6 5 4 3 2 1

For every Jane Doe

From time immemorial the rule has been not to punish the male offender, but to get the victim out of his way.

—Susan B. Anthony, 1896

Contents

Introduction

The term "rape culture" has been in use at least since the late 1970s, but for obvious reasons, it's been slow to enter mainstream parlance. It sounds so extreme at first that I confess even I, a proud feminist, initially balked at the term. *Rape culture?* Isn't that overstating things just a smidge?

And isn't such overblown terminology the kind of thing that makes people call feminists "humorless" and "strident," and accuse us of holing up in our ivory towers, theorizing about human behavior without ever witnessing much of it?

I mean, granted, we live in a culture that claims to abhor rape yet adores jokes about the prisoner who "drops the soap," the trans woman who discloses to a date that she has a penis and gets punished for it, the altar boy who follows a priest into a back room. A culture in which laws and norms prohibiting sexual harassment in the workplace have been strenuously opposed by folks seeking to protect that fundamental civil liberty: objectifying and humiliating your subordinates.

And sure, yes, it's a culture that rewards men for bagging as much anonymous pussy as possible, while condemning women for expressing any sexual impulses at all. A culture in which a young woman's supposed friends will videotape her being violated and then use it as evidence that she's a "slut." A culture in which most victims of sexual assault and rape never report it because they fear they won't be believed—and know that even if they are believed, they're likely to be mortified and harassed, blamed and shamed, throughout a legal process that ultimately leads nowhere.

Also, we live in a culture in which a lot of people think we're too rough on "tortured geniuses" like Roman Polanski, who pled guilty to raping a thirteen-year-old girl, and Woody Allen, who at the very least took naked pictures of his long-term partner's teenage daughter when he was in his fifties, and whose own daughter has consistently maintained that he molested her. Both men have continued to have long, wildly remunerative and award-winning careers since those pesky facts came to light, all the while enjoying the support and company of our cultural elite. But one of them had to do it all outside the United States, and the other has frequently been the victim of jokes and criticism by people who have no power to interfere with his life, liberty, or pursuit of happiness. So haven't they suffered enough?

Fighter Mike Tyson was convicted of rape and served time for it, but jeez, that was all such a long time ago—did you see his cameo in *The Hangover*? Or maybe the episode of the sitcom *How I Met Your Mother*, in which he was portrayed as a kind, gentle soul with whom you'd gladly leave your baby? Or how about the episode of *Law & Order: Special Victims Unit*—a show about how difficult it is to catch and convict sex offenders—in which Tyson played a *victim* of sexual abuse? What an amusingly ironic bit of casting! Wink, wink.

Surely, like all criminals who pay their debt to society and must overcome the stigma of a felony conviction upon their release, Tyson has *earned* Hollywood's extensive efforts to rehabilitate his image, while paying him lots of money just to show up in front of cameras.

I could go on. I will go on, in fact, for the length of a book. But I trust you're getting the picture.

A Crime Unlike Any Other

In the preamble to their 1993 anthology *Transforming a Rape Culture*, feminist scholars Emilie Buchwald, Pamela R. Fletcher, and Martha Roth write, "In a rape culture, women perceive a continuum of threatened violence that ranges from sexual remarks to sexual touching to rape itself. A rape culture condones physical and emotional terrorism against women and presents it as the norm."[1]

Terrorism. Again, it's a bold, shocking choice of words, but not much of an exaggeration. We tend to imagine rapists, like terrorists, as an omnipresent and often unidentifiable threat, everywhere and nowhere at once. Since we don't know exactly who will strike or when, we agree that the best we can do is try to avoid victimhood. We put pressure on potential targets to volunteer for safety rituals that create the illusion of security while quietly eroding our freedom: airline passengers submit to groping by strangers for the sake of thwarting terrorism, and average women restrict their movements and clothing for the sake of thwarting strangers who aim to grope them. Like post-9/11 exhortations for passengers to fight back against skyjackers or die trying, our ostensibly empowering advice to women is to learn self-defense, to plan on disabling potential attackers at the first sign of any impropriety.

The part we'd prefer not to talk about, the part that's much less "empowering" than praising the twin pillars of feminine vigilance and martial arts, is that there will still be victims in this scenario. (Not all of them women, by the way.) Our culture is not equipped to prevent their being attacked, and adding insult to injury, our system is not equipped to bring all of their attackers to justice. Hell, our system isn't even entirely sure what that would mean at this point.

To an extent, this is merely a reflection of harsh reality. You can't prevent every crime or catch every criminal. A certain number of murders, muggings, and aggravated assaults will also occur each year, and not all of those offenders will be arrested, charged, or convicted. But the difference is that prosecutors won't say it's too risky to charge a mugger because the jury will hear that the victim carried her purse in plain sight, and thus vote for acquittal. People who stand around watching and filming a barroom brawl will not later say on the stand that they thought it was okay because only punches to the face count as "assault," not elbows to the kidneys or kicks to the shins. Jurors will not tell reporters, "Based on the evidence presented, we believe she killed him, but she says she didn't, so we're at an impasse."

Who Deserves Our Sympathy?

Rape culture manifests in myriad ways—I'll get to several of them in the rest of this book—but its most devilish trick is to make the average, non-criminal person identify with the person accused, instead of the person reporting a crime. Rape culture encourages us to scrutinize victims' stories for any evidence that they brought violence upon themselves—and always to imagine ourselves in the terrifying role of Good Man, Falsely Accused, before we "rush to judgment."

We're not meant to picture ourselves in the role of drunk teenager at her first college party, thinking, "Wow, he seems to think I'm pretty!" Or the woman who accepts a ride with a "nice guy," who's generously offered to see her safely home from the bar. Or the girl who's passed out in a room upstairs, while the party rages on below, so chaotic that her friends don't even notice she's gone.

When it comes to rape, if we're expected to put ourselves in anyone else's shoes at all, it's the accused rapist's. The questions that inevitably come along with "What was she wearing?" and "How much did she have to drink?" are, "What if there was no rape at all? What if she's lying? What happens to this poor slob she's accusing? What if he goes to prison for a crime he didn't commit?"

Don't get me wrong—I completely understand why many men feel a visceral terror at the thought of being falsely accused of sexual violence, given how theoretically difficult it would be to prove your innocence. But as it is right now, we behave as though we live in a society where innocent men are accused thousands of times a day, while real rapes are few and far between. We swiftly presume that nearly all people who report rape must have some secret, twisted motivation to lie, while ignoring the strong, straightforward motive an actual rapist would have. We look for ways to rationalize sexual violence as a big misunderstanding—she was flirty; he thought the sex was consensual—without questioning why we can easily believe there are people who deliberately murder, steal, and beat the crap out of strangers, yet not people who deliberately rape.

Or rather, we believe there's one very specific type of rapist—the kind who wields a weapon, attacks strangers with no warning, and leaves abundant evidence of violence on the victim's body—but not that some people deliberately rape their friends, girlfriends, wives, children, colleagues, or drunk new acquaintances. We can talk about how that sort of rape exists, and even about how it's the most common sort, but when pressed, we're almost never willing to acknowledge that those *rapists* exist. Not when the accused are people we know, or even just people who remind us of people we know. Not when they remind us of *us*.

Nor do many of us like acknowledging that genuine rape victims might just remind us more of ourselves than some other, more vulnerable, less savvy person. Even calls for increased awareness too often implore the listener to empathize with the feelings of an impotent bystander, not a victim. "Imagine it was your wife who was raped," we suggest. "Imagine it was your mother or daughter or sister."

Picturing a female loved one enduring a violent crime may be a good way to work up anger against a hypothetical criminal, but it doesn't create genuine identification with and compassion for victims. In many cases, it will just send somebody off on a hero fantasy about beating the rotten hypothetical bastard up, or shooting him dead, before they've even had time to wonder how their wife, mother, daughter, or sister is hypothetically feeling.

With this book, I'm asking you to do better than that. I'm asking you to imagine it's *you* who was raped. And I'm asking you to get angry about it.

Placing Blame Where It Belongs

Maybe you don't have to imagine. At some point in their lives, one in five women and one in seventy-one men in this country will find out what it's like to be raped.[2] Among the most vulnerable and marginalized populations—people of color, bisexual and transgender men and women, children, prisoners, sex workers—the numbers are even more nauseating. A whole lot of us already know.

In the pages that follow, I'll ask you to empathize with many different types of people, but above all, with women. (Specifically, Western women, because exploring rape cultures worldwide would turn this into a lifelong, multivolume project.) Women are no more important than any other potential victims, but we are the primary targets of the messages and myths that sustain rape culture. We're the ones asked to change our behavior, limit our movements, and take full responsibility for the prevention of sexual violence in society. Anyone can be raped, but men aren't conditioned to live in terror of it, nor are they constantly warned that their clothing, travel choices, alcohol consumption, and expressions of sexuality are likely to bring violations upon them.

Even if you are a Western woman, empathizing with others of that cohort might not be as easy as it sounds. After all, it was a female judge,

Teresa Carr Deni of the Philadelphia Municipal Court, who described the armed gang rape of a twenty-year-old sex worker as mere "theft of services," and told a reporter that such a case "minimizes true rape cases and demeans women who are really raped."[3] Another female judge, Jacqueline Hatch of Arizona, told the victim of a sexual assault that took place in a bar, "If you wouldn't have been there that night, none of this would have happened."[4]

Less publicly, women call each other "sluts" and "whores," doubt each other's stories, and help perpetuate the myth that if we always dress modestly, drink responsibly, and avoid dark alleys and dangerous-looking men, we'll be effectively rape-proofed. We are part of the problem.

But the problem—the larger context in which all of that occurs, aka rape culture—is what we'll be considering throughout this book. To blame women for it would be as wrongheaded and shortsighted as blaming men or the justice system or Hollywood or the news media or religious institutions or sports culture or celebrity worship or popular music.

Each of those is also *part* of the problem, but the Problem itself is the cumulative effect of so many people, working through so many organs and institutions, to deliver a constant stream of sexist bullshit that trivializes the crime of rape and automatically awards the benefit of the doubt to the accused.

> *If she hadn't been drinking, it would never have happened.*
> *If she's had sex before, how do we know she didn't want it this time?*
> *Why did she go out wearing that, if she didn't want to have sex?*
> *Why was she there at that time of night?*
> *"Date rape" is just sex that a woman regrets the next morning.*
> *An attractive guy like that doesn't need to rape anyone.*
> *Oh, no, it can't be him—he'd never do that.*

I elaborate on (and debunk) these pernicious beliefs throughout the first section of this book, "Slut Shaming, Victim Blaming, and Rape Myths." In the second section, "Law and Order," I consider why successful prosecutions of rapists are so rare, and in the third, "The Culture of Rape," I detail how those myths and stereotypes reproduce like a nasty virus. In each chapter, just when you're thinking this book is so relentlessly bleak that you'd rather read the obituaries for fun, I'll keep the promise of the book's subtitle and offer suggestions as to what we can actually do to make change happen. Sometimes the only honest answer is "not much"—but current research, the work of dedicated activists, and increased awareness of issues surrounding sexual violence are all cause for a guarded optimism, at the very least. Finally, I'll wrap up with some promising examples of new attitudes and legislation on the horizon, in hopes that you'll put this book down feeling energized to join in the struggle for change.

As a culture, we got ourselves into this mess, so it stands to reason we can get ourselves out of it. But the first step, as they say, is admitting we have a problem.

Author's Note

When I sold the proposal for this book in late 2012, I foolishly agreed to finish the manuscript in six months, because my agent, editor, and I agreed that rape culture was having a moment, as it were. News of the Steuben-ville, Ohio, gang rape case was picking up steam, and the memory of Missouri Representative Todd Akin's "legitimate rape" gaffe was fresh in all our minds. Sexual violence was suddenly a popular topic, but—based on national conversations about rape in the 1970s and 1990s that started strong and dissipated quickly—we feared that if we waited too long, this book might be released to a public that was already over it.

The bad news is that it took me way longer than six months to finish the manuscript. The good news—amazing, wonderful, really sort of mind-blowing news, actually—is that years later, Americans are still talking seriously about rape and rape culture. The topic outgrew that initial rash of trend pieces and took its place in the Zeitgeist of the twenty-first century. Sexual violence is in the news every day, and pressure is increasing on colleges to protect students, on police departments to take reports seriously and process all relevant evidence, on the media to stop blaming victims. It looks a lot like the culture is moving in the right direction, which, quite frankly, I never anticipated when I began writing *Asking for It*.

Thrilled as I am about this development, there are a few side effects worth noting here. Primary among them is the likelihood that, by the time you read this, countless new stories will be on our collective mind, and there will have been new developments in some of the ones covered here. Between the time I turned in the manuscript and the time I got the first round of edits back, Bill Cosby was accused of umpteen sexual assaults, and a long *Rolling Stone* story about a gang rape at University of Virginia was lauded as a devastating exposé of campus rape culture, then swiftly reframed as a devastating failure of fact checking. The news moves much faster than a book, and one of the most difficult challenges I faced in writing was simply *stopping*. Every day there is new information I could add.

Speaking of which, even with the depth and nuance a book allows, I have left many facets of rape culture uncovered or only lightly covered. I have no doubt I'll hear about oversights and omissions in reviews and on social media, and I look forward to learning more about aspects I haven't fully considered in these pages.

Asking for It is my best effort, however ephemeral, to contribute to this miraculously ongoing conversation about a subject that's historically gone unremarked. My hope is that all who read it will be moved to join that conversation, too.

Kate Harding
Chicago, Illinois
April 16, 2015

PART I

SLUT SHAMING, VICTIM BLAMING, AND RAPE MYTHS

CHAPTER 1

The Power of Myth

I n his 2011 article "Understanding the Predatory Nature of Sexual Vio-lence,"[1] psychologist David Lisak highlights the paradox of American society's professed intolerance for sexual violence and terribly low rates of convicting offenders: "Ultimately, only a tiny handful of rapists ever serve time for rape, a shocking outcome given that we view rape as close kin to murder in the taxonomy of violent crime."

Theoretically, that's how we view rape. In practice, we tend not to treat it as a serious crime unless there's simultaneously evidence of another one. If you're assaulted badly enough to leave physical evidence, or kid-napped, or murdered, you stand a far better chance of people believing your rape was an unspeakable crime. If the only thing that happens, how-ever, is someone decides to use your body without your consent, well—it's not like he *hurt* you. It was basically just bad sex, wasn't it?

Whatever we may say, it's clear that this is how most of us *really* view acquaintance rape—the most common kind of rape. Why else would we spend so much time assessing the victim's behavior, trying to determine to what degree she invited the crime? Why do we demand to know if the victim physically fought his attacker, if he has bruises and scrapes to prove it? Why are we so ready to believe that the rapist was just a well-meaning young man who got confused by "mixed signals"?

If we all abhor rape, how did people working on Belvedere Vodka's social media accounts in 2012 come to agree on the tagline "Unlike some people, Belvedere always goes down smoothly," superimposed over an image of a frightened-looking woman trying to escape a man's clutches?[2] If we've come so far from the 1950s social mores that demanded women "play hard to get," why do online T-shirt retailers sell tops emblazoned with "No means yes," "No means no—well, maybe if I'm drunk," and "No means eat me out first," among other things? Why was one of the biggest hit songs of 2013 Robin Thicke's "Blurred Lines," the chorus of which includes "I know you want it / But you're a good girl"? (And for the love of Dean Martin, can we please retire "Baby, It's Cold Outside" one of these days? Like "Blurred Lines," it's catchy as hell, but lines like, "Say, what's in this drink?" do not put me in the holiday spirit.)

Before we can talk about how much we, as a society, detest rape and believe in severe punishment for those who commit it, we need to agree on what "rape" actually entails. What, specifically, makes it a crime?

If the real crime of rape is the violation of another person's autonomy, the use of another person's body against their wishes, then it shouldn't matter what the victim was wearing, if she was drinking, how much sexual experience she's had before, or whether she fought hard enough to get bruises on her knuckles and skin under her fingernails. What matters is that the attacker deliberately ignored another person's basic human right to determine what she does with her own body. It's not about sex; it's about power.

This is the message feminists have been trying to get across for years.

But if the real crime of rape is sullying a pure woman with the filth and sin of sex—making her "damaged goods" in the eyes of other men—then of course it matters whether she was a virgin, and what kind of situations she willingly "put herself" in, and whether she deliberately risked further physical injury to demonstrate her refusal. What matters is that she displayed a clear pattern, in both her everyday behavior and her reaction to a man overpowering her, of not wanting sex. Not ever, from anyone. Because once your vagina is open for business, it's not like having a penis in there is anything new or shocking! If he didn't beat you or hold you at knifepoint, if he didn't kidnap you or steal anything, and if your hymen was already broken, what is "rape," really, but a few minutes of unpleasantness? Surely, you can't send a man to prison for that.

This is what we act like we believe, deep down.

Men Are from Earth; So Are Women

In the early 1990s, just as Americans' awareness of "date rape" started increasing, we collectively lost our effin' minds over two books that purported to explain why heterosexual relationships are so confusing. Georgetown University linguist Deborah Tannen's *You Just Don't Understand Me: Women and Men in Conversation* spent four years on the *New York Times* best-seller list, eight months at number one. Soon after that arrived, John Gray—a psychologist with a PhD from the nonaccredited (and since closed) Columbia Pacific University—also hit number one with *Men Are from Mars, Women Are from Venus*. Perhaps you've heard of it? It's the best-selling relationship book of all time. (Go ahead and take a minute to cry, if you need to.)

The idea that men and women's brains are "wired" to think so differently that we practically speak different languages (Tannen coined the term "genderlect") is understandably seductive to straight people who are in lousy relationships—or no relationships at all. It can be perversely comforting to tell yourself that even if you *did* make more of an effort, people of the "opposite sex" wouldn't really get you anyway, so you might as well keep sitting on your ass feeling sorry for yourself. (So I've heard.) And to be fair, misunderstanding and miscommunication certainly do cause snags in relationships of all kinds, because human beings cannot read each other's minds.

Unfortunately, Tannen and Gray's runaway success helped to lay the cultural groundwork for a simplistic and dangerous understanding of what causes acquaintance rape. As British social scientists Hannah Frith and Celia Kitzinger put it in 1997:

> Psychology's dominant explanation for this extensive and continued sexual violence against women is "miscommunication theory." This theory has been described [by psychologist Mary Crawford] as "The bandwagon of the '90s," and is widely used to explain date rape, stranger rape, sexual assault, and sexual harassment....
>
> As applied to sexual violence, miscommunication theory is used to argue that rape and other forms of sexual abuse are often the outcome of "miscommunication" between partners: he misinterprets her verbal and nonverbal communication, falsely believing that she wants sex; she fails to say "no" clearly and effectively.[3]

In other words, the guy made an honest mistake, and the woman failed to protect herself, as usual. It all fits so neatly with our cherished, practically religious beliefs about male-female interaction. Men, we tell ourselves, are bumbling, sex-obsessed fools who can barely speak their own native languages when they come within ten feet of a pretty lady. Women, meanwhile, are weak-willed, incapable of saying what they mean, and utterly unreasonable to expect respect from people with boners. So of course men get carried away, and women fail to successfully shut it down! It's just science.

The problem is, it's not true. As it turns out, men are from earth, women are also from earth, and earthlings communicate indirectly *all the time.*

Pop quiz: Do the following responses mean yes or no?

1. I'd love to, but I already have plans.
2. Sweet of you to offer, but I'm afraid I won't be able to make it.
3. Oh, geez, maybe another time?
4. I so wish I could!

Without knowing what your answers were, I can tell you with complete confidence that if you have the capacity to read this book, you just got 100 percent. A+. Good job!

Human beings do not have to say the word "no" to be understood clearly in any number of social situations—but when it comes to sex, rape culture tells us that *only* "no" can possibly mean no. Them's the rules.

So Frith and Kitzinger assembled some focus groups of men and women and did experiments that demonstrated this point. In fact, men have no trouble understanding indirect refusals. Along the way, they also found that young women "characterized explicit refusals of sex as having negative implications for them."

In other words, women rightly perceive that they'll come across as rude bitches if they refuse a man in no uncertain terms.

One wonders if these guys who believe women must issue a clear, unmistakable (and preferably documented) "NO!" to indicate their lack of interest in a given sexual act would truly like to live in a world where that happened regularly. A world where "Thanks, but I have a boyfriend" was swapped out for "Ew! Go away!" and "I think we should take things slowly" was replaced by the woman barking, "Stop! No touching below the waist! Perhaps we will have sex on a subsequent date, but as for tonight, *no, no, no, no, no!"*

One also wonders if even that would deter them. For their 2014 paper "'Blurred Lines?': Sexual Aggression and Barroom Culture," researchers led by Kathryn Graham of the University of Western Ontario observed 258 "aggressive incidents involving sexual advances" at Toronto bars and clubs. About one-third of incidents involving male aggressors and female targets (which were 90 percent of all incidents observed) were rated as "intentional aggression." That is to say, "the initiator engaged in sexual actions that he knew were unwanted." As for the rest:

> Aggression by the remaining two-thirds of initiators was rated as probably intentional—that is, initiators probably knew that their actions were unwanted and unwelcome by the target, but they may have misperceived the situation, despite the invasiveness of the act or refusals by the target. For example, one man seemed to be genuinely surprised when the female target did not find it humorous when he grabbed her blouse and peeked down it.[4]

Women! No sense of humor at all.

Listen, if these researchers were conservative enough to give *that* guy the benefit of the doubt, I think we can assume they aren't going too hard on the one-third whose aggression was judged "intentional." And when we take a look at some of the specific incidents described, it becomes clear that the problem here is not gender differences in communication style. Consider:

> A man and woman were facing each other dancing. The man moved very close and firmly grabbed the woman's behind with both hands. She immediately pushed both his hands away. The man looked at his male friend and they both laughed. About 10 seconds later, he grabbed her breasts.[5]

Or:

A man grabbed a woman's arm as she was walking by and said something to her. She shook her head no, but he continued to hold her arm and say things. She looked directly at the man and pulled her arm away. He finally let her go.[6]

Bars and clubs are loud places. When it's even hard to hear someone yelling, shaking your head and pushing someone's hands away are, in fact, very direct ways of expressing that you don't welcome the uninvited touch you've just been subjected to. The problem is not that some guys don't get it; it's that some guys don't want to hear it. And some guys do it precisely because they like watching women get flustered.

I went out dancing a lot in my early twenties—probably in some of the same establishments researchers went to for the data this study was based on—and I can't count the number of times I suddenly felt hands around my waist, or someone grinding against me, when I was just trying to enjoy the music and the company of whomever I was with. (So much for the stereotype that Canadians are polite.) Occasionally, I threw an elbow in response or screamed "Fuck off!" loudly enough to be heard over the music—or both. Mostly, though, I did what 55 percent of female respondents in the Graham study did: moved just out of reach and hoped the dude wouldn't keep trying. Sometimes, like another 27 percent, I walked away from the dance floor, whether I wanted to keep dancing or not.

These are things our society normalizes: Women feeling the best way to protect themselves is to walk away and let a predator keep doing his thing, because further confrontation isn't likely to produce any outcome besides more stress. Men thinking they're entitled to grope women who are moving their bodies, or wearing revealing clothing, or simply existing in a bar or club. Men knowing *they can get away with it*, because yes, the broader culture supports—or at least, does precious little to discourage—this behavior.

If you grabbed a strange woman's breast at the office, or her behind at the zoo, or her wrist as she walked past you in Starbucks, you would expect some sort of shocked vocalizations, the open disapproval of bystanders, and possibly a visit from security or police officers. But in a club, where people are drinking, wearing fewer clothes than they might otherwise, and moving their bodies in arguably suggestive ways, no one's going to call it sexual assault if you help yourself to a handful of boob.

They *should* call it that, because that's exactly what it is. But instead, we all just accept that this is the price of women wanting to drink and dance in public. Even if she's gay, even if she's only wearing a camisole and short shorts because clubs get to be 9 billion degrees over the course of an evening, even if she's had several beers because she's having fun hanging out with her bestie and is fully intending to sleep it off alone, we agree that those circumstances are too inherently sexualized to really fault a man who spontaneously puts his hands on her.

And if we agree that dancing is too sexual for bright lines to be drawn, imagine how we feel about sex.

I Know You Want It—but If You Don't, I'm Completely Confused

Going back to the 1990s, somewhere around the time the Mars/Venus thing hit, Ohio's ultraliberal Antioch College issued guidelines for student sex that involved seeking verbal permission from the other person at every step. As the writer Meghan Daum wryly described it in a 2007 *Los Angeles Times* article about the school's closing, "Dorm room make-out sessions were being punctuated by steamy questions like, 'May I kiss you now?', 'May I remove your (Che Guevara) T-shirt now?' and 'May I . . . ' (you get the idea)."[7]

Antioch was roundly ridiculed for the policy, and not totally without reason. Recent history suggests they were merely ahead of their time— "affirmative consent" policies have been voluntarily adopted by many colleges and even made law for universities in California—but it's understandable that people were skeptical at first. It was a well-meaning effort to foreground consent, but with its emphasis on verbal permission, it didn't quite track with how human beings actually behave. Generally, people can tell if their sexual partners are enthusiastic about what's happening without asking in so many words, and we all know it.

The rules we're taught are simple: Consent can be conveyed effectively by moans, gestures, movements, eye contact, and facial expressions. If things are going well, expecting people to verbalize that they want the sex to continue is absurd! Conveying a lack of consent, however, must involve desperate hollering, a good-faith attempt at martial arts, and preferably video documentation of same. Expecting people to understand more subtle messages that someone wants the sex to stop—such as "I'm not feel-ing it tonight" or "I really need to get to sleep" or "Please stop"—is asking too much. What, is the guy supposed to be a mind reader?

I suppose some people who worry that if they check in with a part-ner, the mood will die and everyone will go home sad instead of having mind-blowing sex, simply have little to no sexual experience. They might have no reference points other than movies and TV shows, where any minor interruption will make one partner think better of it and scramble to find their underwear. If that's the case, good news! Drama thrives on conflict, but in the real world, if you have any doubt that your partner is into it, you really *can* just stop and ask. If everything's good, you can imme-diately resume sexing, and trust me, a couple minutes later, you will have completely forgotten that it wasn't all perfectly choreographed and silent like fake sex.

But there's an equally plausible and far more troubling explanation for this insistence that a momentary pause is an unreasonable burden to put on a person having sex: to wit, that those objecting have a good rea-son to expect their partners, given a window, would verbalize their lack of consent. It's not that they don't want to risk killing the mood; it's that they benefit from the misconception that consent is a murky, complicated thing. If we, as a society, actually expected people to be 100 percent certain they had enthusiastic consent from all sexual partners, then we might not be so quick to accept "She wanted it" as a defense. And where would that leave folks who like to rape?

Either way, the misguided idea that confirming consent is an auto-matic boner killer needs to die. If it comes down to lack of experience, why are we letting virgins dictate the terms of a healthy sexual encounter? And if it's not that, why are we letting *rapists*? The rest of us need to be fighting back against this nonsense whenever we see it, because it's among the most pernicious rape myths there is. Not only does it drive the perception that rape happens by accident ("Oopsie!"), but it affects where we direct our money and efforts to prevent rape, increase reporting, and help survivors.

In their 2010 paper "Young Heterosexual Men's Use of the Mis-communication Model in Explaining Acquaintance Rape," psychologists Susan Hansen, Rachael O'Byrne, and Mark Rapley reaffirmed Frith and Kitzinger's findings that "young men ... can and do display a sophisticated understanding of subtle verbal and nonverbal means of communicating sexual refusal."[8] But despite a strong and growing body of evidence against it, "the miscommunication model has been adopted by many contemporary rape prevention programs."

A 2006 campaign by the British Home Office, for instance, used ads in men's magazines that said things like, "Have sex with someone who hasn't said yes to it, and the next place you enter could be prison." (The researchers note that this slogan was "superimposed on an image of a woman wearing white panties printed with a 'No Entry' sign." In case you weren't creeped out enough by the $25,000 *Pyramid*-esque filing of both "prison" and "women's bodies" under "Places You Can Enter.") Another showed bunk beds in a prison cell, with the caption "If you don't get a 'yes' before sex, who'll be your next sleeping partner?" That's right, folks—a rape awareness campaign brushed right up to the edge of a prison rape joke.

I will give one tiny jot of credit to the British Home Office for framing consent as the presence of yes rather than the absence of no. But so very much is wrong with those ads, from their reliance on the "miscommunication model" to the implication that rapists are likely to be arrested, tried, and convicted (most rapists know damn well they won't be), not to mention the suggestion that "you don't want to go to prison" is the best rationale for not raping. As opposed to, say, "you don't want to be a horrible fucking human being who rapes people."

When we try to reduce the frequency of rape, this is too often the kind of thing we spend money on: messages to men explaining what they already know, and messages to women that avoiding assault is a matter of constant vigilance, uninterrupted sobriety, and a degree of assertiveness that we know will instantly mark us as arrogant bitches.

"A crucial upshot of this rhetorical strategy," write Hansen, O'Byrne, and Rapley, "is that the onus for the clear communication of sexual refusal is placed squarely on young women's shoulders."

Who's the Real Victim?

Even in circumstances where some sort of documented, singularly vehement refusal isn't necessary to prove a crime—for instance, statutory rape—some people inevitably still want to argue about whether the victim invited the attack or somehow misled the rapist. One of the most appall-ing recent examples involved a Jane Doe from Cleveland, Texas, who was gang-raped repeatedly by over twenty men on numerous occasions in late 2010, when she was just eleven years old.

Unfortunately for this girl's reputation in both her hometown and the national press, she developed early, liked to wear makeup, isn't white (she is Latina, already subject to "hot and spicy" stereotypes), and didn't have a lot of parental supervision. All of which added up to reasonable doubt, according to a defense attorney for one of her rapists.

"Like the spider and the fly," said Steve Taylor, representing accused rapist Jared Len Cruse, to former Cleveland police sergeant Chad Lang-don on the stand. "Wasn't she saying, 'Come into my parlor,' said the spider to the fly?'"[9]

Actually, I think it was more like, "'Come into my parlor,' said the sixth grader to the group of older boys and men, who would take turns penetrating her vaginally and anally in an abandoned trailer, while some-one filmed it with his phone. More than once." Tomayto, tomahto.

According to the *Houston Chronicle*, after Langdon replied, "I wouldn't call her a spider. I'd say she was just an eleven-year-old girl," Tay-lor "snapped back": "I hope nothing like this ever happens to your two teenaged sons."[10]

Being on trial for rape, you see, is a random tragedy that could befall any young man, as it did Cruse and his cohort. Cruse was in his late teens at the time of the attack, his attorney reminded us, *just a kid*—unlike that eleven-year-old temptress!

This notion that the rapists' lives were tragically ruined by a child's feminine wiles wasn't merely a slimy defense move. An article by James C. McKinley in the *New York Times* described the mood in Cleveland after details of the rapes became known: "The case has rocked this East Texas community to its core and left many residents in the working-class neighbor-hood where the attack took place with unanswered questions. Among them is, if the allegations are proved, how could their young men have been drawn into such an act?"[11] "Drawn into" it. These young men took advantage of a girl on the cusp of puberty, abused her trust, brutalized her body, and we're all supposed to wonder how they were somehow suckered into doing it? A local person McKinley interviewed lamented the effect the crimes had had on the town, but her chief concern wasn't for the victim's welfare. "These boys," she said, "have to live with this the rest of their lives."[12]

It was the same with the famed gang-rape case that rocked Steubenville, Ohio, in 2012. Despite photographic and video evidence of a sixteen-year-old girl being assaulted multiple times over several hours, few witnesses would come forward—although many took to social media to shame the drunk, passed-out girl for being a "slut." ("If you could charge people for not being decent human beings, a lot of people could have been charged that night," Steubenville police chief William McCafferty told the *New York Times*.[13]) The victim was harassed, and her family received death threats. Although some locals joined in the call for a thorough investigation and prosecution, others just wished it would all go away. One, a volunteer coach at the high school, told the *Times* he believed the girl had made it all up, and "now people are trying to blow up our football program because of it."[14]

Aw, jeez, how difficult the whole ordeal must have been for high school football fans—all because some little slut made up photos and videos of herself being dragged around like a blow-up doll.

Similarly, in May 2014, *Time* published a section on campus rape, including an op-ed by criminal defense attorney Matthew Kaiser, who wrote: "When my son goes to college, I want him not to risk his future whenever he has sex after a party. And, based on the cases I've seen, I'm more concerned for my son than my daughter."[15]

Kaiser is more concerned that his son will be accused of rape—a problem he can almost certainly avoid by only having sex with conscious, enthusiastic partners—than about the one in five chance that his daughter will be raped. He is more concerned that his son will have sex with a partner who suddenly wakes up and decides, "Hey, after breakfast, I'm going to charge that guy with rape!" than he is about the one in five chance that his daughter will be raped. Father of the year, right there.

Speaking of charming defense attorneys, despite Steve "Spider to the Fly" Taylor's best efforts, a jury gave Jared Len Cruse a life sentence. Still, the fact that Taylor felt the best strategy for keeping his client out of jail was to paint an eleven-year-old child as the aggressor should give us pause. To say the least.

Seven Basic Rape Myths

If we can't even agree that an *eleven-year-old* gang-rape victim wasn't on some level asking to be abused, what hope is there for other victims? What of the grown woman who's had plenty of consensual sex prior to her rape? The gay man who went out to a club expecting both to hook up and to maintain control over his own body? The sex worker who has the audacity to believe she's a human being with rights?

No matter how much we as a culture claim to despise rape and rapists, we just can't seem to shake the feeling that certain types of people, who engage in certain types of behavior, deserve on some level to be assaulted. For that, we have rape myths to thank.

Like "rape culture," the concept of an identifiable set of "rape myths" first arose among feminists in the seventies, and has been refined and studied by social scientists ever since. In a 2012 paper published in *Aggression and Violent Behavior*, researchers Amy Grubb and Emily Turner explain, "Rape myths vary among societies and cultures. However, they consistently follow a pattern whereby, they *blame the victim for their rape, express a disbelief in claims of rape, exonerate the perpetrator*, and *allude that only certain types of women are raped*"[16] (emphasis in original).

Grubb and Turner then note that in 1999, University of Illinois psychologists Diana L. Payne, Kimberly A. Lonsway, and Louise F. Fitzgerald expanded upon those four characteristic functions, identifying seven categories under which (American) rape myths fall:

1. She asked for it.
2. It wasn't really rape.
3. He didn't mean to.
4. She wanted it.
5. She lied.
6. Rape is a trivial event.
7. Rape is a deviant event.[17]

It's almost funny—almost—that some of the most popular myths complicate and contradict each other. Look at coverage of any rape case that doesn't fit the "stranger jumps out of the bushes" stereotype, and you'll see people arguing strenuously that it never happened *and* that she asked for it *and* that he didn't mean it. (If you want to see the full panoply of rape myths in action, look at the online comments beneath the article.)

That's because rape myths, like all myths, are designed to serve up psychological comfort, not hard facts. As Grubb and Turner put it, "To believe that rape victims are innocent and not deserving of their fate is incongruous with the general belief in a just world; therefore, in order to avoid cognitive dissonance, rape myths serve to protect an individual's belief in a just world."[18]

In other words, that list of seven myths is like a flow chart that begins with "Someone has reported a rape," and proceeds as follows:

1. Did she ask for it? If no, go to 2. If yes, go to 8.
2. Was it really rape? If yes, go to 3. If no, go to 8.
3. Did he mean to do it? If yes, go to 4. If no, go to 8.
4. Did she want to have sex with him? If no, go to 5. If yes, go to 8.
5. Is she lying about whether she consented? If no, go to 6. If yes, go to 8.
6. Was it really such a big effing trauma? If yes, go to 7. If no, go to 8.
7. The kind of rape you're describing is very, *very* rare. Like, so rare that it's practically nonexistent. Go back over steps 1 through 6, until you find your error and end up at 8.
8. Everything's fine! No need to be upset!

If you're the person who was raped, you might find you're still upset after all that. But the rest of us can breathe easy, knowing that it never happened, you wanted it, he didn't mean it, and it was no big deal anyway.

Miscommunication Mythbusting

If rape myths are the engine of rape culture, how do we begin to break them down? Well, the same way we deal with any other pernicious and damaging myths: by repeating the facts of the matter as widely and as often as possible. Let's take those myths one by one.

MYTH: She asked for it.

FACT: It is literally impossible to ask for rape. Rape, by definition, is sex you did not ask for. So either you mean that a woman who dresses a certain way, or flirts, or otherwise expresses her sexuality on her own terms somehow *deserves* to be raped—which would make you a monster—or you are wrong, and she was not asking for it.

MYTH: It wasn't *really* rape.

FACT: There aren't different categories like *rape*-rape, sort-of rape, gray rape, real rape, and not-really rape. If a person was forced to have sex against their will, it was rape. So either you're calling the putative victim a liar, or you're wrong, and it was really rape.

MYTH: He didn't mean to.

FACT: Rapists like to rape. Most of them do it more than once. In "Understanding the Predatory Nature of Sexual Violence," David Lisak cites a study in which 120 college men admitted to a total of 483 acts that met the legal definition of rape. Forty-four of those were one-off crimes. The other 439 rapes were committed by 76 serial rapists, who "had also committed more than 1,000 other crimes of violence, from non-penetrating acts of sexual assault, to physical and sexual abuse of children, to battery of domestic partners."[19] Rape is not an accident.

MYTH: She wanted it.

FACT: See "She asked for it" and "It wasn't really rape." Either the person was raped, *or* the person wanted it; both cannot be true at the same time. And if you want to call someone a liar, you should have the decency to be forthright about it.

MYTH: She lied.

FACT: This is the only rape myth that has the ring of partial truth—somewhere between 2 and 8 percent of the truth. That's how many reports of rape are estimated to be false, based on an analysis of several rigorous studies that attempted to answer that question.[20]

According to the cultural myth, though, women lie about rape *all the time*, for practically no reason at all—to get revenge on men who cheat, or punish men who didn't call afterwards, or minimize their own shame over saying yes. I discuss this at length in Chapter 4, but for now, here's what you need to know: the vast majority of people do not lie about being victims of violent crime, especially since filing a false report is a crime itself. Come on, now.

MYTH: Rape is a trivial event.
FACT: This goes back to our retrograde views about sexual purity and how they get tangled up with consent. *Maybe rape is really traumatic for a young virgin, but for someone who's had lots of sex before, what's one more dick in the hole?* But again, the problem is not the sexual aspect of rape, but the willful rejection of another person's right to decide who may touch, let alone enter, their body. Being penetrated without your consent is a big effing deal.

MYTH: Rape is a deviant event.
FACT: This is the myth that props up most of the other six. *Rape hardly ever happens, and it's only committed by mentally ill monsters, not people who resemble—or are—my friends, coworkers, and family members.* As long as you believe this, it makes sense that she must be lying, or he must not have meant it, or it must not have been *real* rape (see myth #2). As long as this is true, everything is fine, and there's no need to be upset.

Unfortunately, it's not true. The fact is at least one in five women and one in seventy-one men will be raped in their lifetimes. The fact is most rapists are known to their victims. The fact is rapists rape deliberately and repeatedly, not because they like sex, but because they like rape.

The fact is the world is not just, and every day, people with friends and loved ones and jobs and kids and fine reputations commit violence against people who don't deserve it.

The fact is no one deserves it.

CHAPTER 2

Simple Safety Tips for Ladies

One summer night, while I was working on this book, my friend Molly, also an author, walked her greyhound over to my house for a writing date. Earlier that day, my husband had driven to Indianapolis on business, so Molly and I sat in my living room with our dogs and our laptops, drinking tea and clacking away for hours. It was lovely.

Around eleven p.m., Molly asked me for a lift home, per our usual routine when she visits my apartment, about a mile away from hers. But when I went to grab the car keys, they were missing. I checked all of my pockets and a couple of purses, to no avail.

Let's cut straight to the Encyclopedia Brown reveal: Did you remember that my husband *drove* out of town? Because I sure hadn't! And we only have one car.

So there Molly was, late at night, a fifteen-minute walk from home and saddled with a gangly, sixty-five-pound dog who isn't allowed to ride city buses (and who, it should be noted, would be utterly useless in the event of an attack). The mood in the room suddenly shifted from pleasant and companionable to "Oh, shit."

I mean, we weren't going to panic. Panicking would be stupid. Weak. An overreaction. You can't live in fear! You must refuse to be a victim!

Molly was new to the neighborhood, but I'd lived there for eight years without incident. It was home, and I almost always felt comfortable walking around there. Still, during the month that this happened, twenty-six violent crimes were reported to police in the two-square mile area where she and I and about fifty-five thousand other people lived. Two of those were criminal sexual assaults; one, a bona fide stranger-drags-a-woman-into-an-alley scenario. So if either one of us had remembered that my car was in another state before it got dark, there's no question she would have left earlier. Who would *plan* to walk a mile through our neighborhood at eleven p.m.?

I mean, besides men.

"Helpful" Tips

"Hi girls!" begins an email that made the rounds when forwarded safety tips from everybody's credulous aunties were all the rage. More recently, the same information has spread on social media, with a link to a page claiming that what you're about to read is the result of interviews with "a group of rapists and date rapists in prison." Either way, the anonymous writer tells us she's going to share some helpful rape avoidance tips.

From this document, we learn that women should avoid wearing their hair long, especially in grabbable ponytails ("The #1 thing men look for in a potential victim is hairstyle"). Clothing "that is easy to remove quickly" with scissors is also best avoided, so skip the overalls, gals! (Priceless advice if you were planning time travel to the early nineties.) Also, no talking on your cell or rooting around in your purse in public—a distracted lady is just asking for some lurking criminal to crack her over the head and drag her off somewhere. You must be alert at all times!

Oh, and FYI:

- The time of day men are most likely to attack and rape a woman is in the early morning, between five and eight thirty a.m.
- The number one place women are abducted from or attacked at is grocery store parking lots.
- Number two is office parking lots and garages.
- Number three is public restrooms.

If you're thinking, "Gosh, I never knew any of that before!" don't feel bad: I've been reading about rape for twenty years, and I had never heard those things before the first time someone passed along the email. Probably because none of them are true.

Barbara Mikkelson, of the invaluable urban legend–debunking website Snopes.com, researched every claim in that chain email and pronounced the whole thing "codswallop."[1] Noting that the message originated in 2000 with a St. Louis woman, who said it was her takeaway from a recent self-defense class, Mikkelson painstakingly punctures each assertion: No, long hair isn't a risk factor for rape. No, rapists do not typically carry scissors. Most rapes occur between evening and dawn, actually. Parking lots and garages are only more likely to be the site of rapes or abductions if they're empty and poorly lit; you can still go grocery shopping without fear of being attacked. Et cetera, et cetera.

"So, to sum up," she writes, "is avoiding rape a matter of wearing your hair short and eschewing overalls? Hardly. And anyone who attempts to characterize it as such ought to be whomped over someone's knee."

My sentiments exactly.

Back in my living room at eleven p.m., I was furious at myself for having a mental lapse that put my friend in a shitty situation.

"I'll call you a cab, tell them to send someone who doesn't mind dogs, and I'll pay," I offered—but even as I said it, I was thinking of other possible scenarios: Molly could leave her dog overnight with me and grab any old cab home. She and the dog could both spend the night. She could go home in a cab, get her own car, and come back to pick up the dog. Or maybe one of my neighbors was still up and would let me borrow their car…

Running through this index of alternatives seemed completely normal to both of us. This is the stuff women are thinking about all the time, even as we brazenly strut through grocery store parking lots at eight in the morning, wearing overalls, with our hair in ponytails. *How can I go about my life without risking my safety?*

Marching into Battle

In a January 2013 op-ed for the *Dallas Morning News*, Robert Jensen, a University of Texas journalism professor and anti-violence activist, writes of talking with two freshman sorority pledges about the specter of sexual assault in the campus Greek system. The young women impatiently explain to him that they have a strategy to ensure it won't be an issue for them: "We always go to those parties as a group, and we never leave anyone behind."

Jensen points out to them that "leave no one behind" is the language of soldiers going into battle, not teenagers going to a party.

"I do not enjoy saying that, they do not enjoy hearing it, and we are all quiet for a moment," he writes. "It is important, but not always easy, to recognize what is 'normal' in our culture."[2]

Ultimately, Molly insisted that she would be fine walking home—taking the most populated, best-lit route—and she was. That wasn't a surprise to either of us. We both knew the whole time that she had a very good chance of making it home alive and unmolested. The problem wasn't that we thought an assault was *likely*, but that as women, we've been taught never to rule out the possibility. We've been taught that it's never safe to *assume* we'll be perfectly fine, walking around our own neighborhoods after dark, like normal people.

This is why I have no patience for anyone who insists that women must learn self-defense moves and memorize lists of specious advice to prevent our own victimization. We're already calculating risks and taking reasonable precautions every day. We don't often talk about that in public, though, lest we be accused of letting fear control our lives, of being completely irrational about the relatively minor statistical risk of being attacked by a stranger.

It's a maddening catch-22. If we get assaulted while walking alone in the dark, we're told we should have used our heads and anticipated the danger. But if we're honest about the amount of mental real estate we devote to anticipating danger, then we're told we're acting like crazy man-haters, jumping at shadows and tarring an entire gender with the brush that rightly belongs to a relatively small number of criminals.

No one will ever specify exactly how much worry is the right amount, the amount that will allow women to enjoy all of the freedoms typically afforded to North American adults in the twenty-first century, while reassuring judgmental strangers that we aren't stupid and weren't asking to be raped.

"Better Safe Than Sorry!"

Think back to that list of "don't get raped" tips—and *really* think this time. Grocery store parking lots are the number one place women get attacked? Are you kidding me? How did that ever sound logical to so many concerned relatives? It's patently ridiculous.

But when you ask someone who's just shared that list on Facebook, or suggested a self-defense class to a woman concerned about rapes in her neighborhood, they're likely to respond with something like "Better safe than sorry!" Translation: "Even if what I'm telling you to remember is a pile of stinking horseshit, you should still engage in this ritualized expression of anxiety with me, because it makes me feel slightly better about things I can't control. What's so wrong with that?"

Well, nothing, if you're just recommending simple, reasonable measures like locking doors, looking both ways before crossing the street, and carrying cash in purses or pockets, as opposed to walking around, waving it in the air, screaming, "I'm rich! I'm rich!" But there is something very wrong when you're telling women (and only women) to keep their hair short, only dress in ways that no one could consider "provocative," only dress in clothing that is difficult to cut off with scissors (so, Kevlar jeans, I guess?), and never use their phones or search through their purses in public.

There's something wrong with expecting women to remember that they should always go for the groin, or the eyes, or the armpit, or the upper thigh, or the first two fingers (I am not making any of these up), and that it only takes five pounds of pressure to rip off a human ear, and if you hit someone's nose with the palm of your hand and push up just right, you can drive the bone into their brain and kill them.

There's something wrong with acting as though it's perfectly reasonable to tell women never to drink to excess—and, when drinking to nonexcess, never to let their drinks out of their sight—and not to walk alone at night and definitely not to travel alone, and not to jog with earphones, and not to approach a stoplight without locking the car doors, and not to respond to the sound of a crying baby, and not to get into their cars without checking both the backseat and underneath the car first, and not to get in on the driver's side if there's a van parked next to it, and not to pull over for unmarked police cars until they're in well-lit areas, and, and, and.

I just did that off the top of my head, by the way. A bunch of those recommendations are manifestly useless, but they are *all in my brain*, a full catalog of two and a half decades' worth of "helpful tips." Even the ones that are based in some sort of recognizable reality still ultimately send the same message: As a woman, you must live in fear and behave impeccably. If you fail at either charge, you will most likely be raped—maybe even murdered—and it will be at least partly your fault.

"Please forward this to any woman you know," says the end of that email. "It's simple stuff that could save her life."

Actually, there's nothing simple about it.

Kangaroo Signals

In *The Gift of Fear*, his popular 1997 book on violent crime, security expert Gavin de Becker tells of an exercise he once did during a presentation at the Central Intelligence Agency. He informed his audience that a small but significant number of people per year are killed by angry kangaroos and then listed the three unmistakable signals a kangaroo will give before it attacks: a wide "smile," compulsive pouch-checking, and a glance over its shoulder.

Only after audience members demonstrated that they'd memorized all three signals did he reveal that he'd made them all up—and in fact, he knows zilch about kangaroo behavior. Nevertheless, he predicted, everyone who witnessed that presentation would remember the fake indicators of an imminent kangaroo attack forever.

"In our lives," writes de Becker, "we are constantly bombarded with kangaroo signals masquerading as knowledge." The whole point of *The Gift of Fear* is that inaccurate information—along with denial about who's most likely to be the perpetrator or victim of a crime—can interfere with our natural ability to intuit and react usefully to danger. Those handy "don't get raped tips" that keep turning up on the internet like bad bitcoin are just more kangaroo turds for the pile that Western women are expected to carry around in our heads all the time.

By the time we finish high school, our brains are already filled with such rape-proofing basics as the appropriate skirt length for discouraging violent attacks (long); the number of alcohol units that can be consumed before one is thought to have invited sexual assault (one, tops); a list of acceptable neighborhoods to visit alone in daylight; another of acceptable neighborhoods to visit alone after dark (just kidding—there are none); and a set of rudimentary self-defense moves ("Solar plexus! Solar plexus!").

This ubiquitous idea that by controlling our behavior, appearance, and whereabouts we can keep ourselves from being raped does nothing to help women (let alone potential victims who aren't women). It merely takes the onus off the rest of society to seriously consider what we can *all* do to prevent sexual violence. It keeps our focus on what the victims did "wrong" instead of on what type of person rapes, or how he chooses his victims, or how we can prosecute sexual assaults more effectively. It trades on reductive, sexist ideas about how "good" and "bad" women behave and strongly suggests that some victims, frankly, had it coming.

Playing by the Rules: A Case Study

Following a series of sexual assaults in late 2012, Minneapolis police issued a crime alert, encouraging residents to exercise extra caution. In the *Star Tribune*, Paul Walsh and Nicole Norfleet described its contents:

> The crime alert issued to residents in the latest attack included strong advice from police on what women need to do to protect themselves. That includes pay attention to strangers, avoid travel-ing alone (especially after dark), stay away from isolated areas, and switch directions and seek a safe place if you think someone is fol-lowing you.[3]

All sensible advice, to be sure! Now, let's compare it to what Walsh and Norfleet tell us in the same article about the behavior of the third vic-tim, a thirty-three-year-old woman who was sexually assaulted on her way home from a club. We'll call the woman "Jane Doe," the first of many in this book.

Jane called her friend Sheila as she walked out of The Gay '90s, an enormous, laid-back, straight-friendly downtown gay club, where I person-ally have gotten plastered and danced until the wee hours without inci-dent, so anyone who has a problem with that part of the story can move along. She told Sheila that she was concerned about a man following her. Jane was *paying attention to strangers.*

Then that creepy man stole her phone and coat. It's unclear where he went after that, but Jane got on a city bus headed toward her home, and the man did not immediately follow her. *She avoided traveling alone (especially after dark).*

Two stops later, the man got on the bus. Jane stayed on board, probably assuming it was safer than getting off in an unfamiliar neighborhood. *She tried to stay away from isolated areas.*

At that hour, waiting for another bus would be even more dangerous than remaining in an enclosed space with a man who had already robbed her and might continue following her, so "switching directions" wasn't really a viable option. But at the bus stop nearest her home, where she knew the territory, Jane got off. *She tried to seek a safe place.*

Unfortunately, the man followed her, overpowered her, and attacked her.

While Jane was riding the bus home, Sheila called the police to report that her friend had been followed by a strange man and was no longer answering her phone. Sheila was told they could do nothing. She called Jane's stolen phone again and again, until she finally talked to the rapist himself. Eventually, she called her ex-husband and asked him to go over to Jane's neighborhood and look for her. Sheila's ex found the victim not long after it happened and took her to the hospital.

So, to recap: The victim was suspicious enough to call a friend and tell her there was a creep around—and wise enough to choose a friend who would go all out trying to send help in time. She got on a well-lit moving vehicle that the creep wasn't on. After he boarded it, she chose to stay there, rather than get off and risk him following her in an area where she'd have nowhere to run. She only got off the bus when she was close to the promise of safety. (And let's keep in mind, she didn't know this guy was definitely planning to assault her. If he hadn't, all of the above behavior would have been dismissed as "paranoia," if she'd told anyone.)

In other words, she followed nearly all the "strong advice" the police had to offer, and yet somehow, she didn't magically ward off the sexual assault this criminal planned and executed.

Were there still other things she could have done differently, which might have led to a different result? Sure. A commenter at the website for Twin Cities alternative paper *City Pages* did some Monday-morning quarterbacking that was highlighted in a separate post as "good advice for people riding the bus by themselves late at night."

There's no excuse or mitigation of the fact that the man is a violent, dangerous rapist who needs to be stopped. But I did use this awful incident to talk to my early-teen daughter about how to handle a situation like this on the bus. Don't get off the bus. Go up to the front and sit next to the bus driver, and tell the bus driver that the man in back has already attacked you and is following you and has your coat and cell phone. Do Not Get Off The Bus.[4]

"I'm not saying it's her fault, but {reason why it's her fault}" is a bog-standard response to stories about sexual violence. There's always someone who knows exactly what a victim like Jane should have done, even without a whole lot of important information. Information like: Did the man say anything to Jane as they rode the bus? Was the bus driver also a woman? Were there other people on the bus? Was Jane perhaps concerned for others' safety? Did she think the man had a weapon? If he did, or she thought he did, was she concerned that moving or asking someone for help might escalate the situation?

It's easy to work backwards from an attack and see things that the victim could have done differently. And it's really, really easy to sit at home and imagine ourselves as the heroes of our own stories—outwitting criminals, saving the day, making all the right choices and no false steps.

What's not easy is being alone on a bus in the early morning, probably exhausted and a little drunk, with no phone, looking at the man who stole it from you and then reappeared after you thought you'd escaped to safety. You can talk all you want about preparing for the worst, but how can you truly prepare for that? Don't even tell me you know what you'd do in that situation.

Also, let's keep in mind that in the versions of the story where we do everything right, the happy ending is that no crime occurs. You might not even know that you saved yourself.

What About the Men?

Putting the onus on women to prevent our own rapes isn't just an unfair burden. It also reinforces a concept of sexual assault that sex educator Twanna A. Hines describes as "the invisible hand of rape" (with apologies, or not, to Adam Smith). Rape is presented as an abstract threat to women, the way climate change is a threat to the earth—it's a frightening specter we all live with, and we must change our own behavior in hopes of warding it off, but you can't really pin it on anyone in particular.

You've heard of "victimless" crimes. Rape is perhaps the only perpetratorless crime, in our collective imagination.

Or, as Jackson Katz, author of *The Macho Paradox: Why Some Men Hurt Women and How All Men Can Help*, puts it, it's "amazing how this works, in domestic and sexual violence—how men have been largely erased from so much of the conversation about a subject that is centrally about men."[5]

Before you ask, let's acknowledge that women have been known to commit every crime under the sun, including rape. And the boys, men, girls, and women who have been victims of female sex offenders have intense stigma piled on top of their trauma. They all deserve support, concern, and justice as much as any other survivor.

Still, the best available evidence suggests that nearly 98 percent of rapists are men[6]—regardless of the victim's gender—so Katz is absolutely correct that a discussion of rape should be centrally about men. "Calling gender violence a women's issue," he says, "is part of the problem."

In any case, the fact that rape is always committed by individual human beings who chose to behave violently usually gets pushed so far to the side in discussions of sexual violence that people start to forget it exists. Rape is a thing that happens, sure, but it's not really something people *do*. Certainly, not that nice boy, that star quarterback, that beloved priest, that trusted babysitter, that troop leader, that teacher, that dear family friend.

It's as though none of us ever learned about "passive voice" in freshman comp. *She was raped. Local woman raped. Girl, 11, raped in abandoned trailer.* Who's doing all the raping here? Incubi? If nobody's actually committing rape, how are we supposed to address it as a public health and safety issue?

Oh, right, by giving women endless lists of acceptable behaviors and warnings about personal responsibility, for as long as it takes until those dummies get it together and quit becoming victims.

What Are We Teaching Our Boys?

In fact, we know who's at risk of committing rape and what group of people could most benefit from an intervention geared toward preventing sexual violence at the source. Are you ready? Because this is where I make the statement that anti-feminists will trot out as evidence of what a man-hating crackpot I am, whenever they hear my name, until the end of time: every American boy is at risk of growing up to become a rapist.

No, I'm not kidding. But first, let me clarify what I do *not*—*not*, not, not—mean by that:

- Every American boy, left unchecked, will grow up to be a rapist. I do not mean that!
- Every American boy has a fundamentally rapey nature. I do not mean that, either!
- Boys and men are icky and evil, so we should just keep a few around as sperm donors, kill all the rest, and turn America into a radical political-lesbian separatist paradise.

Okay, maybe that's not a bad idea.

No! I kid, I kid. I do not mean that either!

I am really quite a fan of boys and men. I love a great many of them, including my husband, father, brother, and four nephews, so you can put that stereotype back in its holster for now. If you want to prove I'm a man-hater, you're going to have a hell of a time marshaling any real evidence.

So here's what I do mean by "every American boy is at risk of becoming a rapist": we live in a rape-supportive culture, and boys have to grow up here, too.

They grow up in the same atmosphere as girls, absorbing all the same messages about the difference between good girls and sluts, about what certain types of clothing signal, about "real" victims and the ones who were "asking for it." And on top of that, they're reared in a culture of aggressive masculinity that reviles the feminine, demanding conspicuous heterosexuality and rejection of all things queer, while granting social power to young men who have as many semi-anonymous sexual encounters as possible (or at least develop a reputation for doing so). They grow up in a culture where people stand around and take video of popular football players rap-ing a sixteen-year-old girl, instead of stepping in to stop it.

In light of all that, every boy who doesn't grow up to rape anybody deserves a big gold star—and the really good news is, that's most of them! As I discussed in Chapter 1, research shows that a relatively small number of serial predators commit the majority of rapes, and most guys have no trouble figuring out that a willing sex partner is far preferable to one who's not interested.

So why should we bother teaching boys about meaningful consent, the legal definitions of rape and sexual assault, or the double standard that makes guys who have sex "studs" and girls who join them "sluts"?

Well, naturally, I believe we *should* be teaching kids of all genders those things. But I stand by framing this as "We need to teach boys not to rape." For starters, that statement makes a lot of people furious—which to me is evidence that our culture doesn't want to deal with the facts about sexual violence and who's committing it.

In March 2013, the writer, political analyst, and rape survivor Zer-lina Maxwell appeared on Fox's *The Sean Hannity Show* to argue against encouraging women to arm themselves in anticipation of encountering a rapist. Because that would end well, especially for women of color! Police, prosecutors, and juries already think women lie about rape all the time—I'm sure victims would have zero trouble proving they shot sexual pred-ators in self-defense. Just ask Marissa Alexander, an African American woman who fired a warning shot into a wall after her husband attacked and threatened to kill her. She was sentenced to twenty years in prison. That conviction was overturned, but Alexander then faced a new trial and possible sixty-year-sentence before entering a guilty plea that awarded her freedom after three years' time served. For a warning shot.

Asked what we should be telling women about rape prevention, if not "Carry a gun," Maxwell replied, "I don't think we should be telling women anything. I think we should be telling men not to rape women and start the conversation there for prevention.... You're talking about it as if there's some faceless, nameless criminal, when a lot of times it's someone that you know and trust."[7]

Well. From the reaction those remarks got, you'd think she'd said, "We should castrate every male baby, and start there for prevention."

Writing for *RH Reality Check*, Tara Murtha summed up the fallout: "For her audacity, Maxwell received a torrent of abusive tweets. These Twitter users said she should be gang-raped and that her throat should be slit. They called her a 'n——.' Many others simply insisted on perpetuating a false, twisted representation of her argument: Zerlina Maxwell believes women should be raped instead of using a gun on a rapist."[8]

"So it's come to this," Murtha adds wryly. "We now must add carrying a gun to our victim-blaming checklist. 'She wasn't carrying a pistol; she must've wanted it.'"

Critics who say, "You can teach kids whatever you want—that won't stop criminals from committing crimes," aren't necessarily wrong. But educating our young people about consent—especially our boys, who wield the responsibility that comes with both cultural and physical power—might just prevent some of them from becoming criminals. If nothing else, it sends a message that eliminating sexual violence is important to us, as a society. It sends the message that we take every individual's bodily autonomy seriously and that we really *do* believe rape is an abhorrent crime.

Beyond that, it's one of the only things we know of that works.

In April 2014, the Centers for Disease Control released a report on preventing sexual violence on college campuses. After reviewing 140 studies that measured the effectiveness of various prevention techniques, CDC researchers found that "only two primary prevention strategies, to date, have demonstrated significant reductions in sexual violence behaviors using a rigorous evaluation design."[9] Both were interventions aimed at junior high school students.

One of those programs, Safe Dates, "includes a 10-session curriculum addressing attitudes, social norms, and healthy relationship skills, a 45-minute student play about dating violence, and a poster contest." A description of Safe Dates on the website of the curriculum's publisher, Hazelden, explains that it begins with a lesson on "defining caring relationships," followed by one on "defining dating abuse." Later lessons include "overcoming gender stereotypes" and "equal power through communication." The final session before a review of all the material is on preventing sexual assault.

And it seems to help. From the CDC report: "Results from one rigorous evaluation showed that four years after receiving the program,

students in the intervention group were significantly less likely to be victims or perpetrators of sexual violence involving a dating partner."[10]

To be fair, it's true that casually suggesting people don't rape, especially once they're already adults, isn't particularly useful. The same report
notes that a one-off attempt to change hearts and minds works just about
as well as you'd expect:

> Brief, one-session educational programs conducted with college
> students, typically aimed at increasing knowledge or awareness
> about rape or reducing belief in rape myths, comprise the bulk of
> the sexual violence prevention literature. However, across dozens
> of studies using various methods and outcome measures, none have
> demonstrated lasting effects on risk factors or behavior.[11]

What actually creates lasting effects is talking to adolescents about
consent and boundaries, over a longer period of time. In other words,
teaching kids what rape is and not to do it. These programs challenge the
lazy assumption that a "good boy" couldn't do something that falls under
the legal definition of rape, even if he's never learned what actually constitutes consent. They give all young people, not just girls, the information they need to take responsibility for choices they'll make down the
line. They present sexual violence as a widespread problem that men and
women can work together to solve, not a rarity perpetrated by monsters
on victims who fail to protect themselves adequately.

Whether or not such interventions reduce the number of men who
eventually go on to commit sex crimes, they help create an environment
where sexual violence isn't tolerated and victims aren't isolated. They
offer young teens reasonable guidelines for holding themselves and others
accountable for their behavior. A criminal (someone else's kid, surely) will
do what he's going to do, but will your son stand up to him? Will your
son even know that what that guy's doing is wrong? Will he know that a
passed-out drunk girl can't give consent or that penetrating someone else
with any object against their will constitutes rape in many jurisdictions?

Will your son use his phone to call 911 if he witnesses a rape or to
take a video of it?

Rape Jokes and the Social License to Operate

"It's not easy, in male culture, for guys to challenge each other," says Jackson Katz, in a TED talk that condenses his main arguments from *The Macho Paradox*.[12] But the guys who have the guts to do it can start to shift the conversation in important ways. Young people, Katz points out, are deeply concerned with their status among their peers. (So are all human beings, to an extent, but if you're currently older than a high school student, you know how much worse it is in adolescence.) A crucial element of changing destructive cultural norms—whether you're talking about the culture of high school athletics, college campuses, or the entire Western world—is to associate the negative behaviors with a loss of status and desired behaviors with a gain.

As things are now, it's the other way around. In his extremely popular 2009 blog post "Meet the Predators," feminist attorney Thomas MacAulay Millar argues that our culture offers sexual predators a "social license to operate," by trivializing and denying their crimes, and reassuring them that they're unlikely to face any serious consequences. Rape jokes, for instance, are not always as lighthearted as the teller claims. Writes Millar:

> Woman-hating jokes are not jokes. These guys are telling you what they think. When you laugh along to get their approval, you give them yours. You tell them that the social license to operate is in force; that you'll go along with the pact to turn your eyes away from the evidence; to make excuses for them; to assume it's a mistake, or the first time, or a confusing situation. You're telling them that they're at low risk.[13]

If you think jokes about rape are a small-time concern with little real-world impact, you probably weren't paying attention to what went down in the summer of 2012, after comedian Daniel Tosh made a beyond-the-pale crack at an audience member's expense. During a stand-up set at a club, the Comedy Central star did a bit about rape—specifically about rape jokes being funny—which at least two of his female audience members objected to. One of them was moved to interrupt his act, calling out, "Actually, rape jokes are never funny!"

She later explained her decision to heckle in a blog post:

I did it because, even though being "disruptive" is against my nature, I felt that sitting there and saying nothing, or leaving quietly, would have been against my values as a person and as a woman. I don't sit there while someone tells me how I should feel about something as profound and damaging as rape.[14]

Although I love her politics and her moxie, I disagree with that woman about rape jokes being uniformly unfunny. I believe it depends entirely on the joke in question, and specifically, on who the butt of that joke is. Satire that shines a light on rape culture, or wisecracks that release some of the tension women live with all the time, are not making fun of survivors. They aren't built on the premise that victims of sexual violence are a powerful group that deserves to be lampooned.

But then there are jokes like the one Tosh reportedly made to retaliate against his feminist heckler. It's important to note that Tosh did later apologize on Twitter (and referred to "out-of-context misquotes," so it's unclear if he fully admits to having said this), but here's what that female audience member writes that she heard: "Wouldn't it be funny if that girl got raped by like, five guys right now? Like right now? What if a bunch of guys just raped her … "

Yeah, that would actually not be funny.

I'm not an expert on comedy or anything, but I'm pretty sure that for that to be funny, we'd need to live in a country where Cheryl Araujo wasn't gang-raped on a pool table at a bar in New Bedford, Massachusetts; where Jane Does in Steubenville, Ohio, Glen Ridge, New Jersey, Cleveland, Texas, and Richmond and Corona Del Mar, California, weren't raped in front of cheering crowds—in the more recent cases, on video.

We'd also have to live in a country where a woman who finds herself a mile from home on a beautiful night doesn't think twice about walking. One where sorority girls don't talk like soldiers going into battle, because Ivy League frat boys don't go around chanting, "No means yes! Yes means anal!"

For the image of a spontaneous public gang rape to work as a joke, we'd need to live in a world where rape isn't routinely used as a weapon of war, where a young Indian woman wasn't raped and fatally beaten by seven men on a moving bus, where more than 130 rapes aren't reported every day in South Africa, and where that's not thought to be a small fraction of the true number. For starters.

If all of that weren't happening in the world where Daniel Tosh and you and I live, then the thought of a young woman being gang-raped in a comedy club might at least contain an element of the unexpected, enough to elicit a few uncomfortable titters. It still wouldn't be funny, but at least it wouldn't be a scenario that's all too easy to imagine, for those of us who don't have the luxury of considering rape at a safe remove.

As it is, in that moment, Tosh failed as a comic and a human being. He forgot several crucial points, starting with the fact that the guy who's onstage, with a microphone, is not actually the underdog in this scenario; he might affect that persona for the sake of comedy, but clearly, standing in a room full of people who have paid money to see him, he is the guy with the most power.

Similarly, he forgot—or never really understood—that we live in a culture where men, as a group, have more power than women.

This isn't a controversial statement, despite the protestations of guys who funnel their frustration that not all extremely young, conventionally attractive women want to sleep with them into an argument that women, as a group, have "all the power." (Bill Maher, repping for his fan base, famously jokes that men have to do all sorts of shit to get laid, but women only have to do "their hair.")

The really great thing about this argument is how the patently nonsensical premise—that some young women's ability to manipulate certain men equals a greater degree of gendered power than, say, owning the presidency for 220-odd years—obscures the most chilling part: in this mindset, "all the power" means, simply, the power to withhold consent.

Let that sink in for a minute. If one believes women are more powerful than men because we own practically all of the vaginas, then women's power to withhold consent to sex is *the greatest power there is.*

Which means the guy who can take away a woman's right to consent is basically a superhero. Right?

Okay, let me reel this back in now. Do I believe that most of the men saying, "Waaah, women have all the power because my boner is sad" are thinking this through to its logical conclusion? The question answers itself. I do not believe those men are thinking much at all.

But if you subscribe to this bizarro worldview, wherein women are vastly outnumbered by men in politics and business yet still hold "all the power," then a joke about gang-raping a mouthy woman makes a twisted sort of sense. It's about taking a frightening, dominant figure down a notch and awarding moral authority to the oppressed and ignored. That's what good comedy is supposed to do.

Back here on planet Earth, though, women as a class are not frightening, dominant figures. We are not the gender with the vast majority of cultural influence, the generally greater physical strength, or a legal system stacked in our favor when it comes to sexual violence. If the best comedy speaks truth to power, what is the truth in "Wouldn't it be funny if she got raped?" That is not even a joke by any rational comedic standards; it's something you blurt out in a moment of insecurity, when you're brought up short, you panic, and you forget that you're the one, literally and figuratively, holding the microphone.

As feminist writer and bona fide hilarious person Lindy West wrote in an instantly viral *Jezebel* post about rape jokes: "The world *is* full of terrible things, including rape, and it *is* okay to joke about them. But the best comics use their art to call bullshit on those terrible parts of life and make them better, not worse."[15]

Teach Your Children Well

We teach children not to steal, not to hit other people, not to bite. A lot of us specifically teach boys that they're likely to grow up larger than many women, and beating up on someone smaller than you is a really lousy thing to do. But then we act like only a filthy-minded monster would think boys need to be taught to recognize and respect the difference between consent and nonconsent: a crucial part of dismantling rapists' social license to operate.

As I argued in Chapter 1, most people old enough to be having sex are perfectly capable of recognizing nonconsent—but as long as we refuse to teach our kids about it, we support the rapists' plausible deniability. We support the misguided notion that consent is a thorny, complicated issue and sex is an impossibly delicate operation that will self-destruct if one partner breathes the fatal words: "Is that good? You doing okay?"

To be honest, I can't really understand why anyone would object to teaching kids not to rape—that is, teaching them that consent is black and white, and that genuinely enthusiastic consent is both ideal and down-right unmistakable. My best guess is that people are conflating nonconsensual sex (rape!) with the lousy sex that is sometimes a part of healthy sexual experimentation. They fear that marauding feminists are coming for their boys' masculinity, self-esteem, and/or God-given right to an awkward hand job under the bleachers. But I *promise*, in the new world order, our feminist overladies will let your sons keep all those things.

In fact, all of the feminists I know want your sons to have great sex, when they decide they're ready. We want them to have happy, healthy sex lives, with consenting partners who care about their pleasure.

We also want that for your daughters, though. A lot of people can't quite handle that part.

In a rape culture, girls are supposed to be the pure ones, the responsible ones, the ones putting the brakes on *all* adolescent sexual overtures, regardless of their own desires. Boys and men have a natural, biological sex drive, you see, but when girls and women express sexuality, it's because they've been led astray by music videos or vampire movies or something. Never mind that this is both demonstrably false and inimical to good sex.

"Making women the sexual gatekeepers and telling men they just can't help themselves not only drives home the point that women's sexuality is unnatural, but also sets up a disturbing dynamic in which women are expected to be responsible for men's sexual behavior," writes feminist author Jessica Valenti in *The Purity Myth: How America's Obsession with Virginity Is Hurting Young Women.*[16] Everyone loses in this scenario—it prevents women from saying "yes" when they want to and men from saying "no." And it means rape is always, on some level, the woman's fault.

Essentially, the "girls as gatekeepers" construct suggests that adolescence is like a zombie invasion: as soon as the pituitary gland virus starts making its way around our children's classrooms, half of them will lose all rational thought, compassion, and assorted other markers of humanity, while the other half must learn to live in a state of fear and battle readiness. Boys—and later men—are not only relieved of any responsibility for sexual aggression but robbed of the ability to define their own sexuality, which may or may not naturally involve pushiness, selfishness, or female partners. Girls and women, meanwhile, learn to frame being violated as a personal failure, a battle they inadequately prepared for.

Our daughters deserve better, and our sons *are* better than that. For as much as feminists are painted as "man-haters," we're not the ones suggesting that boys and men lack the ability to think rationally, control their own behavior, or act kindly toward other human beings—even with a boner. We're the ones who want all of our children to know about meaningful consent, healthy sexuality, and honoring each other's bodies and boundaries, instead of teaching them that one gender is responsible for managing the other's helpless animal lust.

That's what I mean when I say, "We should teach boys not to rape." We should teach them they're worth more and capable of more than this narrowly defined caricature of sexuality that favors dominance and aggression over genuine human connection.

CHAPTER 3

Not-So-Innocent Bystanders

Y ou've heard the story a hundred times already. This one and a hundred like it.

It starts with a sixteen-year-old girl, at a party with a bunch of other high school students. She's had a lot to drink, and she's not feeling so good. A couple of guys—popular ones, stars of the town's beloved football team—decide to leave the party and bring her along to another one. There, she vomits, and other people notice how disoriented she seems. This will be the only part she remembers later.

The guys take her with them to someone else's house, and in the car on the way, somebody removes her shirt, and one guy puts his fingers inside her vagina, while others take pictures and videos. They take her to the basement of the third house and strip her naked. One of the football stars puts his penis in her mouth. She's passed out at this point. Another star decides to penetrate her vagina with his fingers.

People take more video and more pictures—including one of the two football stars, Trent Mays and Ma'lik Richmond, holding the girl just off the floor by her hands and feet, her limp, unconscious body swinging between them. Her face will be blurred out when this photo makes her national news, but everyone she knows will recognize her.

The town is Steubenville, Ohio, and the girl, like so many others before and since, will henceforth be known as Jane Doe.

In a dorm room at Ohio State University on the same night, a young man named Michael Nodianos watches a twelve-minute video of Jane Doe being assaulted and narrates what's happening onscreen to yet another camera. According to his play-by-play, he believes the video shows her being anally raped ("He's puttin' a wang in the butthole, dude") and urinated on ("They peed on her!"), and that she's unconscious through all of it ("That's how you know she's dead, because someone pissed on her").

None of those charges, specifically, will be proven in court—although Mays and Richmond will eventually be convicted of rape, it's for the digital penetration seen on the only video that wasn't destroyed—but the salient point is, that's what Nodianos apparently believes he's watching: the gang rape and dehumanization of an unconscious sixteen-year-old.

And on and off throughout the entire twelve minutes, he's laughing.

"She's so dead" becomes his refrain throughout the first several minutes. The one-liners he cracks about her unresponsiveness seem to titillate the guy holding the camera, so Nodianos just keeps piling them on, all the way up to, "She's deader than O.J.'s wife," and "She's deader than Trayvon Martin." Then: "She is so raped right now.... They raped her harder than that cop raped Marcellus Wallace in *Pulp Fiction*.... They raped her quicker than Mike Tyson raped that one girl.... They raped her more than the Duke lacrosse team."

About halfway through, some of the other young men in the room also start using the R word, but not in quite the same way.

"That's, like, rape," says one of the other observers, before correcting himself: "That *is* rape."

This only inspires more jokes from Nodianos and corresponding laughter from the cameraman.

The first conversation in which someone tries to do the right thing goes like this:

Offscreen Guy 1: No, this is not, like, funny.
Camera Guy: I'm sorry, but Nodi's funny.
MN: It isn't funny—it's hilarious!
OSG1: What if that was your daughter?
MN: If that was my daughter, I wouldn't care. I'd just let her be dead.
OSG1: Listen to yourself.

MN: I'm listening to myself fine.

Moments later, there are two young men offscreen speaking up for the cause of "not being totally evil."

Offscreen Guy 2: Dude, this is not cool. They're raping a girl.

MN: They're not raping her, 'cause she's dead.

OSG1: Y'all don't understand how it is, all right? I got a fuckin' little sister. What happens if that was my little sister, who just turned, like sixteen?

OSG2: Right.

MN *[sounding, for one second, genuinely chagrined]*: You're right.

OSG2 : What if it was Amanda?

MN: It wouldn't be, though. 'Cause she's not dead.

OSG2: Neither is that girl![1]

What if it were your daughter? What if it were your sister? Obviously, those questions are enough to make some young men think twice, but Nodianos doesn't appear bothered. Even when someone presumably close to him is named, he reverts to his position that the girl being raped on camera is "dead," and therefore not like any of those real, living, breathing people he's supposed to care about.

"Is it really rape?" Nodianos asks at one point. "Because you don't know if she wanted it or not. She might have wanted it."

Even though penetrating an unconscious person—that is, someone physically incapable of offering consent—meets the legal definition of rape in every state, for reasons that should be blindingly obvious, this is an incredibly common argument. What if the victim somehow made it clear that she really wanted to have sex with the perpetrator(s) *before* she fell asleep or passed out? What if the men using her unconscious body were under the impression that she had *volunteered* to be their lifeless fucktoy?

Nodianos cracks himself up as another riff on the "dead girl" theme comes to mind: "It might have been her final wish."

Stepping Up

I didn't watch the Nodianos video for months after it was first leaked to the internet by hacktivist group KnightSec (an offshoot of the better-known

Anonymous) because I didn't have the stomach for listening to this kid laugh and laugh about a "dead girl" getting raped. Reading about the high-lights seemed like more than enough to get the gist.

But the tiny part of me that believes in progress, believes the future *could* bring liberty and justice for all—if it doesn't become a scorching dystopian hellscape where women are kept on breeding farms—was actu-ally heartened by watching the video. Because even if Nodianos's laughter and rotten jokes dominate, at least those other guys are *there*, saying, "You know that's not cool, bro."

"If more men spoke up before, during, or after incidents of verbal, physical, or sexual abuse by their peers, they would help to create a climate where the abuse of women—emotional, physical, sexual—would be stig-matized and seen as incompatible with male group norms," writes Jackson Katz in *The Macho Paradox*.[2] "That is, a man who engaged in such behav-ior would lose status among his male peers."

On the video, Nodianos seems to expect that his unspeakably crass and cruel comments will raise his status among all the other young men in the room—and at first it seems to be working. But as those twelve minutes wear on, and his peers begin speaking up, we see the dynamic shift a bit. Michael Nodianos is not quite the successful comedian he believes he is, and parts of his audience are increasingly vocal about their revulsion. One voice gingerly suggesting he knock it off becomes two voices explaining to the whole room (and anyone who watches the video) why jokes about the actual rape of a "dead girl" are beyond fucked up. That's promising.

Still, despite those dissenting voices, the Nodianos video demon-strates just how far we have to go. Because someone saying, in so many words, "Bro, he raped a girl. Really raped someone," isn't enough to make the "star" or the cameraman stop laughing. It's clear that Nodianos, emboldened by the camera (and sycophantic encouragement of the guy holding it), feels no threat to his status when his peers try to reason with him. He's the focus of attention, the guy making everybody (or at least him-self and one other kid) laugh. The bystanders who try to intervene are just a couple of losers trying to ruin the fun.

We need to change our culture so that young men who toss around casual pro-rape sentiments are the ones regarded as buzzkills, wrecking everyone else's good time with their hateful crap. This, once again, is a big part of what I mean when I talk about "teaching boys not to rape." It's not a matter of Dad sitting down with his preadolescent son and incorporating "Don't be a criminal!" into the "birds and the bees" talk. (I mean, that couldn't hurt, probably. But it's not the point.) It's about teaching our boys to *actively* oppose sexual violence.

It's all well and good to say you're against rape and would never rape anyone, end of story. But somewhere in that crowd of guys laughing about an unconscious girl getting "a wang in the butthole, dude"—and the one listening to Daniel Tosh say, "Wouldn't it be funny if she got gang-raped right now?" and the one reading an op-ed in the *Washington Post* that puts "sexual assault" in quotation marks, as though it exists only in the eye of the beholder—somewhere in all of those crowds is the guy who *would* rape someone. The guy who *will* rape someone. The guy who *has* raped someone.

And could you blame any of those guys for thinking that rape is not a serious crime, or even something to be particularly ashamed of, when so many "good" guys around them are laughing at the same jokes?

"A Powerful Manhood"

Changing young men's perception of what sort of rape-related discourse will win them the admiration of their peers is about much more than cleaning up offensive language. The celebration of pro-rape rhetoric and elevation of men who degrade all things feminine also lays the groundwork for some "good" young men to participate in group acts of sexual violence. Frequently, these are attacks on a girl or woman, but as increasing reports of military sexual violence and "hazing" rituals make clear, it can as easily be a lower-status male.

In her 1990 book *Fraternity Gang Rape*, anthropologist Peggy Reeves Sanday describes the purpose a multiple-offender assault serves: "The event operates to glue the male group as a unified entity; it establishes fraternal bonding and helps boys to make the transition to their vision of a powerful manhood—in unity against women, one against the world."[3] (The author uses "fraternity" in the title and elsewhere to describe any bonded unit of men, not just those in the university Greek system.)

In *Our Guys*, his classic account of the 1989 gang rape of a developmentally disabled girl in Glen Ridge, New Jersey, the late journalist

Bernard Lefkowitz describes the rapists in a way that tracks precisely with that description:

> Much of the sexual behavior by the leaders of the clique revolved around acts that put them at an emotional distance from individual girls, acts that reflected an unrestrained enthusiasm for pornography and voyeurism. These acts allowed them to escape judgment on their sexual performance and also allowed them to avoid ongoing relationships of any intimacy with girls. And they wanted to avoid such intimacy because only one relationship meant anything to them: the close ties with their male buddies.[4]

Although Sanday focuses on crimes with female victims, I would argue that the "unity against women" part holds true even when the victim is another young man. Homophobia and misogyny are thoroughly intertwined, and boys making "the transition to their vision of a powerful manhood" through rape are looking to degrade and punish anything perceived as weak and feminine—or gay, which is basically the same thing to a lot of high school kids (and adults).

A chilling example of this occurred in 2012, when a group of small-town Colorado teen boys were away for their state high school wrestling tournament. On a bus before a meet, three older boys—two of whom were sons of the wrestling coach and president of the school board—bound a thirteen-year-old with duct tape and used a pencil to anally rape him. Similar incidents at New York's Bronx High School of Science and suburban Chicago's Maine West High School have made national news in recent years. Finding someone smaller and weaker, and putting your own body parts or other objects inside that person, is officially a Thing among high school students—especially male athletes. And the point of these rituals is the same whether the victim is male, female, or gender-variant: they are a perverse celebration of stereotypically masculine power, at the expense of anyone who is in some measure stereotypically feminine.

The thing about gang rape is that it should be the kind of assault that genuinely outrages and appalls us all, even if we have our doubts about other rapes. By definition, it involves witnesses—it's fundamentally a performance for other guys in the room or, increasingly, anyone with an internet connection.

It's not about sex gone wrong, because most perpetrators aren't oriented toward sexual activity with other men—or with their own brothers, as in the Colorado case. And it's certainly not a matter of one hapless, inexperienced guy being confused about whether somebody consented. When multiple people get together to hold a kid down, or take turns penetrating a kid who's drunk enough to appear "dead," it is not a misunderstanding. It is a deliberate act of violence and humiliation.

So you'd think we could at least all agree on *that* being a terrible thing, right?

Of course not.

As in Steubenville, when word of the Colorado crime spread, the town's response was to rally in support of the *rapists*, who were eventually charged as juveniles with kidnapping, sexual assault, and false imprisonment. Denver district attorney spokeswoman Lynn Kimbrough told *Bloomberg News*, "They blamed our victim. There was a huge backlash, and everybody turned against this boy and his family for bringing trouble to their town."[5]

Eventually, the victim's father took a job elsewhere, making far less money, to spare his family the town's vitriol. Robert Harris, the wrestling coach and father to two of the rapists, kept his job and status in the community. The perpetrators all pled guilty to lesser crimes and received sentences of community service, probation, and minor fines.

The problem, according to the townspeople, was not that three star athletes had raped a boy barely in his teens. It was that the boy had told on them.

Scapegoating the "Other"

Such a callous response from the community would be shocking if it weren't so common. The 2009 gang rape of a fifteen-year-old girl in Richmond, California, on school grounds during a homecoming dance, was witnessed by up to twenty people—about half of whom participated in the assault—over the course of more than two hours. By the time police got there, the girl was lying unconscious under a bench. "She looked wet. She looked really clammy white. I thought she was dead when I saw her," police officer Todd Kaiser would eventually testify.[6] The girl was taken by helicopter to a hospital, in critical condition.

Salvador Rodriguez, a twenty-one-year-old who witnessed the crime (and was arrested for participating, before being released for lack of evidence), told local news station KGO-TV, "People say, 'Why didn't I call the cops,' but at the same time, I live in Richmond, a neighborhood like this, snitching is something you don't do, you know, I mean I have to walk down the streets now in fear of my life."[7]

Remarks like that—and the fact that most of the people eventually arrested were not white (nor is three-quarters of Richmond High's student body) led people all over the country to pin the attack on their favorite racial scapegoats and the overall *otherness* of this community. "Take the poverty-driven frustration of inner-city Richmond, a youth street culture that glorifies thugs and applauds degradation of women, and the desensitization of young men through violent video games, music and language, and you have a template for trouble," fretted a writer for the *San Francisco Chronicle*.[8]

If you somehow missed the racial implications of "inner-city… thugs," there are always internet commenters to spell out the hatred for you. Concerned citizens commenting on one AOL article couldn't seem to choose between the usual victim blaming ("Anyone want to bet this 15 year old girl knew some of these guys and hung around with this low life crowd by choice prior to this rape") and actually holding the young men responsible—because they're brown ("Black and Spic rapists, no white boys involved, Wanna bet?"). And then there were those charmers who covered both at once: "Any white girl who hangs with mexicans deserves this."[9]

But the focus on race, gangs, and the urban environment of Richmond as explanations for the crime is clearly wrongheaded if we take a look at all the similar scenes that have played out across the country. Steubenville, Ohio, and Norwood, Colorado. Corona del Mar, California, where an assistant sheriff's son was convicted in 2005, along with two friends, of raping a sixteen-year-old girl. Glen Ridge, New Jersey.

In all of those cases, white criminals attacked white victims, who were then bullied and shamed by white communities. (Not all of the defendants in these cases were white, but the communities overwhelmingly were, and high-status white boys were involved in all of them.) They might not have talked in terms of "snitches" and fatal retaliation, but those towns made sure that the victims and whistle-blowers paid a price.

Be a Good Friend—or Else

Our cultural obsession with victims' appearance, behavior, and rape-preventative actions shows up not only in the hostility of communities shaken by high-profile gang rapes (not to mention media coverage of same) but in government-sponsored public health messaging.

A 2011 campaign by the Pennsylvania Liquor Control Commission, for instance, held women responsible for their *friends'* safety. The interactive campaign at now-shuttered website ControlTonight.com showed pictures of disembodied, underwear-wrapped ankles superimposed with scolding entreaties to visit their educational website, like, "Date rape: See what could happen when your friends drink too much." Or my personal favorite, "She said no, but he kept going. And now your friend is on his bathroom floor, bruised and victimized. See how you could have prevented this."[10]

Why not just go with, "Rapey the Bear says, 'Only YOU can prevent your friend's violent assault'"?

Listen, when I'm asked what young women can do to feel safer, I often suggest that they focus on making good friends, and then look out for each other's best interests, because that advice will serve them well throughout their lives. Surely, some number of potential rapes have been averted, and many more eventually will be, because a woman had her friend's back when it counted. But to add this to the list of responsibilities on girls' and women's shoulders, to hold us accountable for rape-proofing not just ourselves but all of the women we care about, is appalling.

And it's doubly so when you consider the specific advice the Pennsylvania Liquor Control Commission had to offer at the campaign's website. You got three tips when you clicked on "Keeping Away the Creeps."[11]

First was a redundant suggestion to use the buddy system. A fine idea, though not always feasible, and certainly something we don't warn men to do when they go out for drinks. Next, you were warned that rapists don't generally announce themselves. "You might meet someone who is very attractive and well-dressed, but is a creep nonetheless. Evaluate a person's character by their words and actions—not by their looks." (Important advice for when an attractive, well-dressed man says, "Would you like to come back to my apartment, where I plan to rape you?" You wouldn't want to miss that subtle clue.)

Finally, if you were concerned that you hadn't yet learned anything that would help you prevent your friend's rape, there was this mind-bomb: "Most sexual assaults are by acquaintances." Gee, you don't say.

So basically, here is a thing that people spent a lot of taxpayer money to make, and all it offered—by way of teaching us how to protect our loved ones from devastating attacks—is, "Anyone could be a rapist. Maybe try not to be alone?"

Bystander Intervention

The PLCC's "Keeping Away the Creeps" campaign was a clumsy attempt to promote a useful message: When lots of alcohol is being consumed around you, think about the well-being of your friends—and of strangers. If you see something rapey, say something.

During my freshman year of college, after I was raped, I became extremely vigilant at parties. Twice, I saw my friend "Ann" in situations that made me nervous, and I intervened. The first time, when she was about to leave a party with an older guy she barely knew, I pulled her aside for a second and asked if she was sure about him. She assured me that nothing bad would happen—in fact, he was gay, so I had nothing to worry about. (In fact, he wasn't, but he was a respectful person.) I felt mortified, they left together, and she was perfectly fine.

The second time, I came back from a trip to the bathroom and saw Ann bouncing in the air, legs wrapped around the belly of a cheerful drunken behemoth, skirt hiked around her waist. They were both laughing, just dancing—or something like it—and I don't think either one of them even realized where her skirt had ended up. I had very little impression of who the behemoth was as a person, but knew some people who thought he was nice. I certainly had no particular reason to suspect he was a rapist, and for all I know, he absolutely was not. Nevertheless, I grabbed Ann's arm and announced that it was time to go home.

Neither Ann nor the behemoth was at all happy to see me, but I kept pulling and insisted that Ann get down and talk to me before I would leave them alone together. Once she had her feet back on land, she soon stopped complaining, and five minutes later, she was thanking me for intervening. She was so drunk, she wasn't even totally sure how she'd ended up in his arms, and I was correct that she had no idea she was flashing the whole room. In other words, she was in no position to consent to anything except going home and getting tucked into bed.

The behemoth disappeared. Twenty-odd years later, Ann and I are still friends. The end.

I offer these examples to demonstrate that playing the hero is not necessarily fun, even when it works out for the best. You won't always be sure that you strictly need to intervene, and you might get it wrong, and even if you get it right, you might have to endure a lot of anger before you're ever thanked for the effort. It's awkward as hell at best, and at worst, it can be dangerous.

At that point in my life, I didn't care what anybody thought of me, if it meant I could save one friend from going through what I had, so I was uncharacteristically fearless about looking like Ann's meddling auntie. But I can't blame any young person who hesitates to risk the embarrassment of interrupting two people who are perfectly fine, or the hurt of being yelled at to fuck off and mind your own business—much less the threat of getting punched in the face. Direct confrontation can be an efficient option, but it's not the only one.

The bystander intervention training programs proliferating across the country, most notably on hundreds of college campuses and in the military, take a holistic approach to effecting change. Curricula like University of Arizona's Step UP!, The Green Dot Program, One Student, and Katz's Mentors in Violence Prevention (MVP) are all aimed at dismantling rape culture as well as preventing individual assaults. Several schools begin by teaching incoming freshmen and resident assistants (RAs) the "Three Ds" for taking action: Direct, Distract, Delegate.

"Direct" encompasses actions like yanking your drunk friend off a man-mountain in the middle of a dance floor, simply standing next to someone in a "Don't get any ideas" sort of way, or even just giving unmistakable side-eye to someone whose behavior looks predatory. It also means saying, "That shit's not funny" when people make rape jokes, and "You know that's not cool, bro," when a bro is not being cool.

"Distract" is just what it sounds like—getting in the middle of a scenario that has the potential to turn ugly, without saying outright, "Hello! I am here to perform a bystander intervention!" University of Massachusetts literature on the "Three Ds" suggests asking where the bathroom is, saying someone is looking for one of the people involved, or complimenting an outfit, just to bring everyone mentally back to their surroundings for a moment. Distractions—aka changing the subject—can also be a good tactic for shutting down sexist jokes or dehumanizing conversations without feeling like a huge buzzkill.

Finally, "Delegate." Talk to other people who are around and get backup. Call an RA or security guard to intervene. Call 911, if necessary. There's no shame in asking for help when you aren't sure how to approach a volatile situation. There is shame—or there damn well should be—in standing there taking pictures, not to show the authorities, but to forward around to everyone you know.

The One Student program offers a pledge to take actions including: "If I see someone taking advantage of a person who is intoxicated I will safely intervene," "I will respect my partner's (or anyone I have sexual contact with) boundaries and will expect my partner(s) to respect me," "I will talk with my friends about the importance of consent," and "I will make sure my friends understand that a person cannot consent to sex if they're intoxicated."[12] In a post called "10 Things Men Can Do to Prevent Gender Violence," Katz suggests:

> If a brother, friend, classmate, or teammate is abusing his female partner—or is disrespectful or abusive to women in general—don't look the other way. If you feel comfortable doing so, try to talk to him about it. Urge him to seek help. Or if you don't know what to do, consult a friend, a parent, a professor, or a counselor. DON'T REMAIN SILENT.[13]

All of these approaches make the important connection between everyday disrespect and the potential for violence. It's not just about caping up and saving a damsel in distress, but about creating a general environment in which everyone understands the meaning and importance of consent, sexism and homophobia bring shame instead of status to their purveyors, and victims of sexual assault and rape know they will be taken seriously if they come forward. The more we work on that, the less need there will be to physically get between our friends and people who might mean them harm.

In the meantime, though, it's worth remembering that in every one of the gang rapes I wrote about earlier in the chapter, there were not just people who participated and people who watched: there were also people who walked away, not wanting to be a part of it yet somehow not feeling empowered to stop it.

CHAPTER 4

The Problem of False Accusations

In 2010, a zebra was spotted on an Atlanta highway during rush hour, having escaped from a traveling circus—and that wasn't even the first time local commuters witnessed such a sight. Two years earlier, an injured baby zebra had been found near Interstate 75. And In Staten Island, New York, two years later, another baby (adorably named Paparazzi) escaped from a maybe-not-totally-legal petting zoo and went for a trot around town. The loose zebra problem in this country is so bad, in fact, that the twenty-fifth season of the TV show *COPS* kicked off with a high-speed chase after one of the stripey equids.

There are zebras in this country, and sometimes they end up where they don't belong. These are facts. A wild animal on the loose is something the authorities should always take very seriously: also a fact. Still, you've heard of the med school adage about hoofbeats, right? As in, if you hear them—and you're not currently at a zoo or on a game reserve in Africa—you should assume they're coming from a common horse, an animal that actually exists in large numbers in North America.

Even though zebra escapes *do* happen, and they *do* put people's lives at risk, treating every report of hoofbeats as a probable zebra would obviously be a terrible waste of resources and a recipe for investigative failure.

Based on the best available data, we can assume that somewhere between 92 and 98 percent of the time, a person reporting a rape is telling the truth—which means *false rape reports are zebras.* Just as a patient presenting with bad headaches most likely doesn't have a brain tumor, a person who reports sexual violence to police most likely is not an attention-mongering, man-hating liar. It is safe—and logical, and ethical—to presume that person is a victim, unless there are specific indications that this is one of the rare false reports.

Rape and sexual assault are unusual, if not quite unique, in that often, the only real evidence of a crime is the victim's testimony. Physical evidence might demonstrate that a sexual encounter took place between two people, but even cuts and bruises can't definitively prove lack of consent on one person's part—especially if the accused is the alleged victim's friend, lover, or spouse, or someone with whom they freely chose to leave a party. Ultimately, in the absence of photographic or video evidence, it comes down to one person's word against another's.

The most obvious tragic result of this fact is that nearly half of rapes are never reported, few are prosecuted, and even fewer lead to a felony conviction. Victims wonder what the point of reporting uncorroborated sexual violence is, and they're not wrong; the relatively tiny chance of bringing their rapists to justice must be weighed against the near certainty that they'll be suspected of lying and treated accordingly, as part of law enforcement's due diligence.

But equally devastating and shameful—if far, far less common than unreported attacks—is the prosecution of innocent people. How does this happen? When so many guilty rapists go free, how do people end up charged with rapes that other people committed—or worse yet, rapes that never happened?

First, Let's Agree on a Definition of "False Report"

Just kidding! Nobody can!

In a 2009 report for the National Center for Prosecution of Violence Against Women, researchers discuss the difficulty with pinning down a single definition of "false report." The FBI Uniform Crime Report Handbook says a report can only be classified as "unfounded" if it's "determined through investigation to be false or baseless. In other words, no crime occurred."[1] That seems straightforward enough, but Kimberly Lonsway,

Joanne Archambault, and David Lisak, authors of the NCPVAW report, warn that "it does not typically reflect the way investigators, prosecutors (and their supervisors) tend to think of sexual assault investigations."

"In fact," they write, "at virtually every training we offer on this topic, we hear from law enforcement professionals who unfound cases—and prosecutors who reject them—either because they do not believe the victim's account or they failed to prove it conclusively."

That's right: many law enforcement officers are skipping over the "determined through investigation" part and basing their official statements that no crime occurred on either a *gut feeling* that the victim is lying or the (probably accurate) sense that prosecution will be futile.

This is one reason why there can be no conclusive agreement on what percentage of sexual assault reports are false, except to say that the most credible, verifiable studies find results between 2 and 8 percent.[2] Researchers who have recently sought solid data on false accusations have been frustrated not only by inconsistent definitions but by poorly designed studies and indeed by the stereotypes we all absorb.

Take one of the men's rights movement's* favorite citations, for example: a 1994 study by Eugene Kanin of 104 sexual assault complaints made to a single police department in the Midwest. Of those, Kanin declared that 41 percent were false.

Forty-one percent! Holy smokes, that's almost half! If they're that common, how could you ever trust that *any* given claim of rape is the truth?

Exactly.

Here's how Lisak critiqued that study in 2007:

> Kanin describes no effort to systemize his own "evaluation" of the
> police reports—for example, by listing details or facts that he used
> to evaluate the criteria used by the police to draw their conclusions.

---

* If you're fortunate enough to be unfamiliar with the current incarnation of the men's rights movement—as opposed to the benign, woodsy, drum-circle type of yore—you should be aware that this lot's primary form of activism is writing blog posts about how feminists ruin everything. For more than you could possibly want to know about them, I refer you to David Futrelle's equally hilarious and depressing website, "We Hunted the Mammoth: The New Misogyny, Tracked and Mocked," at wehuntedthemammoth.com. I'll also discuss men's rights activists more in Chapter 11.

Nor does Kanin describe any effort to compare his evaluation of those reports to that of a second, independent research—providing a "reliability" analysis. This violates a cardinal rule of science, a rule designed to ensure that observations are not simply the reflection of the bias of the observer.[3]

In other words, all the Kanin study teaches us is that the detectives in one police department in one Midwestern town believed fewer than 60 percent of the people who reported rapes to them. And there are a lot of reasons why that might be.

One reason, for instance, is that it was standard practice at this department to offer to polygraph everyone who reported a rape, so the victims had an opportunity to prove they weren't just scheming liars. But a 2003 National Academy of Sciences report found not only that "almost a century of research in scientific psychology and physiology provides little basis for the expectation that a polygraph test could have extremely high accuracy," but "there is evidence suggesting that truthful members of socially stigmatized groups and truthful examinees who are believed to be guilty or believed to have a high likelihood of being guilty may show emotional and physiological responses in polygraph test situations that mimic the responses that are expected of deceptive individuals."[4]

So a genuine victim who submitted to a lie detector test to bolster her story could, in fact, undermine her own case, all because Americans still really like and trust this incredibly unreliable technology.

That's one reason why offering to polygraph anyone who reports a sexual assault is a terrible idea. Additionally, say Lonsway, Archambault, and Lisak, "many victims will recant when faced with apparent skepticism on the part of the investigator and the intimidating prospect of having to take a polygraph examination. Yet such a recantation does not necessarily mean that the original report was false." It will probably, however, lead to police "unfounding" the original report.

Another very good reason why an entire small-town police force might disbelieve over 40 percent of rape reports is that police, like all the rest of us, grow up in a rape culture. And as we'll see in Chapter 5, that has devastating effects on their treatment of victims.

Who Makes a False Accusation?

I have to concede one point to antifeminists: the series of events that lead to a man being imprisoned for a rape he didn't commit often begins with a woman lying to police. (Often, but not always. Sometimes it's the police who accuse the wrong person, as we'll see later in this chapter.) I certainly don't want to downplay how that choice can devastate innocent lives—and believe me, I'm not interested in making excuses for fraudulent victims, who make it that much harder for real ones to get justice.

I do, however, want to complicate the unrealistic and inhuman picture many people have of the false accuser: an evil minx who wraps the entire justice system around her little finger, just to hurt some poor, innocent man. It's fine to think women who lie about rape deserve to be punished for it, but let's not act as though one woman's false testimony is, by itself, sufficient to create the Kafkaesque hell of a wrongful prosecution—especially when a genuine victim's credible testimony is still often not enough to merit even an arrest. The idea that any given vengeful, embarrassed, or simply bored woman can "cry rape" and automatically send an innocent man to prison is pure fiction.

Consider the following hypothetical false report of rape—a composite of characteristics and choices typical in these cases—and pay special attention to all the places where someone could intervene to stop a miscarriage of justice.

Start with a young woman without a lot of family support—we'll call her Brianna, because it's a popular name in the United States across races, and she could have any ethnic background. Brianna probably suffers from depression or some other form of mental illness that isn't being treated. She feels like nobody cares about her and desperately craves attention. She might be going through an especially difficult time right now—romantic problems, money problems, job problems, family problems, or all of the above. She's frustrated, angry, and scared, and she just wishes the unreliable people in her life would reach out and offer some comfort. She's not thinking long-term, to say the least.

So Brianna makes up a story about being raped. Because she doesn't want to get anyone she knows in trouble, she says it was a stranger who grabbed her—and come to think of it, he had a gun. That will head off questions about why she didn't run away! She decides she'll tell people she didn't get a very good look at the guy, can't describe much more than his race and build. (Which race the imaginary assailant is will probably depend on what Brianna expects her own community to find most believable and infuriating. The notion of interracial rape still tends to capture the public imagination, even though most rapes are intraracial.) She doesn't want to hurt an innocent person; she just wants people to act like they give a damn about her for once.

Brianna decides she fought back as hard as she possibly could but doesn't think to cause any serious injury to herself, to bolster that part of the story. (If she does go as far as faking injury, maybe she writes or cuts some kind of message or slur on her body, somewhere easy to reach, like her stomach.) She'll probably keep her description of the attack pretty simple, although she might choose to embellish with details lifted from a recent sex crime in the news, or even a fictional story.

Once she's got all that hammered out, she shares it with a friend or family member and basks in their shock and sympathy. It feels great, and it's just what she needed. That's as far as she's thought any of this through.

But then the person Brianna shared the story with—let's say it's her mom—insists on reporting the rape to the police. If Brianna comes clean at this point, she'll lose this newfound sympathy and attention, and as long as she keeps saying she doesn't remember much about what the guy looks like, it's not as if she'll get anyone else in trouble. So she goes to the police station and tells her story again, tentatively, through tears. You'd cry, too, if you painted yourself into a corner like that.

The detective assigned to her is used to dealing with typical rape cases, which are really difficult to prove: the assailant knows the victim, the physical evidence doesn't show anything except that these people had sex, the victim was drunk at the time, the accused insists it was consensual. Witnesses probably saw them flirting with each other (or dating each other for months or marrying each other). They're around the same age, the same race, and the alleged victim telling her story is so composed and matter-of-fact, you wonder if she's been rehearsing. If you can even get an indictment for something like that, no jury is going to convict. It sucks, but that's the way it is.

But *this*, an obviously traumatized young woman who says she was abducted by a stranger with a weapon? This is a case with legs. This is a real chance to get a couple of rapists off the streets. So our detective is instantly pumped to do whatever it takes to find the bastard who hurt this girl. As he questions Brianna, an irritating little voice in his head says there's something off about her story, but he can't put his finger on it. And what if he accuses her of lying, and he's wrong? He'll come off as a sexist jerk (and possibly a racist one, depending on what races you've decided he and Brianna are).

Multiple interviews with the victim follow, in which police beg her to remember something, anything they can use. A sketch artist. Photo arrays. Lineups. Finally, a suspect! An indictment. Victory for our intrepid detective.

Predictably, the media eats this story up.

Brianna feels guilty but also terrified of what will happen if she admits now that she made it all up. Will she go to jail? Will anyone ever forgive her or love her again? It's best to stay quiet. A jury's not going to convict an innocent man, after all.

The prosecutor is up for reelection soon, and she needs a high-profile win like this. She can get around the fact that there's no DNA evidence (or any evidence at all) linking the suspect to the victim—he probably used a condom. The suspect has an alibi for the night Brianna says she was raped, but it's far from bulletproof. He doesn't own a gun, but his brother does. He swears he's never met Brianna, but don't they all? Who's going to say, "You got me! I raped her!"?

The cops and the victim say he's the one, and our prosecutor is so tired of not being able to help sexual assault victims. Yes, the win will be big for her career, but it will also legitimately feel good to convict a rapist for once. Never mind the old joke about the guy who drops his keys in one place, but looks for them half a block away because that's where the best light is. She is going to get this guy!

And the jury—well, they're the suspect's peers. They're American citizens, who are outraged by the thought of a man raping a young woman at gunpoint. They'll imagine themselves, their daughters, their sisters being abducted off the street and subjected to such a terrifying violation. They'll see Brianna crying on the stand—mostly because she can't believe it's gotten this far but doesn't know how to stop it—and want to string the guy up by the balls.

Of course, if the suspect were Brianna's classmate, if she'd been drinking and smoking pot when it happened, if she left some embarrassing detail (like the fact that she was drinking and smoking pot) out of her initial report to police and was later called out on it by the defense, if the accused took the stand in a nice suit and explained with controlled indignation that they had consensual sex and she's just mad that he didn't call her the next day, that same jury would have a lot of trouble convicting a nice young man of rape. Maybe he even got a little rough with her, but what did she expect? Why did she drink so much? Why was she wearing a short skirt, if she didn't want someone to take it off, or pretty underwear if she didn't want someone to see it? How do we know she's not lying about this, too? And if we aren't sure, how can we possibly find him guilty?

This guy, though! This stranger, with some kind of record (we know she picked out his mug shot, after all), with a flimsy alibi and access to a gun, he sure *seems* like a rapist. The police and the prosecutors seem sure they found the right guy. And that poor, innocent girl broke down sobbing as she described how hard she tried to fight him—she is definitely acting as if she were raped. How can we deny her justice?

We find the defendant guilty.

Who Is the Imaginary Rapist?

For as long as there's been an America, there have been high-profile instances of false rape reports—especially, it bears repeating, false reports of interracial rapes. A 2015 report on lynching by the Equal Justice Initiative is blunt about what the tragic consequences have been for black men in this country:

> Nearly 25 percent of the lynchings of African Americans in the South [between 1888 and 1950] were based on charges of sexual assault. The mere accusation of rape, even without an identification by the alleged victim, could arouse a lynch mob. The definition of black-on-white "rape" in the South required no allegation of force

because white institutions, laws, and most white people rejected the idea that a white woman would willingly consent to sex with an African American man.[5]

Much as we might like to believe that's all in the past, some white women still fabricate violent crimes committed by imaginary African American men, and their stories are fueled by ongoing stereotypes of black men as insatiable predators.

In 2001, an Iowa State University student named Katie Robb reported to the college that she'd been raped by four large, armed black men and then recanted the next day.[6] In 2009, Pennsylvania mother Bonnie Sweeten called 911 to report that she and her nine-year-old daughter had been kidnapped by two African American men; meanwhile, Sweeten and her daughter were at Disney World.[7] In 2008, Ashley Todd, a volunteer for Republican John McCain's campaign for US president, feigned a mugging by a six-foot-four black supporter of Barack Obama, even going so far as to cut the letter B into her own cheek. (The fact that the B was backwards, because she'd carved it while looking in a mirror, was the first clue that something was amiss.)[8] And in 2011, a Brooklyn nun—or at least, a Brooklyn member of a cultish Christian sect, who identified herself as Sister Mary Turcotte—told detectives she was attacked and raped by a "6-foot, 250-lb. Black man."[9] She later blamed an "emotional break" for her decision to send police out looking for a racist caricature.

Why those women chose to concoct claims of violence is a puzzle I don't have enough information to solve. Why they all chose to blame large African American men, however, is a no-brainer: centuries of systemic racism have primed us all to fear the black brute with a ceaseless drive to possess white women.

But two of the highest-profile false accusation cases in my lifetime have involved African American victims accusing white men of rape, evoking a legacy of sexual domination of black women by white men that goes back to the horror of slavery. By the late twentieth century, US culture had progressed on such matters to approximately the point where we remain today: simultaneously deeply racist and deeply ashamed of being called racist. So, in their rush to be perceived as supporting victimized African American girls and women, public figures ranging from black preachers to white feminists, from news reporters to prosecutors, threw their muscle behind two people who were just plain lying. And that, boys and girls, is why every internet discussion of false accusations now involves some white dude bleating "Tawana Brawley!" or "Duke lacrosse!" as though nothing else needs to be said.

Whether or not you're already familiar with these cases, *plenty* more needs to be said. Both are high-profile examples that have a lot to teach us about who makes a false report, whom we imagine to be capable of rape, and how other people's agendas can work to compound a single, terrible lie.

Tawana Brawley was just fifteen in November 1987, when she went missing for four days and then turned up in a garbage bag with feces in her hair and racial and sexual epithets written on her body. Brawley wasn't suffering from exposure after her ordeal in the New York cold, nor was she malnourished, after four days ostensibly spent in the woods. The crotch of her jeans was burned, but her body was not. Her only injury was a bruise that did not seem all that recent. There was no physical evidence that she'd been raped.

At the emergency room, Brawley pretended to be unconscious but flunked a reflex test that said otherwise. She resisted medical professionals' attempts to force open her eyes but eventually opened them herself when a doctor said, "I know you can hear me."

According to a grand jury report published in the *New York Times*, "Tawana Brawley never provided a detailed account of her allegations, a detailed description of her alleged attackers, or named her alleged assailants to anyone."[10] The girl was largely uncommunicative, answering questions by nodding and shaking her head. At some point, she reportedly wrote a note that said, "white cop," and from there, a story emerged that she'd been abducted by two white men, one of them blond, with a light mustache, a badge, and a holster.

All of that detail became "fact" without Brawley opening her mouth. On top of the racial slurs written in charcoal on her body, it was enough to get the FBI involved.

It was also enough to get Reverend Al Sharpton involved. In concert with lawyers Vernon Mason and Alton C. Maddox, Sharpton "[used] the case for various purposes, from raising black consciousness to raising cold cash," wrote journalist Edwin Diamond in *New York* magazine.[11] The story of a pretty, young black woman raped by white cops was irresistible to the media. Brawley's legal advisors took full advantage of that fact.

After a white police officer in the area coincidentally committed suicide, he became the focus of an investigation that would bring several innocent men—friends of the deceased—under intense suspicion in the long months before the grand jury concluded that no abduction and rape had taken place.

According to a boyfriend of Tawana's who gave an interview to *New York Newsday*, Tawana and her mother, Glenda, fabricated the story together but never intended for it to become public. The boyfriend said they went to such extremes to keep Glenda's husband, Ralph King, from beating Tawana for staying out all night. Allegedly, King had done so in the past, and his wife and stepdaughter had good reason to fear him: King's documented history of domestic violence includes a conviction for killing his first wife.

But once the police, the FBI, and the Sharpton-led legal/PR team got involved, a self-protective lie that was meant to stay within Tawana's troubled family instead thrust her into the national spotlight for months. And it all happened without her saying a word.

Crystal Mangum, the woman who in 2006 accused three members of the Duke University lacrosse team of raping her after a party at which she'd performed as a stripper, said a lot more than Brawley, but her own words were suspicious and often contradictory. Without the single-mindedness of prosecutor Mike Nifong propelling it forward, the case would have died out long before becoming a cause célèbre of feminists and, later, men's rights activists playing "gotcha" with anyone who suggests that rape victims are subjected to excessive scrutiny.

Today, it should be noted, we know a whole lot about Crystal Mangum that wasn't known in 2006. We know, for instance, that in December 2010, when Mangum was thirty-two, she was convicted of misdemeanor child abuse for lighting her boyfriend's clothes on fire in a bathtub, with her kids present in the apartment. We know that in April of the following year, she was charged with fatally stabbing a different boyfriend. And we know there was no evidence that the rape she accused those lacrosse players of ever happened. We know she lied and lied, and when confronted with evidence that would disprove her story, she just kept changing it.

I'm going to go out on a limb and say that Crystal Mangum is *proba-bly* not someone I'd like to hang out with.

But as Akiba Solomon wrote at *Colorlines* after Mangum's indict-ment in the stabbing, the African American mother of three has also received more than her share of pain and criminal violence: "Mangum isn't what TV newsmagazines and tabloids call an 'innocent victim.' But she seems to be a victim, nonetheless."[12]

Solomon goes on to sketch out Mangum's troubled past. At fourteen, she had a boyfriend twice her age, who allegedly "shared" her with three of his friends. (She filed a police report but never followed up on it, only doc-umenting the incident in her personal diary.) Hospital records subpoenaed during the rape investigation show she'd been diagnosed with bipolar dis-order and prescribed antipsychotic drugs. On the night she alleged she was raped, she was visibly impaired by drugs and alcohol.

All of those things—previous claims of rape, mental illness, intoxication—show up in the profiles of many false accusers *and* many genuine victims. So I actually want to applaud the authorities in Durham County for taking her initial claims seriously. Reports of serious crimes should always be taken seriously, even when they come from imperfect citi-zens who will make lousy witnesses.

But taking marginalized, mentally ill, intoxicated, or generally odious people seriously does not mean abandoning all common sense. According to a "Summary of Conclusions" released by the Office of the Attorney General of North Carolina—following a reinvestigation of the horren-dously botched rape case catalyzed by Mangum's lies—the accuser had (what should have been) obvious credibility issues from the get-go. Not what passes for "credibility issues" in rape culture, like a history of drink-ing and having sex voluntarily, but *actual* credibility issues, like changing major parts of your story, identifying a man who wasn't there as one of your attackers, and showing up to a meeting with special prosecutors so high on prescription medications you're slurring your words and unable to walk in a straight line. *That* kind. As the "Summary of Conclusions" puts it:

> While prosecutors acknowledge that rape and sexual assault victims often have some inconsistencies in their accounts of a traumatic

event, in this case, the inconsistencies were so significant and so contrary to the evidence that the State had no credible evidence that an attack occurred in the house that night.[13]

In May 2006, three men were indicted for first-degree rape, first-degree sexual offense, and first-degree kidnapping. Several months later, after the lacrosse team had been suspended, their coach had been fired, and many feminists had thrown their support behind Mangum, the North Carolina State Bar brought ethics charges against Nifong. They alleged that the prosecutor made inflammatory and inaccurate pretrial statements to the media, positing a "deep racial motivation" for the fabricated crime, and painting the accused as suspiciously uncooperative, among other things. (Over 150 other things, to be exact.) More damningly, the Bar accused Nifong of sitting on potentially exculpatory DNA evidence for months.

Testing of Mangum's rape kit originally showed no evidence of semen, blood, or saliva, which prompted Nifong to request more sensitive testing. On round 2, a new lab "found DNA characteristics from up to four different males on epithelial and sperm fractions from several pieces of evidence from the rape kit," according to the Bar's amended complaint.[14] The trouble for Nifong was, the lab concluded that all of the Duke lacrosse players could be excluded as the owners of that DNA. Undaunted, the prosecutor allegedly requested an abridged report from the lab, pointedly failed to reveal the full testing results to the defense, and then lied about it in writing.

"From his very first involvement in this case, Mr. Nifong weaved a web of deception," said the State Bar's attorney, Doug Brock, in his closing arguments at Nifong's June 2007 ethics hearing. After less than an hour of deliberation, the disciplinary panel voted to disbar him.

Without Crystal Mangum's original lies, none of this would have happened. But without the district attorney's inexplicable obsession with wringing a conviction out of a mentally ill woman's constantly changing story, the case would never have gotten as far as it did. When we treat false arrests, prosecutions, and convictions as problems that can be avoided simply by never trusting a woman who says she was raped, we let serious flaws in our justice system go unchecked. And sometimes, those same flaws send innocent men to prison for rapes that really did happen.

"Wolfpacks and Wilding": The Central Park Jogger

On April 19, 1989, a young white woman jogged into New York's Central Park one evening after work. She left the park hours later, on a stretcher, expected to die. The woman had been raped and beaten so severely, she lost three-quarters of the blood in her body and needed to have one eye removed. With a fractured skull and swollen brain, she remembered nothing, including her own name. Coworkers of hers who learned about the attack on the news would identify her as twenty-eight-year-old investment banker Trisha Meili.

As Sydney H. Schanberg wrote in the *Village Voice* thirteen years later, "The atmosphere surrounding this crime was, modestly put, emotional. The city was crackling with racial aggravation."[15] Against the backdrop of a mayoral race between Rudy Giuliani and David Dinkins—who, when he won, would become the first African American mayor of that great "melting pot"—police rounded up five black and Latino teenagers, who were connected to a group of about thirty young men who said they'd been out "wilding" that night.

Neither the New York City detectives on the case nor the average American in 1989 knew what the hell "wilding" meant, but the teens' slang fit perfectly with persistent stereotypes of dark-skinned men as uncivilized savages. Within days, the term would enter the national lexicon via breathless news reports about roving gangs of young men of color, committing property crimes and violent assaults with no apparent motivation, method, or remorse. In her 2011 book *The Central Park Five*, Sarah Burns writes that it was just one example of the "blatantly racist language and imagery" journalists routinely used to describe the crime.

> Animal references abounded. When referring to the suspects, the words *wolfpack* and *wilding* were used hundreds of times and came to be emblems of the case, a shorthand that nearly everyone used and that still elicits memories of the Central Park Jogger's rape in many minds. The term *wilding* came to embody the coverage.[16]

It also came to embody the attitudes of police and much of the public toward the five young men accused: to wit, they were dangerous animals who needed to be put down.

Under harsh questioning, those five adolescents, the oldest of them just sixteen, broke down and confessed to raping and nearly killing Trisha Meili. Not long after, all five recanted, but the damage was done.

The Central Park Five's coerced confessions "were factually wrong; and one police officer testified that the wording in three of the written confessions was his own,"[17] according to Columbia University law professor Patricia J. Williams, who sat in on the trial. Writing in the *Nation* in 2013, she recalls that "the footprints and semen didn't match; there was no blood or mud on the defendants' clothing," and of course, there's the pesky fact that the defendants recanted their confessions.[18] None of that slowed things down.

Despite a total lack of physical evidence connecting them to this unspeakably violent crime, the Central Park Five were convicted—four as juveniles and the sixteen-year-old, Kharey Wise, as an adult. The younger boys served out sentences of five to seven years; Wise was released from prison in 2002, after a convicted serial rapist and killer named Matias Reyes apparently found Jesus and confessed to the crime. That confession, unlike those of the Central Park Five, was backed up by DNA evidence.

In 2014, the Central Park Five settled a civil rights lawsuit against the city of New York for a reported $40 million.

Reassessing Our Red Flags

Just as one rape is too many, so is one false conviction of an innocent person. Unfortunately, the chief strategies we employ to avoid trying and convicting innocent people accused of rape—distrust of women's testimony, victim blaming, trivialization, and denial—neither prevent false convictions nor offer survivors of sex crimes any real hope of justice. We need to change the way we think about sexual violence to better protect the rights of both victims and the accused.

First, we must fight the myth that false reports of rape are common. The fact is, men are far more likely to be victims of sexual assault than of lying, vindictive women. Nearly 2 percent of American men report having been raped in their lifetimes, and a full 20 percent report having been victims of other sexual violence.[19] Those numbers might very well be low, given the stigma associated with being a male survivor. That's a real public health and safety crisis for men, but it's one of many problems that are obscured when so much of our focus remains on the relatively small prospect of false accusations.

We also need to remind ourselves that when friends, family, police, prosecutors, and juries choose not to believe a victim—or when the justice system railroads the wrong suspect—*a rapist goes free to rape again*. As a society, we probably won't get that through our collective thick skull until we stop thinking of rape as an accident, a moment of sexual incontinence easily provoked by revealing clothing and flirtation. As long as we see rapists as average men overcome by lust in a particular moment, as opposed to the opportunistic predators they typically are, we will keep giving criminals a pass to commit more violence in our communities.

Our refusal to be realistic about rapists' behavior leads to a terrific irony: women who do file false reports, wanting to be believed, usually fabricate a scenario that sounds not like the typical rape but like our cultural idea of "rape-rape." The imaginary rapist is a stranger with a weapon; the angelic imaginary victim fought back as hard as she could; the imaginary rape consisted of rough penis-in-vagina sex. You know the drill.

The tidiness of this fiction then appeals to police and prosecutors, who more often encounter rape cases that involve imperfect victims assaulted by people they know, who leave no physical evidence of violence and claim the sex was consensual. It's much easier to indict, try, and convict someone if the narrative of the crime matches our cultural concept of what that sort of crime looks like; because our concept of rape is so divorced from reality, most of us are actually more likely to believe the made-up story than the real one. The woman who admits she was drinking and wearing a tight dress, that she willingly danced or even went to a second location with her rapist, that in the moment, she never even *thought* to try gouging out his eyeballs with her thumbs, has a story full of red flags, in the eyes of investigators. All she's giving them is the "she said" part of a "he said/she said" scenario.

But that's exactly what rape is: one person says "I don't want sex right now," and the other says, "You don't get to decide that." It's ridiculous to act as though there's never any way to determine who's telling the truth, when two people have conflicting stories. Imagine if every pedestrian who reported being hit by a car were thoroughly investigated for evidence of suicidality, while the driver's claim of "I didn't see him there" would be reason enough to drop any charges.

"To move beyond this issue of false reporting," write Lonsway, Archambault, and Lisak, "one of the most important steps we can take is therefore to recognize that the 'red flags' that raise suspicion in the minds of most people actually represent the typical dynamics of sexual assault in the real world."[20] When we're all—including investigators—nitpickingly skeptical of stories that sound like real life but foolishly credulous of those that sound mythical, how can we expect justice to be served?

PART II

LAW AND ORDER

CHAPTER 5

To Serve and Protect

"All my bitches, take some shots!"

When Pittsburgh Steelers quarterback Ben Roethlisberger addressed those words to a group of female college students he'd purchased drinks for on March 5, 2010, he probably wasn't expecting them to end up in a police report. That delightful toast disgusted at least one woman enough that she left the VIP room in a Milledgeville, Georgia, bar, where Roethlisberger and his people had invited her to party. But others, including four sorority sisters of the woman who would be referred to in the national press as Jane Doe—stayed in the VIP room the famous athlete had invited them to share.

According to police statements provided by those four friends, after Roethlisberger's bitches took some shots, one of his bodyguards led an extremely drunk Jane out a side door, with the quarterback following soon after. Jane's friends immediately recognized that this was a bad idea, given the young woman's level of intoxication.

A sorority sister named Ann Marie approached the bodyguard. "This isn't right," she said. "My friend is back there with Ben. She needs to come back right now."

The bodyguard, Ann Marie wrote in her statement, said, "I don't know what you are talking about."

Other friends attempted to open the door Jane had disappeared through and to speak with the bar's owner, Rocky.

"I told Rocky that {Jane} was too drunk to be back there," said Jane's friend Nicole in a handwritten statement to police, "and he told me not to worry because Ben would not do anything to ruin his reputation."

Rocky can probably be forgiven for thinking Roethlisberger wouldn't be so stupid as to assault a woman he'd plucked from a room full of witnesses, given that he'd been publicly accused of rape before. In 2009, a Nevada woman sued Roethlisberger in civil court over an alleged 2008 rape, which was still pending on that night in Milledgeville. (The case eventually ended in 2012, with an undisclosed settlement.[1]) The woman, a casino host at a hotel where Roethlisberger was staying for a celebrity golf tournament, claimed the football star called her to his room to fix a broken television and then overpowered and raped her.[2]

According to Ann Marie's and Nicole's statements, Jane emerged from the locked room about ten minutes later, crying, and immediately told them Ben Roethlisberger had penetrated her, despite her repeated pleas with him not to. (Ann Marie's statement says Jane told her that "he had unprotected sex with her," while Nicole's says flatly, "He raped her.")

Jane's own statement fills in the details. After the bodyguard escorted her to the empty hallway, he told her to wait there. Roethlisberger arrived shortly thereafter, with his penis hanging out of his pants. Jane told him that wasn't okay and tried to leave, but the door she opened led into a bathroom. The rest of her statement reads:

> He followed me into the bathroom & shut the door behind him. I still said no, this is not OK, and then he had sex with me. He said it was OK. He then left without saying anything. I went out of the hallway/door to the side, where I saw my friends. We left {the bar} and went to the first police car we saw.[3]

Bystanders Revisited

Before I tell you about the police officer they found, can we take a moment to celebrate Jane Doe's sorority sisters, and how hard they tried to look after their drunk friend? This is what gets lost in pearl-clutching articles about "hookup culture," binge-drinking college kids, and overtly sexual sorority girls.[4] Jane's friends were well aware that she was too drunk to be left alone with a guy, and they worked very hard to intervene when she was—pleading for help from the bodyguard and club owner, trying their best to get past the door Jane had disappeared behind. They immediately believed her when she told them what happened, and they went with her to find help. During a night of bar hopping, they remained aware of the risks and worked together to keep each other safe while enjoying the same type of partying men can generally do without fear. When the worst happened anyway, they acted swiftly to look after their friend.

It's a perfect example of that simultaneously heartwarming and heartbreaking "Leave no woman behind" approach Robert Jensen wrote about. Sometimes, no matter how prepared you are for battle, a soldier is lost.

But how many rapes *have* been prevented, do you suppose, by young women looking out for each other? We only hear about it when the system breaks down, but young women all over this country, every damned night, are looking out for each other at parties, dragging friends out of dicey situations, following their guts, walking away, and putting their besties to bed with a stuffed animal and a puke bucket. They may not accept finger-wagging, Puritanical bullshit about abstaining from alcohol and sex to protect themselves from violent crime, but young women are *trying*.

It would be great if they could get a little more help from men.

Sergeant Blash, Superfan

And now we come to the police officer Jane, Ann Marie, and Nicole found when they left the club. Sergeant Jerry Blash, as it turns out, was such a football fan that when he spotted Roethlisberger earlier that night, he'd posed for pictures with the star. There's a group shot in which Roethlisberger has an arm around Blash's neck and an apparent selfie of the two with their heads close together, Roethlisberger smiling while Blash does his best imitation of Derek Zoolander's "Blue Steel."

Blash's narrative of what happened after Jane and her friends approached him, a copy of which is available (along with all the other statements) on the *Smoking Gun* website, goes like so:

> She advised me that while in Capitol City (the club), she was sexually assaulted or sexually manipulated by the suspect around 130

hours. She also stated that one of the suspect's bodyguards escorted
her to a back room/hallway area where the suspect was. Once there
she stated the suspect asked her for sex. At this time it is unclear
to what happened after this point due to the complainant's recollection being foggy from to [*sic*] her intoxication. However she did
write a statement of what she thought happened.... The suspect
stated that he remembers the complainant being around him, but
advising her she was too drunk after observing her fall. He then
walked away from her.[5]

That would sound fairly reasonable, if it weren't for a couple of little
problems. First, there's Jane's statement, which is perfectly clear on the
point that Roethlisberger penetrated her after she told him not to. It's not
a matter of what she *thought* happened but what she *says* happened.

And the second problem, as the *New Yorker*'s Amy Davidson put it:
"Blash admitted to investigators that he went straight to Roethlisberger's party... and told them about the accusations in crude and dismissive
terms, calling the woman 'this bitch.'"[6]

Anthony J. Barravecchio, an off-duty police officer traveling with
Roethlisberger's entourage, reported that Blash said words to the effect
of, "We have a problem. This drunken bitch, drunk off her ass, is accusing
Ben of rape. This pisses me off. Women can do this. It's bullshit, but we've
got to do this, we've got to do a report. This is BS. She's making shit up."[7]

An Officer Clay, who accompanied Blash when he went to interview
Roethlisberger, told a Georgia Bureau of Investigation agent that the quarterback "said she probably started it because he wouldn't give her the time
of day, basically... she was rude to him so he kind of ignored her throughout the night. I can't tell what he felt, but it seemed like he felt like she was
the one who instigated it because she wasn't given the time of day."[8]

Instigated what? The penetration she says she didn't want and he
says didn't happen?

Oh no, wait, I get it. She started a *conspiracy* to get Ben Roethlisberger arrested for rape, while she was literally too drunk to stand up
straight. As revenge for being ignored, this theory goes, Jane made up a
story that she was raped *and* convinced her friends to back her up. And

her friends were all, "Sure, we'll totally make false statements to the police, in hopes of sending an innocent man to prison, because you're irritated that a famous athlete didn't pay attention to you! What are friends for?"

Not too surprisingly, prosecutors declined to charge Roethlisberger with anything—in part because the alleged victim expressed that she did not wish for the case to proceed. (Davidson notes wryly, "One issue for her and her family, apparently, was that they didn't trust the police."[9]) Ben Roethlisberger claims he committed no crime that night, and I do not personally have enough information to say any different. Sometimes, as you'll see by the end of this chapter, a bizarre and incredible story *is* the truth. But regardless of what happened that night, the way police handled the complaint reeks like the Steelers' locker room.

Sergeant Blash, the only officer to interview Roethlisberger about these allegations, resigned from the Milledgeville Police Department one day before the Georgia Bureau of Investigation made documents pertaining to the case public.

Do the Police Trust Women?

Sadly, although the fact that the accused was a celebrity makes it an exceptional case, Blash can't be dismissed as an anomaly. A recent study of eleven police and sheriff's departments in the Southeast United States, conducted by sociologist Amy Dellinger Page and published in the journal *Feminist Criminology*, evaluated officers' "perspectives on sexual assault" via two scales: one that measured "rape myth acceptance" and another that measured respondents' perception of victim credibility.[10]

The "rape myth acceptance" scale measured agreement with statements like "Any victim can resist a rapist if he or she really wants to," "Women who dress provocatively are inviting sex," "Many women secretly wish to be raped," "A woman is responsible for preventing her own rape," "Any man can be raped," and the like, on a five-point scale: strongly disagree, disagree, neither disagree nor agree, agree, and strongly agree.

For the most part, the officers responding didn't fall for the most egregious rape myths—93 percent at least agreed, for instance, that any woman can be raped. But then, only 66 percent agreed that any man can be raped, and a full 5.9 percent strongly disagreed with that statement. (One is curious about what kind of men those other 34 percent believe to be rape-proof. Perhaps they have some lessons for the rest of us?)

Meanwhile, 16.6 percent agreed and 6.1 percent strongly agreed with the statement "Any victim can resist a rapist if he or she really wants to." So that's 22.7 percent of cops who apparently think victims just didn't want *not* to be raped badly enough? That they could have gotten away if they'd really tried? Fantastic.

And then there's the statement most relevant to what went down in Milledgeville: "Women falsely report rape to call attention to themselves." The good news: 10 percent of respondents strongly disagreed with that, and another 30 percent disagreed. However, 17.6 percent agreed, and another 2.6 percent agreed strongly. So that's more than 20 percent agreement with one of the most pernicious rape myths there is.

To be fair, the statement is worded somewhat ambiguously; 38.4 percent chose the "neither" option, which is a higher number of fence sitters than there were for any other statement on the "rape myth acceptance" scale. If one reads it as "Some number of women falsely report rape to call attention to themselves," then one would have to agree; the facts bear that out. If, however, one reads it as "Women *often* falsely report rape to call attention to themselves," then a person who knows the facts would have to disagree. As it is, "neither agree nor disagree" probably is the safest bet, and this is why surveys like this can be frustrating.

But. *But.* Let us not forget what this census was measuring: acceptance of rape myths. And the myth, in this case, is not that the very occasional woman will fabricate a sexual assault story to garner sympathy and attention. The myth is that women, as a class, are so likely to do that— so many are "bitches" just "making shit up"—you cannot and should not trust any woman who reports a rape.

"Unfounded" Cases

That interpretation is echoed in research conducted by sociologist Martin D. Schwartz when he was a visiting research fellow at the National Institute of Justice between 2004 and 2006. Working with 428 first respondents from fifteen municipal and campus departments in several states, researchers posed the question: "What percentage of rape reports do you think (your gut feeling) never happened; they are false reports? We don't mean dismissed cases, but flat out never happened?"[11]

The phrasing was meant to keep the focus on the officers' personal feelings, as opposed to giving them an opportunity to mindlessly spit back the department's "unfounded" rate. The FBI requires all US police departments to submit their crime statistics to the annual Uniform Crime Report, including cases deemed "unfounded." As I noted in Chapter 4, the FBI defines "unfounded" cases as "determined *through investigation* to be false or baseless" (emphasis mine), but individual police departments often have different definitions.

Happily, 27.3 percent of Schwartz's respondents said their gut estimate of the false rape report rate was between 0 and 10 percent—consistent with the most reliable data we have.

Unhappily, "a similar number, 28.8%, came up with an estimate that was at 50% or above, and some estimated that 95 to 100% were false reports."[12]

Some number of actual, working police officers in the twenty-first century said they believed 100 percent of rape reports are false. ONE HUNDRED PERCENT. What do you even do with that?

Writes Schwartz: "Overall, the 428 patrol officers who answered this question estimated that 32.7% of all reported cases were false. This is an extraordinary finding for a group of people who almost invariably got the questions on a rape myth scale 'correct.'"[13]

Did I mention he tested the same officers on their acceptance of common rape myths, using a scale similar to Page's? Schwartz found, as she did, that most respondents gave the "correct" answers, implying that they didn't subscribe to victim-blaming stereotypes. But it's unclear whether that shows a genuine decline in sexist attitudes or is simply a matter of "impression management"—which is sociologist for "lying to make someone think the best of you." Schwartz's interviews with detectives point toward the latter.

We learned earlier that police were quick to say all of the right things, including and especially the fact that all cases were investigated dispassionately by the detectives, written up objectively, and passed on without prejudice. Yet when the microphone was off (or

even while the microphone was on), again and again these detectives admitted that there were a large number of cases where they
"unfounded" the case rather than continue with it. Evidently if they
just plain didn't believe the victim, then this did not count as a case
of "real rape" that would be turned over to the prosecutors. If the
victim was treated poorly, and she chose not to continue with her
complaint, this was another sign that the case could be ignored.[14]

So basically, if police make the process of reporting a rape so dreadful
that victims decide seeking justice isn't worth it, they don't have to do all
the hard work of investigating a case. That's a neat trick.

Worse, it's shockingly common. In 2010, a *Baltimore Sun* investigation of FBI data revealed that over the previous four years, "more than 30
percent of the cases investigated by detectives each year [were] deemed
unfounded, five times the national average."[15] Forty percent of emergency
calls about rape in Baltimore were not even investigated.

After reported data suggested New Orleans had 43 percent fewer
rapes than twenty-four other high-crime cities, the Department of Justice ordered a review of the city's "forcible rape" reporting. The findings
were bleak: "The NOPD misclassified 46% of the offenses tested to sexual
battery, miscellaneous offense or Unfounded (UNF) rather than forcible
rape."[16] *Almost half* of reported rapes were called something else in the
official paperwork.

These were not accidents or misunderstandings. In a 2014 article
titled "How to Lie with Rape Statistics: America's Hidden Rape Crisis,"
University of Kansas law professor Corey Rayburn Yung writes that Baltimore and New Orleans, along with St. Louis and Philadelphia, "lowered
their official counts of rape incidents through three difficult-to-detect
techniques."[17] First, "unfounding" complaints without a thorough investigation; second, reclassifying rape complaints as lesser offenses; and third,
"police officers in those jurisdictions often failed to create any written
record that a victim made a rape complaint to eliminate the incident from
the UCR data."[18]

It's easy to make it look like you've got a remarkably rape-free city, if
you stick to a consistent policy of minimizing sexual violence and manipu-
lating data.

Military Malfeasance

That approach also works nicely for those charged with serving and protecting the entire country.

When I started writing this book, I expected to rely heavily on Helen Benedict's 2009 book, *The Lonely Soldier*, and Kirby Dick's corresponding 2012 documentary, *The Invisible War*, for information on rape in the military. Both are thorough, powerful, and highly recommended; *The Invisible War* even inspired then secretary of defense Leon Panetta to move all military sexual assault investigations up the chain from commanders to colonels, and call for a special victims unit in each branch of the armed services.

But starting in early 2013, military rape suddenly became a hot topic, with constantly updating news. *The Invisible War* was up for an Academy Award, and the Senate Armed Services Committee held its first hearings on sexual assault in the military in a decade. The media exploded with talk about the film, the hearings, the Defense Department's annual report on sexual assaults, and the complex, shocking problems they all highlighted.

An Associated Press report revealed that nearly a third of all military commanders fired between 2005 and 2013 were released because of sexual offenses.[19] Based on anonymous surveys, the Pentagon estimated that 26,000 soldiers were victims of sexual violence in 2012, but only 3,374 of those assaults were reported; 2,610 investigations were completed; 594 courts martial were convened, and 302 went to trial. A mere 238 cases ended in a conviction.[20]

In May 2013 Air Force Lieutenant Colonel Jeffrey Krusinski was charged with sexual battery. Although that charge would later be downgraded to assault, of which he would eventually be acquitted, it's worth noting that Krusinski's mug shot shows scratches and bruises on his face, delivered by a woman who told police that he'd drunkenly groped her in a parking lot. Also worth noting: Krusinski was—wait for it—head of the USAF's Sexual Assault Prevention and Response program.[21]

His arrest came a month after Air Force Lieutenant General Craig Franklin used his authority to overturn a jury verdict that found Lieutenant Colonel James Wilkerson guilty of sexually assaulting a woman in his home after a party. Describing a six-page letter Franklin wrote to Air Force Secretary Michael Donley justifying the decision, the Associated Press reported:

Franklin, commander of the 3rd Air Force at Ramstein Air Base in Germany, said a host of details led to his decision, including that the victim turned down offers to be driven home from the party, didn't accurately describe the house layout and gave a version of events that he did not find credible. He said Wilkerson was a doting father with a good career and it would be "incongruent" for him to leave his wife in bed, go downstairs and assault a sleeping woman he'd only met earlier that evening.[22]

Missouri senator Claire McCaskill, who at the time was working on a bill that would remove commanders' authority to overturn jury verdicts, told the AP, "This letter was like fingernails on a blackboard to me."[23] Girl, tell me about it.

A week after Krusinski's arrest, an army sergeant first class, in charge of *his* battalion's Sexual Assault Prevention and Response program at Fort Hood, was under investigation for two counts of sexual assault and allegedly forcing a subordinate into prostitution. Although he went unnamed in the press at the time, in March 2015, Sergeant First Class Gregory McQueen pled guilty to fifteen of twenty-one charges, including pandering, and received a sentence of twenty-four months. Army reports indicate that McQueen recruited female privates who were desperate for money into a prostitution ring.[24]

Suddenly, it made a lot more sense that military sexual trauma was so ubiquitous—if victims were reporting their assaults to sexual predators, no wonder they weren't getting justice.

And even when it wasn't *that* bad, it was still pretty bad. Writing in the *Atlantic*, Garance Franke-Ruta outlines the hurdles victims face:

The basic problem with the military justice system in cases of sexual assault—as outlined in horrific detail by the military women and experts featured in *Invisible War* and by members of Congress during hearings—is that it combines the dynamics of the workplace with the problem of crime investigation. A woman who is assaulted and wants redress has to report the crime to her commanding officer—her boss—and press charges against one of her colleagues in the military, often someone who also works for her boss, all the while continuing to live near her attacker in a thick soup of overlapping interpersonal and professional relationships between her and his friends.[25]

Beyond that, the commanding officer has a strong incentive to decide allegations of rape are unfounded—it will reflect poorly on his leadership if crimes are happening under his nose—and women who report rape can find themselves penalized for "adultery."

New York senator Kirsten Gillibrand, who spearheaded a bill to remove sexual assault prosecutions from the chain of command entirely, told *PBS Newshour* in July 2013:

> For those victims who have been courageous enough to report these cases, 62 percent have said they have been retaliated against for reporting those cases. Of the tens of thousands who didn't report incidents of sexual assault, rape, and unwanted sexual assault contact, the reason they give us is they don't trust the chain of command, that they think nothing will be done, or that they fear retaliation, or they have seen someone else be retaliated against.[26]

I believe the correct military terminology for this situation is "FUBAR."

On the upside, legislators saw in this an opportunity for bipartisan progress—because everybody loves the military and hates rape, right?—and got cracking on reforms. On the downside, Gillibrand's bill eventually failed, and conservatives were quick to blame the military rape crisis on young men and women living in close quarters. When Senator McCaskill interfered with the nomination of Lieutenant General Susan Helms for vice commander of the Air Force Space Command, citing concerns about Helms's judgment in a past sexual assault case, *Wall Street Journal* columnist James Taranto declared it evidence of "a war on men—a political campaign against sexual assault in the military that shows signs of becoming an effort to criminalize male sexuality."[27]

Once again, I can't help but notice that it's not feminists who equate "male sexuality" with the desire to rape any woman who wanders by.

Setting that aside, what these "if you let women in, it's bound to happen" arguments leave out—besides everything decent and reasonable—is the fact that, owing to sheer percentages, more than 50 percent of military sexual assaults involve male victims. Just over 6 percent of women serving have reported sexual violence, and less than 2 percent of men have. But as of 2010, there were 210,000 women on active duty and about 1.2 million men. A far greater proportion of women are being assaulted, but a greater number of individual men are suffering sexual trauma. The crisis has nothing to do with horny young people in close quarters and everything to do with a culture of toxic masculinity and institutional secrecy.

Extreme Victim Blaming

What all of this tells us is that soldiers and law enforcement officers are just as affected by rape culture as laypeople—only, when they don't believe a victim's story, they have the power to punish her. Just as being falsely accused of rape can plunge an innocent victim into a nightmare journey through the criminal justice system, so can reporting a real one. When we talk about sexual violence and false accusations, we must also remember the stories of women who were arrested and prosecuted for reporting their own rapes.

In 1997, a legally blind Madison, Wisconsin, woman named Patty was raped at knifepoint in her own bed. She called police and underwent a hospital examination but was unable to identify her attacker. Patty had been sexually abused as a child and had reported two attempted rapes to police when she was younger. Pressed to think of anyone who might have done this, she named her daughter's boyfriend, who resembled what she could make out of the rapist. But that young man had a solid alibi.

Because she suggested he investigate the wrong man, and because he apparently didn't believe her vision was as substantially impaired as she claimed, Detective Tom Woodmansee became convinced that Patty had made the whole thing up. In his report of her questioning, Woodmansee writes, "I told [Patty] that her vision does not even appear to be noticeably bad to me and she stated 'I don't think it is that bad.'"[28] Patty's ophthalmologist would later submit a court brief explaining that her vision is 5/200 in both eyes, "considerably worse than legally blind."[29]

The Madison district attorney's office told journalist Bill Lueders, author of the book *Cry Rape: The True Story of One Woman's Harrowing Quest for Justice*, that she "behaved in a manner wholly incompatible with" their image of a rape victim.[30] Perhaps that explains why Woodmansee and another detective, Linda Draeger, encouraged Patty to confess that she'd invented the rape story. She eventually did, telling the detectives, "I'll say whatever you want."

Here's a taste of how that conversation went, from Woodmansee's own report:

> I asked her, "Do you believe that I know this is a lie," to which she responded by saying, "yeah." [Patty] then responded by saying, "Okay, I'm lying." I asked her why and she stated she did not know why. I told her I found it difficult to believe she would not have a reason for making this up and she stated, "I'm honest, I don't really know why." I asked [Patty] at what point did she decide in her mind to make this up or was it spontaneous. [Patty] stated, "I'm sorry, I'm very sorry, I didn't mean for this to happen." I asked [Patty] if she has ever told anyone else that she was lying about this incident and she stated she did not. I asked her, "Did you ever consider telling me that you're lying" and she stated, "no."[31]

Patty recanted her confession the next day but was charged with filing a false report—a charge later dropped when DNA tests failed to produce a match between semen found in her bed and any man she knew. Patty sued the city of Madison and underwent a lengthy, humiliating series of depositions. A judge dismissed the case.

In 2001, the Wisconsin State Crime Laboratory reexamined the DNA and found a match on file: Joseph Bong, who was by then in prison for robbing a hotel and sexually assaulting the clerk. Convicted of raping Patty, Bong was sentenced to an additional fifty years in prison.

The city of Madison eventually apologized to Patty and offered her $35,000 for her trouble.

Sara Reedy was nineteen and working alone at a Cranberry Township, Pennsylvania, gas station when an armed man came in and held up the store for $600. He then held a gun to Sara's head and demanded that she perform oral sex on him.

For reasons best known to himself, the detective who took her statement in the hospital, Frank Evanson, almost immediately decided that Sara had fabricated the sexual assault story to cover up her *own* theft of the

$600. Despite knowing of another recent assault under similar circumstances, Evanson simply dismissed the possibility that Reedy was telling the truth. A rape kit was collected but never tested.

Reedy was charged with theft, receiving stolen property, and filing a false report. Pregnant at the time, she was turned away by a local victims' services center, and lost the trust of friends and even some family members, who took the police's word over hers.

After several months—and only a few weeks before Reedy's trial was scheduled—a man named Wilbur Brown was arrested for another convenience store sexual attack. During the interrogation, he confessed to orally raping Reedy and assaulting a third young woman; eventually, he would plead guilty to ten sexual assaults and be sentenced to life in prison.

Reedy sued Cranberry Township. The case was thrown out. On appeal, though, she was awarded $1.5 million.

In a January 2013 interview with *Vice* magazine, reporter Natalie Elliott asked Reedy what she'd do differently, if she could go back to that first encounter with Evanston. "I don't think that, in that position, after having been sexually assaulted and robbed at gunpoint, there is necessarily anything that I could have done differently," she said. "I was just in so much shock, and I guess they had a certain expectation of a person who was sexually assaulted. And I didn't live up to that expectation."[32]

Frank Evanson still has a job with the Cranberry Township Police Department.

Fancy Figueroa of Queens, New York, was two weeks pregnant on her sixteenth birthday, in 1997, when a man followed her home from school and snuck into her home. The girl grabbed a knife to defend herself, but her assailant took it from her, chased her into her basement, and raped her.

As with Reedy, authorities went through the motions of taking a rape kit but didn't expect anything to come of it. Because of the pregnancy—by her boyfriend at the time—they assumed she made up the rape story to avoid getting in trouble with her parents. Their belief in this theory was so strong, in fact, that they charged the traumatized high school sophomore with filing a false report, convicted her, and sentenced her to community service. By that point, even her parents didn't believe her.

Nearly seven years went by before a DNA match would identify Vincent Elias as the man who did, indeed, break into the Figueroa home and rape Fancy on her birthday. Elias confessed and was sentenced to twenty-two years, on top of the fifteen he was already serving for two other rapes.[33]

He committed those two rapes after he raped Figueroa—while the city was busy prosecuting her for making it up.

Stranger Than Fiction

As horrible as all of those women's experiences were, New York's Seemona Sumasar endured a post-rape miscarriage of justice that tops them all.

On March 8, 2009, Sumasar tried to get her abusive boyfriend, Jerry Ramrattan, to leave her Far Rockaway home, where he'd been living. Ramrattan took her down to the basement, covered her mouth with duct tape, and according to the *New York Times* account of her testimony at his trial, "held her captive for hours, ordering in Chinese food, watching television and putting a gun to his own head before raping her."[34] When he was gone, Sumasar showered and called 911.

Later, after Sumasar refused to recant her report of the rape, Ramrattan plotted elaborate revenge. He recruited friends to claim they'd been robbed at gunpoint by Sumasar. He showed them pictures of his ex so they could identify her to law enforcement, created fake crime scenes, and coached his friends on how to offer clues that would lead the authorities where he wanted them to go. The plot had such range and depth, it convinced police to arrest Seemona Sumasar and charge her with multiple armed robberies.

Immediately, she told them that Jerry Ramrattan had to be behind the frame-up.

Although Sumasar had alibis for all of the nights in question—including security video that showed her at a casino when one of the robberies supposedly took place—her bail was set at $1 million. Unable to afford it, she spent seven months in jail, separated from her child, awaiting trial for crimes that never happened. The restaurant she owned went out of business. Her home went into foreclosure.

Sumasar was freed only after a police informant tipped off the authorities that her ex-boyfriend was, indeed, connected to the people who claimed she robbed them. Ramrattan was eventually convicted of rape and perjury, and sentenced to thirty-two years in prison.

Notice some distinguishing factors about the women whose stories I've just told. First, they were imperfect victims. Patty didn't tell a completely consistent story and was a survivor of previous sexual assaults. Sumasar had dated her attacker before realizing he was dangerous. Figueroa and Reedy were both young and pregnant—clear evidence that they weren't wide-eyed virgins.

As I hope you've gathered by now, none of these factors should suggest that a person is lying about being raped—in fact, all except the pregnancies are common characteristics of genuine victims. But rape culture tells us that "real" victims don't get confused, misspeak, or tell white lies alongside the description of a true attack. "Real" victims don't make stupid mistakes, have crappy families, or stay with abusive men. And they certainly don't have consensual sex for pleasure, outside of marriage.

Next, note that all of these women were already marginalized in some way. Sumasar and Figueroa are women of color. Patty is disabled, and she and Reedy were both struggling financially. Any one of those details can severely damage victims' credibility in the eyes of law enforcement—not to mention juries and the general public. (For instance, Detective Evanson assumed that Reedy's lack of funds was motive to steal $600, which figured heavily into his refusal to believe she'd been assaulted and robbed.) As long as our image of a "real" rape victim is still a naive, sexually inexperienced, able-bodied, middle-class white woman conked over the head and dragged into an alley by a large, gun-wielding, brown man, other types of people who report rapes are at risk not only of being humiliated and degraded by invasive questioning and a general aura of suspicion, but of being *charged with crimes themselves.*

Think for a moment about how many people believed that Seemona Sumasar, who had no criminal record, was an armed robber who lied about being raped to get revenge on her ex. (For what? Who knows?) Yet they found it easier to believe *that* than to believe that her ex—who did have a record and enough underworld connections to be a paid source for police—went to great lengths to punish her for reporting him and prevent her from testifying.

All of those people believed three separate reports of nonexistent crimes coming from petty criminals but didn't believe a rape victim (previously deemed credible by police on that count, even!) who said her abusive ex-boyfriend and attacker, already a convicted criminal, had set her up.

A catastrophic series of failures like that doesn't happen when you start out believing, in accordance with the statistical probability, that someone who reports a rape is most likely telling the truth. That happens when you start out believing the chance is no greater than fifty-fifty, and if a woman has any possible motive to lie, she will.

That same erroneous belief is at least partially behind the appalling and widespread failure among US police departments to bother testing the evidence they collect from victims.

Missing and Untested Rape Kits

Helena Lazaro was seventeen in 1996, when a man approached her one night at a self-serve car wash in Los Angeles, claiming to have been in a fight, and asked her for a ride to the hospital. Lazaro's instincts told her to flee, and she thought she had time to get into her car and drive away. Before she could, the man held a knife to her throat and demanded that he drive her to a parking lot, where he raped and robbed her.

As investigative reporter Ralph Blumenthal wrote in *Marie Claire* in 2009, Lazaro reported the crime to the first police officer she saw, and submitted to being swabbed, prodded, and combed for a rape kit at a local emergency room, in hopes of identifying her attacker.

Six weeks later, an Indiana truck driver named Charles Courtney raped his wife at knifepoint. She reported the rape but didn't protest when Courtney struck a deal that reduced the charge to sexual battery, a class C felony. Courtney served only five months.

Fortunately, that felony conviction meant his DNA was already on file when he raped a young Ohio woman in 1998, at knifepoint, in a deserted parking lot. Eventually, samples taken from the Ohio victim's rape kit were matched to Courtney via the national Combined DNA Index System, or CODIS, and he was arrested for that rape—three and a half years later.

Meanwhile, Lazaro continued to call the L.A. County Sheriff's Department regularly. In 2007, she was told that her rape kit had been destroyed, along with any hope of catching her attacker. She called a friend at Peace Over Violence, a social service agency that specializes in sexual violence prevention and education, who had a coworker make a call to the sheriff. Writes Blumenthal, "Miraculously, Lazaro's rape kit was found and tested and the DNA results uploaded to CODIS. It matched Courtney's DNA profile."[35] Thirteen years after that evidence was collected.

If Lazaro's rape kit had been tested, and the DNA results entered into CODIS in a timely fashion, authorities could have identified him as a serial rapist after he attacked his wife—instead of pleading him down to a lesser crime that carried a shamefully short sentence.

Now let's take a moment to recall what Page's survey found about law enforcement officers' attitudes about marital rape. That men who rape their wives might also rape other women should surprise exactly no one at this point. But again, as long as we continue to treat rape as an act of sexual incontinence—as opposed to one of deliberate malice—rapists who target their romantic partners will benefit from that misconception. If down deep, we believe the real crime of rape is violating a chaste woman— as opposed to violating another person's bodily autonomy—we'll never take spousal rape as seriously as we do stranger rape. But as the case of Charles Courtney demonstrates, sometimes the same men commit both.

If Courtney had been charged with the crime he actually commit- ted against his wife—rape carried out with a deadly weapon, a class A felony—it's unlikely he would have been free to commit the Ohio rape less than two years later. Or if Helena Lazaro's evidence had been tested fewer than thirteen years after she was attacked, Courtney could have been kept in prison for a very long time. Either one of those actions—and you'd expect both of a functioning justice system—would have prevented at least one more violent crime that we know of.

Instead, Courtney was free after five months for raping one woman at knifepoint and wouldn't be prosecuted for raping Lazaro until more than a decade later. In the meantime, as the Ohio victim told Blumenthal, "He was a trucker driving across the United States. I honestly feel there are more women out there."

Statistically, she's probably right. And that isn't an isolated example. The men who raped Sara Reedy, Fancy Figueroa, and "Patty" all commit- ted more sexual assaults while those victims' rape kits sat untested. A CBS News investigation in 2009 found twelve US cities "said they have no idea how many rape kits in storage are untested."[36] In Detroit that same year, prosecutor Kym Worthy discovered more than 11,000 aging, warehoused rape kits and vowed to process them all. As of early 2014, 1,600 kits had been tested—and 455 suspects identified, with 87 of those serial rapists.[37] In 2011, Los Angeles finished testing a backlog of 6,132 rape kits, which yielded 1,000 matches to DNA already in the system.[38]

In August 2014, *New York Times* reporter Eric Eckholm offered the following explanation for why key evidence in rape cases so often goes ignored:

> The reasons for the backlog, experts say, include constraints on finances and testing facilities, along with a slow recognition among investigators that even when the offender is known, DNA testing might reveal a pattern of serial rapes. And too often, women's advocates say, the kits went untested because of an uncaring and haphazard response to sexual assault charges.[39]

A 2010 article in the *Journal of Community Psychology* by psychologists Debra Patterson and Rebecca Campbell explores why some victims *do* choose to report their rapes to police, despite it all. Both prior research on the topic and Patterson and Campbell's small study of twenty adult female survivors revealed that one of the most common motivations is to prevent the perpetrator from victimizing anyone—including themselves—again.[40] And yet, as we've seen, law enforcement's spotty, suspicious response to sexual assault reports often leaves predators free to attack repeatedly.

This is what happens when rape culture infects the systems we have in place to protect us. Quite simply, we allow violent criminals to go free.

The Right Way to Center an Investigation on the Victim

In January 2013, Human Rights Watch, a nonprofit organization that keeps tabs on abuses of power around the globe, published a policy paper, "Improving Police Response to Sexual Assault." It contains forty pages' worth of recommendations based on the existing literature and interviews with "sex crimes detectives, Sexual Assault Nurse Examiners (SANE nurses), prosecutors, forensic lab chiefs, and/or rape crisis advocates" in four American cities.[41] I strongly encourage you to read it for yourself, if you're into that sort of thing. But right now I want to talk about a subject that takes up nearly half of the document: what it means to investigate sex crimes using a "victim-centered approach."

It means collecting just the basic facts at first, while reassuring the victim that they won't be judged or mistrusted, what the report calls "brief but compassionate initial contact." Pumping someone for details in the immediate aftermath of a trauma is counterproductive, and a "poor inter-action with a first responder can result in the victim deciding not to move forward with the investigation."

It means being mindful of how often a victim is asked to repeat her story and by how many people. The more you're asked the same questions over and over, the more it can start to feel like no one believes you, even if the actual issue is poor communication among investigators. Ideally, the victim should only have to deal with one detective throughout the process, and police and SANE nurses will work together and share information.

It means interviewing victims in a space that's comfortable, safe, and private—whether that's their own home or a room at the police station—and prioritizing their emotional well-being. The report offers some lovely examples of how this plays out in departments that have undertaken delib-erate efforts to improve their interactions with victims:

> The guiding principle for detectives in Philadelphia, according to the former lieutenant in the Special Victims Unit, is "How do you want someone in your family to be treated?" In Kansas City, police start the interview by saying, "We are really glad you are here because you are safe," or "Thank you for being here." They also explain the effects of trauma to victims who may be upset about being unable to remember events chronologically. In Grand Rapids, the sergeant responsible for sex crimes makes a point of regularly reminding her detectives that victims will remember their first con-tact, and that if officers are accusatory, blame the victims, or convey disbelief, "it is all downhill from there."[42]

It's so simple, really: You treat the victim like a human being. You begin with the assumption that this person is telling you the truth about a traumatic event they've experienced, and you treat them as you would like to be treated in that awful situation. You remember that your job is to investigate the crime reported, not interrogate the victim. If your investigation of the crime reveals good reasons to doubt the victim's testimony—as, for instance, the investigations of Tawana Brawley and Crystal Mangum's rape reports did—then you follow that evidence where it leads. But you don't look at a person telling you she's been the victim of a violent crime and immediately start trying to poke holes in her story.

In keeping with this reasoning, the report also recommends that detectives "should be trained to create a non-judgmental environment by reassuring the victim that they are not there to judge the victim's behavior and that nothing the victim did could have given the suspect permission to sexually assault them." This isn't just the nice thing to do; it's also an important part of making sure the victim doesn't leave out crucial information.

When they're worried about being judged, blamed, or punished, survivors of sexual assault don't always include all the pertinent details investigators need to know. They don't want to admit that they were drunk or high, for instance, or that they engaged in some amount of consensual activity before being forced. Later on, though, withholding information like that can come back to haunt them, if a defense attorney uses it to paint them as liars. It's best to get it all out up front, and investigators can facilitate that process by clearly explaining their questions and reassuring victims that they are not on trial.

You'd hope this would go without saying, but "experts also strenuously object to threatening victims implicitly or explicitly with charges for false reporting."[43] Again, a detective is meant to investigate the reported crime, not the person who brings it to their attention. If that investigation supports the conclusion that there was no crime, then sure, police should close the case and maybe even charge the "victim" with false reporting— just as they would if someone lied about being mugged or beaten or burgled. There are systems in place to handle the minority of people who waste police resources for their own inexplicable reasons. Nobody needs to reinvent the wheel for fabricated allegations of sex crimes.

Other things that are helpful in creating a victim-centered approach to investigations: connecting the victim with an advocate, taping the interview, making an effort to follow up as time goes by, and helping the victim access community resources. Collaborating with people outside the department who become involved in an investigation also makes a difference:

> Communication between law enforcement and medical personnel, for example, can assist the investigation by helping the nurse docu-ment and collect evidence. The victim may also be more comfort-able speaking to a nurse in his or her medical capacity and therefore might disclose information that he or she is hesitant to share with law enforcement.[44]

There is much, much more than this to be done, if we want to see the number of reported sexual assaults increase, let alone the number of successfully prosecuted cases. For starters, requiring that all reports of sex crimes be fully investigated, and all rape kits be sent for processing, would be good. Many departments still haven't even gotten that far.

The greatest challenge, though, is changing the culture. Both a law enforcement culture in which one former Philadelphia detective—echoing Milledgeville's Sergeant Blash—reportedly called Special Victims the "Lying Bitches Unit"[45] and the larger society we all live in.

CHAPTER 6

Unreasonable Doubts

The presumption of innocence is a cornerstone of a fair judicial system, ensuring that the state cannot inflict punishment on an accused criminal without a trial, and that the prosecution, not the defense, carries the burden of proof. It helps to protect people who haven't committed a crime—and for that matter, those who have—from being sent to prison (or worse, in states that still have capital punishment) on flimsy or trumped-up evidence. This is an excellent legal standard. I am a fan!

Unfortunately, the *phrase* "presumption of innocence" has been co-opted and corrupted by the general public—and in particular, by people who think it's unfair to *ever* assume that a woman who accuses a man of rape might be telling the truth.

"Whatever happened to 'presumed innocent'?" online commenters immediately ask, whenever someone writes about a high-profile sexual assault case that hasn't yet been to trial. "Whatever happened to 'innocent until proven guilty'?"

The answer, of course, is "nothing." The prosecution will still be expected to prove its case beyond a reasonable doubt, and the jury will be reminded that they cannot vote to convict if the prosecution fails in that duty. What's more, prior to any conviction, reputable journalists commenting on a case will take pains to insure they refer only to the "alleged" criminal, reporting on the fact of an accusation without speculating as to its veracity. And not for nothing, an accused rapist who garners media attention in the internet age will inevitably have hundreds of average-Joe defenders in his corner, reminding us all that nothing has been officially proven yet.

But said average Joes aren't just keeping tabs on government power and journalistic ethics. They're trying to redefine defendants' legal right to the presumption of innocence as a moral obligation for all of society: if a man has not been convicted of rape, we all must presume he didn't do it.

The problem with that, of course, is that automatically offering the accused the benefit of the doubt means automatically denying it to the purported victim.

By the time one person accuses another, either the rape has happened, or it hasn't. The alleged rapist is either guilty or not. Even if we're not privy to the correct answer and never will be, we know that one exists. We also know that the vast majority of the time—over 90 percent, at least—when a police report is made, the answer is, yes, he did it. The victim made the report for the simplest, most obvious reason: because she was raped.

Yet the people who cry, "What about the presumption of innocence?" often behave as though there is no objective answer to "Did he do it?" until the trial is over. As though they think people accused of crimes are *literally* "innocent until proven guilty." I'm not sure how that would work, exactly—once the verdict comes in, would the accused and the victim travel back in time, so the rape in question could either happen or not happen, based on what the jury decided?

If you can't grasp that any person accused of a crime has already either done it or not done it, regardless of what a future jury has to say, you have a very interesting understanding not only of time and space but of the law. How are police supposed to investigate suspects and make arrests if no one is allowed to draw a reasonable inference that someone is guilty until a jury has officially said so? How are prosecutors supposed to meet their burden of proof, so a jury *can* officially say so? In reality, lots of people within the justice system—let alone outside it—start to presume guilt after a certain point, because *that's their job.*

Their job is also to respect the accused's constitutional rights, to make their case in good faith, and to wait for a jury verdict or a guilty plea before they lock anybody up and throw away the key. (They can, of course, still lock people up before trial and set a price for them to rent the key.) But their job is not, in fact, to presume innocence.

It's not our job, either, when we aren't on juries. Sure, it's perfectly reasonable and fair-minded to say something like, "I don't have enough information to know who's lying," or "I believe everyone deserves a fair trial," or "I'm going to withhold judgment until I learn more." It is not, however, reasonable and fair-minded to bleat about the "presumption of innocence" whenever laypeople try to discuss a suspect's possible guilt. It is not reasonable and fair-minded to say, "We can never know what happened, because we weren't there," about *every last report* of rape or sexual assault, and let that be the end of it.

You're not being as objective as possible when you do that; you're betraying a bias against anyone claiming to be a victim. As human beings, we are endowed with discernment, which allows us to make decisions about whom to trust and whom to doubt. We don't always get it right— we fall for urban legends and phishing scams and people who break our hearts, and sometimes, we even sit on juries that collectively come to the wrong conclusion—but we still make those calls every day.

If you're part of a more vulnerable demographic—say, a woman—and someone in your community is accused of rape, your safety might even depend on your personal appraisal of the claim, well before a jury gets involved. If you're living in a college dorm or military barracks, and you hear that another person who lives there has raped someone, you'd do well to avoid being alone with that person, even while the law presumes his innocence. Likewise, a man who finds himself in prison—where his chance of being sexually assaulted is far greater than in the general population— will want to steer clear of inmates and corrections officers rumored to have raped other prisoners, even if those claims haven't been proven in court.

So when you hear that one person has accused another of rape, you most certainly *are* allowed to use your own reason, judgment, and life-time's worth of accumulated social skills to determine whether you believe what the accuser is saying. You are welcome to factor in what you know about the alleged victim and attacker, and form an opinion on who's the more credible party. You have every legal and moral right to decide what *you* think happened, even before there's an official verdict.

Sure, it's important to acknowledge that you're not infallible, with regard to pretty much every question. But if you've been alive longer than a few years on planet Earth, you have some ability to recognize bullshit. You should feel free to use it.

Prosecutorial Discretion, Conduct, and Misconduct

Partly because the prosecution's burden of proof is so great, and rapes so often lack evidence beyond a victim's testimony, few reported rapes ever make it to trial. According to the most recent National Crime Victimization Survey, 64 percent of rapes are never reported, and only 12 percent lead to arrest.[1] So most rapists walk free before a prosecutor even has a chance to get involved.

When one does, the numbers don't improve as much as you might hope.

A January 2014 report by the White House Council on Women and Girls, *Rape and Sexual Assault: A Renewed Call to Action*, sums up the problem:

> One study indicated that two-thirds of survivors have had their legal cases dismissed, and more than 80% of the time, this contradicted her [the victim's] desire to prosecute. According to another study of 526 cases in two large cities where sexual assault arrests were made, only about half were prosecuted.[2]

Sit with that for a minute: even when the victim reported it, the police believed her, *and* they amassed enough evidence to justify an arrest, half the time, prosecutors decided not to take it any further. Half.

In some jurisdictions, rapists are all but guaranteed a walk. A recent review of 270 police reports of rape over a nine-year period in Salt Lake County, Utah, found that only 6 percent were prosecuted. Examining 30 randomly chosen cases per year in which both a report and a rape kit were taken, researchers found two years in which *none* of the 30 ended in prosecution.[3]

In the Salt Lake district attorney's defense, two-thirds of those cases never even made it as far as their office. Erin Alberty and Janelle Stecklein of the *Salt Lake Tribune* report:

West Valley City's new police chief Lee Russo said that he discovered rape investigators in years past had been making some prosecutorial judgments on their own. For instance, he said, some cases raise questions about the victim's level of intoxication and ability to consent to sex. The win-ability of such a case is "subjective," Russo said. In the past, investigators may have decided not to pursue such a case.[4]

Subsequent to the review, the West City Valley Police Department began requiring that all rape reports go to the district attorney's office for screening and all rape kits be submitted to the state's crime lab.[5] But Salt Lake City police chief Chris Burbank told the *Tribune* that "in many cases, prosecutors themselves discourage investigators from sending a case to the D.A.'s office."[6]

In other words, investigators might decide not to send a case for formal review after being told *informally* by prosecutors that the case would be unwinnable. (You know that point in numerous *Law & Order* episodes when an assistant district attorney shouts at the detectives, "I can't go to trial with this! Go get me something to work with"? I like to imagine that's what he's talking about.) Of those that did make it all the way through the prosecutorial screening process, the district attorney's office only chose to file charges in 25 percent.

So, to recap, at every level those meant to represent the victim—the *people*—in a criminal investigation and trial believe that most of the time, it's just not worth putting rape cases in front of a jury.

This shouldn't come as a surprise. In any given rape case, the jury is pulled from the same rape culture we all live in, and the defense will trot out every allowable rape myth to create reasonable doubt in the mind of at least one juror. If there's no rock-solid physical evidence—a video, maybe, or at least severe injuries to the victim—the battle may be simply unwinnable for the prosecution. And prosecutors really don't like that.

A 2012 report by the Vera Institute of Justice examines the reasons why prosecutors choose not to pursue cases—all of them, not just sex crimes.

Researchers found that prosecutors' decisions were guided by two basic questions: "Can I prove the case?" and "Should I prove the case?" The former question was most influential at the outset of a case, at initial screening and charge filing, when an objective assess- ment of the evidence was the dominant factor in moving cases for- ward. Later, other case-level factors—such as the seriousness of the offense, the defendant's criminal history, and characteristics and cir- cumstances of the defendant and victim—assumed an increasing degree of influence as prosecutors evaluated whether a case should go forward.[7]

On the plus side, the report found that most prosecutors were gen- uinely concerned with justice; they wanted to "do the right thing" and aimed for "a balance between the community's public safety concerns and the imperative to treat defendants fairly." When those two priorities were in conflict, though, "survey respondents overwhelmingly considered fair treatment to be more important than public protection."[8]

This, too, is a defining element of our justice system. The famous axiom known as Blackstone's formulation, after the eighteenth-century English jurist who coined it, goes: "It is better that ten guilty persons escape than that one innocent suffer."

In theory, I'm also a fan of this as a legal standard, especially living in a country that still has the death penalty. If you're going to deprive someone of life or liberty, you had better be *sure* you've got the right guy. And since some innocent people still manage to be convicted even under this system, a superabundance of caution is warranted.

But in practice, the combination of Blackstone's formulation and rape myths means we let *nearly all* of the guilty persons who commit sexual assault and rape go free.

Let's look again at the seven main categories of rape myths:

1. She asked for it.
2. It wasn't really rape.
3. He didn't mean to.
4. She wanted it.
5. She lied.
6. Rape is a trivial event.
7. Rape is a deviant event.[9]

Any jury of average Americans is likely to contain folks who believe some or all of those things—and we're among the comparatively enlight-ened societies on this stuff. A 2012 review of the literature on how rape myths affect jurors, commissioned by England's BPP School of Health, noted that: "In general the prevalence of negative attitudes towards rape victims ranges from 18.3% (United Kingdom) to 29.5% (Canada) amongst western countries and 32.9 (Hong Kong) to 51.5% (Malaysia) in eastern countries."[10]

How do you evaluate the question "Can I prove the case?" if you know it's unlikely you'll find twelve people who harbor no negative atti-tudes toward rape victims—and your opponent will be looking to load the jury with people who do?

Worse yet, if you, as a prosecutor who has grown up in a rape culture just like the rest of us, buy into some of those myths, how likely are you to believe a "he said–she said" rape case is worth trying? Is it really such a big deal in the first place? Do you believe it's likely to happen again, to some-one else? Can you be *sure* that the "victim" isn't just making it all up for some mysterious reasons of her own?

The result of all these myth-fed doubts, according to the White House Council on Women and Girls, is that "prosecutors were more likely to file charges when physical evidence connecting the suspect to the crime was present, if the suspect had a prior criminal record, and if there were no questions about the survivor's character or behavior."[11]

Too damned bad if you've ever been in trouble before or your rapist never has. Too bad if you weren't a virgin, your rapist comes across as like-able, and nobody got video. Too bad if you're the victim of a garden-variety acquaintance rape, as I was—one that started with consensual activity, left no scars or bruising, and was committed by a man only rumored, not legally proven, to have raped multiple times before.

In fairness, I was among the 64 percent who didn't even try reporting my rape to police. I just can't imagine I would have gotten far if I had. I went to the hospital the next morning but declined a rape kit because all I could think, at seventeen years old, was that I didn't want my parents to find out. I'd been wearing tight clothes, drinking heavily, dancing provoc-atively. I kissed him, on purpose, because I wanted to. I had no evidence except my word that he raped me after that.

And at seventeen years old, I already knew my word wasn't nearly enough.

A Tale of Two Experts

When a rape trial does go forward, either side might bring in expert witnesses to give testimony that supports its theory of the case. As with so many things regarding the law and sex crimes, this practice is perfectly reasonable in theory, yet sometimes goes horribly wrong in reality—for both accuser and accused.

Later, I'll discuss the spurious belief that a lubricated vagina is evidence of consent, but as it turns out, even body parts not known for self-lubricating can give silent consent, if you ask the right "expert." At the 2005 trial of three Corona del Mar, California, teenagers arrested after they misplaced a homemade porn video that showed them raping a sixteen-year-old, a doctor testified that the unconscious girl's body effectively said yes in her stead. According to an OC Weekly account of the trial, defendant Greg Haidl's father—the assistant sheriff, by the way—"paid a New York doctor to claim with all seriousness that [Jane] Doe didn't need to give oral consent to the gangbang because her rectum had done so when it accepted the insertion of foreign objects."[12]

In their book *Satan's Silence: Ritual Abuse and the Making of a Modern American Witch Hunt*, journalist Debbie Nathan and attorney Michael Snedeker explain how the very same pseudoscience helped falsely convict numerous adults of child rape during the 1980s "Satanic panic." Until the 1970s, it was widely believed that "when a patient is prepared for a rectal examination, if his anus spontaneously opens, this means he is accustomed to being sodomized."[13] This belief has since been debunked as so much homophobic garbage, but many people found it persuasive at the time.

In 1981, Bruce Woodling published a paper about the "anal wink test" he'd developed to determine if children had been anally penetrated. By the time he was asked to examine children involved in the 1982 sweep of Kern County, California, adults allegedly involved in a Satanic ritual sex abuse ring, "his standard exam involved rubbing the anus with swabs, inserting glass test tubes into the rectum, and taking photographs of the genitalia."[14]

That's right: a man hired to investigate claims of children being forced to endure trusted adults penetrating their anuses with foreign objects did exactly that.

"Anal winking" is, to be clear, a common reflex to being touched in the rectal area. But Woodling's testimony that it indicated sexual abuse helped convict some of the more than twenty Kern County residents sent to prison for nonexistent crimes, after which he became a sought-after "expert" in similar child sexual abuse cases around the country.

Woodling wasn't arguing, like the doctor in the Corona del Mar case, that a normal autonomic response equals consent. But in both cases, we see how false beliefs about rape, bolstered by so-called experts, can be devastating—to victims *and* the accused.

In their desperation to produce evidence beyond victims' testimony, too many people charged with bringing justice to our communities expect the human body to perform magic. Unfortunately for them, the vagina and anus are not recording devices or lie detectors. No matter what an "expert" witness might say, the only part of the human body capable of consenting to sex is the brain. And the trauma it sustains from rape can't be photographed and blown up for a jury to see.

When the Right Man Is Convicted of the Wrong Crime

Even when there is unusually strong physical evidence, a rape case can still become hopelessly tangled, thanks to rape myths, racism, bad laws, and confused juries. Genarlow Wilson's story involves all of the above.

Wilson was seventeen years old on New Year's Eve, 2003, when he went to a hotel party in Douglasville, Georgia, with several friends from school. Over the course of the night, Wilson would be videotaped receiving oral sex from a fifteen-year-old girl—who appeared to willingly offer the same service to four other young men at the party—and having intercourse with an intoxicated seventeen-year-old. That tape would radically change the course of his future.

When the seventeen-year-old woke up at three in the morning, she was naked and confused. She phoned her mother and begged to be picked up. Reporting for *Atlanta Magazine*, journalist Chandra R. Thomas describes what happens next (using the pseudonym "Michelle" for the girl):

Once they got in the car, Michelle's mother told her daughter that she reeked of liquor and marijuana and as soon as they got home she needed to take a bath. Michelle got into the tub, but then broke down and told her upset mom, "I think they raped me." She dressed, and mother and daughter headed to the Douglasville Police Department. After they filed a report, investigators ordered Michelle to go to a hospital for an examination.[15]

Police went to the hotel rooms Wilson and his friends had rented and rounded up the boys. Six of them would be charged with raping "Michelle" and committing aggravated child molestation against the fifteen-year-old girl, who always maintained she'd been a willing participant.

At the time, the state of Georgia had no "Romeo and Juliet" law that would exempt teenagers from harsh penalties for having consensual sex with slightly younger teens. Making matters worse for the accused, oral sex was actually deemed a worse violation than sexual intercourse; that's what tacked "aggravated" on to the charge. Finally, the mandatory minimum sentence for anyone convicted of aggravated child molestation was ten years in prison.

All five of his friends took plea deals, but Wilson insisted he was innocent and went to trial. The jury acquitted him on the rape charge but, not knowing about the mandatory minimum sentence, convicted him of molesting the fifteen-year-old. Jury forewoman Marie Manigault told Thomas that when she found out she'd helped send this young man to prison for a decade, "I just went limp. They had to help me to a chair."

Outrage blossomed in the community and throughout the United States on behalf of this bright young man—a football player who'd never been in trouble with the law—imprisoned for consensual oral sex with a girl two years younger than he. Jesse Jackson publicly articulated what a lot of people were thinking: this was, in Thomas's words, "yet another example of excessive sentencing for black and brown youth."

With the political will whipped up by this case and a similar one involving NFL player Marcus Dixon (then, like Wilson, a high school football star), Georgia lawmakers eventually passed a "Romeo and Juliet" provision that would have made the crime Wilson was convicted of a misdemeanor. After serving two and a half years, Wilson was released when the Georgia Supreme Court declared his original sentence "cruel and unusual."

The media embraced Genarlow Wilson as a wrongfully convicted man, and radio host Tom Joyner's charitable foundation helped the young man go to Morehouse College, where he graduated with a degree in sociology in 2013. If you Google him today, you'll find loads of supporters holding him up as an example of what happens when a racist justice system gets a young black man in its talons; an *Ebony* magazine profile, for instance, is called "Notorious to Glorious: Genarlow Wilson Is No Child Molester and Never Was."

But you'll also find a post by Gina McCauley, founder of the blog "What About Our Daughters," which focuses on African American female crime victims usually ignored by the media. The post is called "Genarlow Wilson: The Most Ungrateful and Entitled Child Rapist Ever to Graduate from Morehouse." (Not to put too fine a point on it.) McCauley blasts those who would congratulate Wilson for "beating the odds" to earn his bachelor's degree.

> What odds? Having a college education dropped at his feet? Getting a book deal as a reward for raping two girls? Getting a job in law enforcement despite being a child rapist? Having a State senator and multimillionaire radio show host as his primary benefactors? What odds? Genarlow Wilson was going to graduate from Morehouse if Tom Joyner himself had to come take his final exams for him.[16]

So which is it? Is Wilson the victim of a broken justice system that routinely abuses young black men, imprisoned for a crime that didn't actually happen? Or is he a lucky bastard who was acquitted of a crime he *did* commit by a jury of his peers—i.e., people who also grew up in a rape culture that routinely tolerates the sacrifice of young black women to men's violence—and rewarded with a college education and a book deal?

As far as I can tell, he's both.

I differ from McCauley in that I likely would not have voted to convict Wilson on the charge for which he went to prison. I am strongly in favor of "Romeo and Juliet" laws, because I believe that calling consensual sex between a fifteen- and seventeen-year-old rape only contributes to the impression that rape is something other than a deliberate, violent crime. It also obscures the sexual agency of teenage girls, who are perfectly capable of making an informed decision—even if it's a bad one—to experiment sexually with their peers.

To be clear: If I could meet that fifteen-year-old, I'd want to talk to her about *why* she offered to fellate multiple guys in one night. I'd ask if she felt pressured to do it, if she enjoyed it, if it was her idea, if she could see herself doing it again, and if she fully understood the health risks of unprotected oral sex. I'd talk to her about owning her desires and protecting herself. I'd want to know if she seemed unduly preoccupied with male attention, if she felt good about herself in general, and about whether she had supportive friends and adults in her life. And I'd want to make sure she knew she always had the right to refuse or withdraw consent, and that all parties involved in a sexual act should be enthusiastic participants. But I wouldn't automatically assume it *wasn't* her idea, or that she was an unsuspecting naïf, besmirched by wicked older boys.

"Michelle," on the other hand, was repeatedly victimized in a manner that meets every reasonable definition of rape—yet a jury didn't see it that way. So her violation has been all but erased by the cries of justice for Genarlow, and the stories about what a fine young man he's become since leaving prison. (Maybe he has! I surely hope his days of penetrating semiconscious people are well past.)

Since Wilson was acquitted of the rape charge, we aren't obligated to think any longer about what actually happened, on video, that night. We don't have to consider whether justice was served in the case of the seventeen-year-old girl who woke up naked on a bathroom floor, unsure of what all had happened to her body in the preceding hours. We don't have to grapple with whether attending an all-night party, drinking alcohol, and flirting actually means a seventeen-year-old girl *deserves* whatever a bunch of guys feel like doing to her.

That's how rape culture likes things to be: simple.

Go ahead and shed a tear, if you like, for poor Genarlow Wilson, sent to prison for a consensual blow job—but maybe also spare one for the other young woman he put his penis in that night, the one who *didn't* consent. Wilson is both the victim of a miscarriage of justice and the beneficiary of one. He is simultaneously a tragic figure and a lucky bastard, and the whole case is a grotesque Gordian knot of racism, sexism, and the law gone rogue.

Jury Doody

In May 2011, New York City police officers Kenneth Moreno and Franklin L. Mata—you might remember them as the "Rape Cops" of numerous headlines—were convicted of official misconduct yet acquitted of rape and burglary charges following a night in which they went three times to the home of an extremely drunk woman. In *Confessions of a "Rape Cop" Juror*, a long essay about his time on that jury, writer Patrick Kirkland offers a fascinating and maddening window onto the way in which rape cases are ultimately decided.

The alleged victim originally met the officers after they were called to help her home, because she was intoxicated to the point of being unable to exit a taxi; her blood alcohol level was at least twice the legal limit for drunk driving. The fact that Moreno and Mata returned to her apartment twice that night was never in dispute; there was security camera footage to prove it. (They had, in fact, attempted to shield their faces from the cameras they were aware of.) The officers were even found to have placed a false 911 call, claiming a drunk homeless man was causing trouble near the woman's address, to justify one of those returns. They refused to turn over Mata's "memo book," in which he was supposed to record what they did while on duty.

Moreno admitted on the stand that he'd "cuddled" with the alleged victim, and sang to her while she wore only a bra, as Mata waited in another room. Of Moreno's testimony Kirkland writes, "Truth or fiction, the more he talked, the more incredible his story sounded. And yet as it continued, the more I believed it."[17]

An increasingly incredible story that somehow also becomes more believable as it goes on? Cool. That makes sense.

For the most part, *Confessions of a "Rape Cop" Juror* is the story of a bunch of American citizens trying very hard to do their duty honestly and fairly, without any particular legal or psychological expertise. Although Kirkland walked into the jury room planning to vote "not guilty" on the rape charge and never changed his mind, he takes pains to explain how he got there and remind us that their task was not to determine what happened, but what the prosecution had proved beyond a reasonable doubt. He spells out the tedious process they went through to reach agreement on twenty-six separate charges, after sitting through a trial that included hours spent discussing the layout of the alleged victim's apartment and the pillows on her sofa. It all sounds terribly, painfully methodical.

If you believe—and I do—that everyone accused of a crime deserves a vigorous defense, and that it's better to set a guilty person free than convict an innocent one, you can't help but sympathize with Kirkland. Even if you also believe—and I do—that Moreno and Mata had no business going back to that woman's apartment even once, and there's no obvious reason to doubt the victim's testimony that she was raped.

In our justice system, as we've already discussed, people accused of crimes are granted the legal presumption of innocence. If the prosecution cannot thoroughly demonstrate to a jury that the defendant is guilty, the jury must acquit. You can understand and appreciate all this, even if you strongly suspect the "Rape Cop" jury came to the wrong conclusion.

But then you get to the part where Kirkland describes, not a little smugly, a conflict he had with Juror Number Four.

"She said she woke up to being penetrated," Four repeats.

I turn directly to Four. Hours have passed. We've gone in circles, and Four has seemingly made the penetration line her new mantra.

My elbows hit my knees and I speak slowly. "You do know that penetration can mean sex, right?" I ask.

I can hear her mind racing, speeding toward the light of reason. "Yes."

"And you do know that sex does not equal rape?"

She stares down at her notepad. "She said . . . she felt the penetration."[18]

Now, this scene comes after Kirkland has described querying the judge on relatively tiny matters of law—that's how seriously this jury takes its duty to be accurate and certain on all counts. And yet somehow, they never thought to ask if penetrating a sleeping person is, by definition, rape?

If they had, the answer they would have gotten is yes.

Under New York State law, a person is guilty of rape in the first degree "when he or she engages in sexual intercourse with another person who is incapable of consent by reason of being physically helpless." "Physically helpless" is defined as when "a person is unconscious or for any other reason is physically unable to communicate unwillingness to an act."[19]

In other words, once again: *a sleeping person cannot consent to sex.* This should be the most obvious thing in the world, and yet it seems to be the place where a lot of folks get hung up.

In some cases, it's because people don't want to think of themselves or their lovers as rapists. Every time I've made this point online—*a sleeping person cannot give consent*—commenters have rushed to tell me that they enjoy waking up their partners with penetration or vice versa, or even that they have a standing agreement that it's okay to do so.

But once again: *you cannot prearrange consent.* Even people who wish to be bound and whipped by a partner typically arrange a "safe word" to maintain their right of refusal. Just as the marriage contract doesn't state that spouses eternally surrender their right to say no, an understanding that you're not theoretically averse to sleep sex doesn't actually equal consent to any given act that happens while one party is asleep. Because you need consent at the time, *every* time.

Is it possible to wake a person up by penetrating them, and subsequently have a mutually enjoyable sexual encounter in which neither side feels violated? Yes, sure. Does that mean there was actual consent to that first act of penetration? No.

A sleeping person cannot consent.

A waking person cannot consent to sex that will take place at a time when they're incapable of consent.

Consent cannot be applied retroactively.

Ergo, penetrating a sleeping person is always technically illegal, even if that person wakes up and says he or she feels fine about it.

People who have intimate relationships and a good sense of each other's boundaries can do lots of things to each other that would be punishable by law if they did them to anyone else. A daughter who wears her mother's diamond earrings without advance permission probably won't be arrested for theft, nor will a husband who takes his wife's car to the store while she's asleep, or a brother who doesn't ask if he can carry his sister's laptop with him to a café. But if a stranger did any of those things, the owners of the missing items would immediately call the police. And if an estranged husband took his wife's car while she was asleep, or a forty-year-old junkie broke into her mother's home to "borrow" some jewelry, the owners might very well bust their family members, too.

Illegal acts don't magically become legal just because you're pretty sure the victim of your transgression won't mind. Context matters, but if you misjudge the context, you're still responsible for your actions. So a partner might have *forgiven* you—even enthusiastically—for waking them up with a sexual act, but they did not, and could not, consent to one while asleep. And if you one day did the same to a person who woke up, felt horribly violated, and called the police on you, it would be because you had, in fact, committed rape.

Are we completely clear on this point? Okay, back to Kirkland's argument with Juror Number Four.

Four brings up a point that, if true, means one of the accused is definitely guilty of rape under New York law, and Kirkland dismisses it out of hand—not because he thinks the victim was lying, but because he thinks it's impossible to prove she didn't consent. So certain is Kirkland that penetrating a sleeping person is *not* automatically rape, he bullies Four into shutting up about it, and then writes an essay in which he pats himself on the back for condescendingly helping her "[speed] toward the light of reason." Never mind the tiny, pesky fact that she was right about the law, and he was wrong.

The right to trial by an impartial jury of our peers is one more wonderful thing that can and does go wrong all the time, because our peers are human beings, and human beings have biases. The hope is that twelve of them, working together, can approximate impartiality, but a jury is basically only as even-handed as its loudest, most bigoted member.

Consider that African Americans—already more likely than white people to be arrested and indicted—often face all-white juries, who aren't nearly as impartial as they might like to think. One recent study examined over seven hundred jury trials that took place in Florida between 2000 and 2010, in which almost 40 percent had all-white jury *pools*—let alone seated juries.

"The results of our study were straightforward and striking," wrote lead author Shamena Anwar in a CNN op-ed. "In cases with no blacks in the jury pool, black defendants were convicted at an 81% rate and white defendants at a 66% rate. When the jury pool included at least one black member, conviction rates were almost identical: 71% for black defendants and 73% for whites."[20]

Just as stereotypes and myths about African Americans and criminality can prejudice white jurors toward a guilty verdict, stereotypes and myths about rape can prevent a jury from recognizing that what they're discussing is, in fact, a criminal assault. And if the guy who thinks penetrating a sleeping person isn't necessarily rape happens to shout louder than the woman who thinks it is, the actual law doesn't necessarily matter.

Judge Dread

Even when a jury does get it right, there's still a chance for the judge to screw everything up.

In the summer of 2014, one English jury took only two and a half hours to reach a guilty verdict after hearing the twenty-four-year-old victim testify that she'd woken up on a man's couch to find him having intercourse with her. She and a friend had gone to Lee Setford's place after a night of drinking, because they couldn't get into the friend's house. Earlier in the night, the victim had fallen while outdoors, bruising her face on the pavement. She vomited after arriving at Setford's home, then passed out on the couch. Some time after that, as she slept it off, Setford decided to put his penis in her.

In court, he claimed this was consensual.

Fortunately, the jury didn't buy it. Judge Michael Mettyear sentenced Setford to five years in jail, which is more than most rapists get, but his comments at the sentencing were appalling. "I do not regard you as a classic rapist," the judge told Setford, continuing:

> I do not think you are a general danger to strangers. You are not the type who goes searching for a woman to rape. This was a case where you just lost control of normal restraint.... She was a pretty girl who you fancied. You simply could not resist. You had sex with her.[21]

Mettyear went on to admonish Setford for pleading not guilty, instead of admitting his "mistake" and apologizing to the victim. "That would have made it much easier for her and I could have passed a lighter sentence."[22]

You know what I think would make it easier for the victim? If she didn't have to hear the judge talk about how her prettiness made her irresistible to a rapist. Or about how a man who raped her isn't "a general danger," even though studies of convicted rapists as well as undetected ones—that is, "nice guys" who know better than to say "I've raped someone" but will admit on an anonymous survey that they've forced someone to have sex—have shown that many are serial predators.[23]

I also have to imagine it would be easier on the victim if the judge sentencing her rapist didn't regard the crime as a simple loss of "normal restraint." That, to me, is the most chilling of all Mettyear's remarks, since it implies that under regular circumstances, your average guy must *restrain himself* from raping anyone. As though any healthy, red-blooded man, upon finding a sleeping "pretty girl who {he} fancied," would naturally be overcome by the urge to put his dick in her. As though giving in to that urge wouldn't be so very different from having consensual sex with a married person or going unprotected because you're too excited to go find a condom. Men and their out-of-control sex drives!

I am once again astonished to learn how little some men think of their own gender.

Genuinely wanting to fuck a person who can't consent is not normal male behavior. There is an enormous difference between thinking, "Wow, that sleeping person is hot—I sure would like to have sex with her," and wanting to penetrate an unconscious or semiconscious person's body so badly that it takes real self-discipline to avoid going through with it.

Most men do not struggle with wanting to rape anyone, sleeping or not. Most men, like most human beings in general, can easily distinguish between an abstract desire for sexual contact and an immediate, urgent desire to possess another person's body without their consent. Most men do not find the thought of an unwilling and/or unwitting partner remotely sexy, for reasons that should be obvious. Rape is not a failure of "normal restraint" but of humanity. It's not a "mistake" but a deliberate decision to treat another person like a soulless object.

If even a ball-busting feminist harpy like me knows that most guys would never do that, why doesn't a man with an extensive legal education know?

Similarly, one could ask why women with extensive legal educations don't know that there's no such thing as "asking for it." I've already told you about Arizona judge Jacqueline Hatch, who told a sexual assault victim, "If you wouldn't have been there that night, none of this would have happened to you."[24] Did I mention the man convicted of that assault was a former police officer, speaking of people who should have known better? Or that he'd had several beers before driving himself to a bar, putting his hand up the woman's skirt, and fondling her genitals?

Judge Hatch, who sentenced the man to two years' probation and zero jail time beyond the four days he'd already served, hoped the victim would consider it a learning experience, advising her, "When you blame others, you give up your power to change."

When you blame *the drunk ex-police officer* who came up behind you and touched your junk, for *coming up behind you and touching your junk*, you give up your power to change. Hey, thanks for the tip.

Retired English judge Mary Jane Mowat seemed to share Hatch's opinion of women who go to bars when she told the *Oxford Mail* in August 2014, "I will be pilloried for saying so, but the rape conviction statistics will not improve until women stop getting so drunk."[25]

She went on to explain:

> I'm not saying it's right to rape a drunken woman, I'm not saying for a moment that it's allowable to take advantage of a drunken woman. But a jury in a position where they've got a woman who says "I was absolutely off my head, I can't really remember what I was doing, I can't remember what I said, I can't remember if I consented or not but I know I wouldn't have done." I mean when a jury is faced with something like that, how are they supposed to react?[26]

Mowat is, of course, correct that a victim who was drunk at the time and can't remember everything that happened presents the jury with a serious challenge. There's no getting around the fact that cases are easier to prosecute when the victim makes a strong, confident witness. Still, let me take this opportunity to "pillory" her, because too many people think remarks like these are just the harsh truth, end of story.

The real harsh truth is that if women who were raped while drunk can never be regarded as credible witnesses, then it actually is "allowable to take advantage of a drunken woman." No matter what the law says on paper, we've created a gargantuan loophole for any rapist who chooses an intoxicated victim.

The even harsher truth is: *Rapists already know this.* This is why anti-rape advocates refer to alcohol as "the number one date-rape drug." It's not just that a guy planning to rape will buy a gal a drink in hopes of lowering her resistance; it's that he'll pick someone who's already visibly intoxicated, knowing that will torpedo her credibility if she decides to report him.

A 2007 report from the Medical University of South Carolina's National Crime Victims Research and Treatment Center spells it out: "The most common rape-risk situation for both adult women and college women is not being rendered intoxicated; it is being taken advantage of by a sexual predator after she has become intoxicated voluntarily."[27]

So sure, in theory, if women would "stop getting so drunk," they might escape a rapist's attention in the first place, and those who weren't so lucky would make better witnesses. But apart from the simple unfairness of that attitude—only one gender is expected to see physical violation as a natural consequence of enjoying alcohol—it gives legal cover to rapists. Blaming women's drinking instead of men's decision to rape means throwing up our hands and saying, "Well, as long as the criminals keep choosing this one sort of victim, there's nothing to be done about the second worst crime there is!" We might as well say outright that it's perfectly legal to rape a drunk person.

We're not ready to say that yet, are we? Please tell me we're not ready to say that.

Taking Victims' Testimony Seriously

Elsewhere in the same interview, Judge Mowat herself makes exactly the right point, slamming pundits who claim there's "no evidence" in cases involving celebrities. Even in the absence of DNA, visible injuries, or video, she scoffs, "to say there was no evidence is just rubbish, because the victim's account is evidence, and it's for the jury to decide if they believe it or not."[28]

Yes! *The victim's account is evidence.* Even when she was drunk. Even when she's accusing a celebrity. Even when she's a sex worker. Even when she's trans. Even when the victim is not a woman. Testimony is a real and admissible form of evidence.

It's not the kind of evidence prosecutors like to hang a case on, and on its own, it's probably not enough to persuade a jury to convict. But we must stop putting the burden of proof on *victims* of sexual assault and rape.

As soon as someone says, "I was raped," we cannot say, "There is no evidence that it happened." Regardless of whether investigators are able to corroborate the story, prosecutors are able to present a compelling case, or a jury agrees that the defendant is guilty, there *is* evidence, just as soon as a victim dares to tell someone what happened.

We should remember, too, that in the United States, the prosecution represents "the people." The purpose of putting rapists on trial is not just to punish someone who's committed a crime but to remove him from society, so he cannot do the same to others.* When investigators "unfound" a case because they don't think the victim's acting "victimy" enough, or fail to send a rape kit to the crime lab; when prosecutors decline to file charges because there's no physical evidence to corroborate the victim's account; when a judge gives a convicted offender a suspended sentence or probation and lectures the victim on personal responsibility, they're all tacitly accepting that they've set a rapist free to do it again.

You can almost understand why they'd tell themselves that a high percentage of rape reports are false. How could you live with yourself if you knew you failed so many genuine victims, so routinely?

Blackstone's formulation can only justify so much blatant neglect of rape survivors and potential victims. At some point, if the people in charge of separating violent criminals from the rest of us can't manage to convict more than a very few, we must demand that they do better.

---

* As I've mentioned elsewhere, rates of rape inside prisons are tragically high, so arguably, incarcerating a rapist is only changing his pool of potential victims, not preventing him from doing it again. Not for nothing, prison also vastly increases a man's risk of being raped, which we should never accept as an appropriate punishment. All that said, prison currently remains our best bet for limiting serial predators' ability to victimize the public.

In the United States, many of those people are elected officials—judges, sheriffs, prosecuting attorneys. The next time these positions come up for vote in your community, resist the temptation to blow off that part of the ballot. Take the time to Google the candidates beforehand, and see how they've handled past sex crimes. We might not be able to fix the fundamental problem of cases that boil down to one person's word against another's, but we can at least vote out the worst victim blamers, slackers, and rape apologists in positions of power.

Meanwhile, as long as the criminal system remains an unlikely source of justice for survivors of sexual assault and rape, we should remember that civil courts have a lower standard of proof and don't require a prosecutor's sign-off for a victim to get her day in court. In her book *Rape Is Rape*, legal scholar Jody Raphael points out that "if publicized, civil lawsuits are a way to protect others from harm from the same predator."[29] You may not be able to get him off the streets, but at least you can warn other people to be careful around him.

Raphael acknowledges that victims who go this route are often maligned as "gold-diggers who want to cash in," particularly if the defendants are wealthy or famous. What else is new? But in addition to helping other vulnerable people be on their guard around an accused rapist, media coverage can encourage any other victims he might have to come forward. As we saw in late 2014 with mounting accusations against Bill Cosby, eventually, if enough women report that you assaulted them, reasonable people will start to believe them.

CHAPTER 7

The Politics of Rape

T here is no good way to begin this chapter.
I don't want to write a book about the abortion debate (right now, anyway), and you presumably didn't expect to read one when you picked up a book on rape culture.

You might even agree with me that rape culture is real and terrible, while vehemently disagreeing with me on reproductive rights (I'm for 'em). One of the most surprising things I've observed as a liberal feminist writing publicly about sexual assault is that this issue can sometimes unite people like me with the staunchest conservatives. When I wrote a piece for *Salon*—not exactly a right-wing publication—criticizing the journalists, actors, and ordinary citizens who came out in support of Roman Polanski after his arrest in 2009, I was quoted approvingly not only by feminist blogs but by the *Wall Street Journal* and even the far-right-wing tabloid *World Net Daily*.

After a couple days of unaccountably fawning Polanski coverage, people of every political persuasion were relieved to hear someone say, "Hey, wait a minute, didn't this guy rape a kid and flee the country to avoid sentencing? Are we really supposed to see him as some kind of victim?" Of course, it only needed to be said because so many people of every political persuasion were coming to his defense, trying to minimize or erase the fact that he had pled guilty to drugging and then vaginally and anally penetrating a thirteen-year-old girl in 1977. But for a brief, shining moment there,

I was a darling of the right, the left, and everyone in between who claimed membership on Team Wait a Minute, This Is Really Fucked Up, You Guys. It was so nice to agree on at least one thing!

That's never going to happen with abortion.

But I can't bring up the subject of politicians and rape without talking about reproductive justice, because our elected officials keep intertwining the issues. It's not just that both rape and severe abortion restrictions spring from the same fear of women's sexual autonomy, although they do. Nor is it just that antiwoman politicians sometimes go as far as stripping funding from rape crisis centers if they offer information about abortion.[1] It's that the (mostly older, white, male) politicians who keep trying to effectively overturn *Roe v. Wade* by legislating increasingly severe abortion restrictions are inevitably asked if they support exceptions for women who become pregnant through rape or incest. And then they answer those questions, out loud, and it's all downhill from there.

Legitimate, Emergency, Honest, Forcible Rape-Rape: Could It Be God's Plan for You?

Previously unknown Missouri representative Todd Akin became the most famous of these in August 2012, when he shared his scientific understanding of conception: "If it's a legitimate rape, the female body has a way of shutting that whole thing down." That single sentence is breathtaking in its ignorance of basic biology—if sperm meets egg, pregnancy can occur—and of forty years of scholarship and activism that's sought to disabuse Americans of the notion that distinctions like "legitimate rape" are anything other than misogynistic bullshit.

Akin's hardly alone. In the last few years, several American politicians—mostly focused on restricting or removing rape exceptions from antiabortion policy—have given us a host of awkward phrases that reveal how they think about sexual assault, and it ain't pretty.

In 2011, 214 Republicans sponsored a bill, the No Taxpayer Funding for Abortion Act, which specified that exceptions would only be allowed for victims of "forcible rape"—just to make sure no shifty women were getting away with abortion after gentle and well-meaning rapes. (To be fair, it was only in 2013 that the word "forcible" was struck from the definition of rape in the FBI's Uniform Crime Reporting program.) Then there was presidential candidate–cum–OB/GYN Ron Paul's advice, in February 2012, for sexual assault victims concerned about pregnancy: "If it's an honest rape, that individual should go immediately to the emergency room, I would give them a shot of estrogen."[2]

We'd barely had time to recover from that when Todd Akin hit us with the "legitimate rape" doozy, followed by Connecticut Republican senate candidate Linda McMahon's clumsy attempt at walking back her support of Catholic hospitals that refuse to provide emergency contraception: "It was really an issue about a Catholic church being forced to offer those pills if the person came in in an emergency rape."[3] (If a rape victim showed up at a Catholic church, I certainly hope someone there would get her to a hospital.)

And then there was Indiana Republican senate candidate Richard Mourdock, who said—again, *out loud*, with people listening—"I think even when life begins in that horrible situation of rape, that it is something that God intended to happen." This sentiment was shared by former GOP presidential candidate Rick Santorum, who told Piers Morgan, "I believe and I think that the right approach is to accept this horribly created, in the sense of rape, but nevertheless, in a very broken way, a gift of human life, and accept what God is giving to you."[4] *Hey, there, mortal. Sorry about the rape thing—my bad—but please accept this unwanted pregnancy as a token of my esteem. Love, God.*

Eventually, the president of the United States ended up on *The Tonight Show*, reassuring the American public that at least one elected official isn't an ignorant sexist. "Let me make a very simple proposition," said President Obama. "Rape is rape. It is a crime. And so these various distinctions about rape don't make too much sense to me—don't make any sense to me."[5]

Tell me about it.

Forcible rape. Honest rape. Legitimate rape. Emergency rape. These qualifiers call to mind Whoopi Goldberg's now-famous reaction to the news of Polanski's arrest: "I know it wasn't rape-rape. It was something else, but I don't believe it was rape-rape."[6]

Goldberg took a lot of flack for that inelegant turn of phrase, but without a doubt she was only expressing what many Americans—some of them in public office—believe down deep: there's rape, and then there's *rape-rape*. Women who are rape-raped don't deserve to be punished with forty weeks of incubating the product of that assault, followed by the most physically painful experience known to human beings, which also happens to kill several hundred women a year in the United States and causes severe, life-threatening complications in over fifty thousand more. And that's before you have to either give the baby up for adoption or raise your rapist's child. But women who were merely "raped"? Yeah, they should probably have to endure all that.

How the Antiabortion Movement Got It So Wrong

Akin and his buddies are not only insinuating that the thirty-thousand-plus grown American women who become pregnant as a result of rape every year were asking for it, mind you. They're also indirectly blaming twelve- and fourteen-year-olds impregnated by their fathers and uncles. They're suggesting that child victims like Jaycee Dugard and Amanda Berry, who had children by men who abducted them and held them captive for years, weren't victims of legitimate rape. Nor were slave women who had white male politicians' children, apparently.

According to the GOP's finest, ovulating around the time of your rape is sufficient evidence that you're a liar, not a victim. These geniuses have basically created a seventeenth-century-Salem standard for abortion eligibility: if you'd been *legitimately* raped, your Super-Secret Cervix Shield would have activated when it detected the presence of unsolicited ejaculate. The fact that you got pregnant proves you don't deserve to end that pregnancy. (But if you drown, you were innocent, and your reward will be in heaven. I think that's how it works.)

You know, I'm not even saying we *couldn't*, in theory, have evolved physical mechanisms in our ladybusiness to prevent pregnancy from rape. Ducks have! Male ducks have corkscrew-shaped penises and a shocking propensity for rape—apparently, at least a third of sexual encounters between ducks are forcible. But in response, female ducks have developed "cryptic" vaginas that corkscrew in the opposite direction, and extra pathways that lure sperm to a dead end. The result is that only about 2 percent of duck babies are thought to have fathers the moms didn't choose. Duck bodies are amazing! But human bodies do not have such a mechanism. And it's religion, not science driving the erroneous claims that they do.

In the wake of all these so-called gaffes, journalists like Sarah Kliff of the *Washington Post* and Garance Franke-Ruta of the *Atlantic* identified the work of John Willke, MD, as a likely source for much of the current misunderstanding about pregnancy and rape. Willke, a onetime obstetrician and founder of the International Right to Life Federation, first published these ideas in a 1971 *Handbook on Abortion* coauthored with his wife, Barbara. According to the Associated Press, "The book became an instant touchstone for the anti-abortion movement, selling 1.5 million copies at the height of the sexual revolution."[7]

In a 1999 essay published in *Christian Life Resources* and beloved by conservative opponents of abortion, Willke argued that the emotional trauma of "assault rape"—again, distinguishing the bad kind of rape from the good is a priority among this crowd—could prevent ovulation. In a 2012 interview with the *Los Angeles Times*, he reiterated this belief and pronounced it "downright unusual" for a woman to become pregnant by rape, guessing the instance to be "one or two" in a thousand.[8]

(It's more like fifty in a thousand, but who's counting?)

The American College of Obstetricians and Gynecologists issued a scathing statement in response to Akin's regurgitation of Willke's stunningly incorrect assessment, which read, in part:

> Each year in the US, 10,000–15,000 abortions occur among women whose pregnancies are a result of reported rape or incest. An unknown number of pregnancies resulting from rape are carried to term. There is absolutely no veracity to the claim that "If it's a legitimate rape, the female body has ways to shut that whole thing down." A woman who is raped has no control over ovulation, fertilization, or implantation of a fertilized egg (i.e., pregnancy). To suggest otherwise contradicts basic biological truths.
>
> Any person forced to submit to sexual intercourse against his or her will is the victim of rape, a heinous crime. There are no varying degrees of rape. To suggest otherwise is inaccurate and insulting and minimizes the serious physical and psychological repercussions for all victims of rape.[9]

Inaccurate, insulting, and in contradiction of basic biological truths: that about sums it up. But one suspects the scientific facts are lost on people who believe God chooses some women not only to be raped but to carry their rapists' children.

The Built-In Polygraph

Contrary to the idea of the Super-Secret Cervix Shield, there's actually some scientific evidence that women's bodies may be designed to *facilitate* rape, in a manner of speaking. Not because we "want it," but because our genes have a better chance of surviving if we don't succumb to massive infections, like the ones that might follow having our vaginas torn up.

In the early 2000s, researchers at Northwestern University measured physical sexual responses like erection in men and lubrication in women as both genders watched three kinds of porn: straight, gay, and bonobo chimp. Regardless of sexuality, the men generally became physically aroused when watching the porn that aligned with their self-reported orientation—and none of them got off on the chimp sex. Women, however, lubed up for *all of it*. (Disclosure: one of those researchers, Dr. Meredith Chivers, is a friend who first told me about this study over drinks in my backyard.)

The researchers theorized that this could have evolved as a protective measure for women; if we can only self-lubricate when mentally aroused, we're vulnerable to far more physical damage from rape. (Or, presumably, from really boring sex.) But pre-antibiotic rape victims who lubricated at the first sign of sex would be less likely to die of an internal wound gone septic.[10]

When the *New York Times* reported on this study in 2007,[11] there was a fair bit of outrage in feminist circles, because lots of people interpreted it as implying that women secretly want to be raped. In fact, though, it implies that there's a significant difference between lubricating automatically and being genuinely turned on. That's actually a useful piece of information for *resisting* rape culture.

Consider: among the many delightful bon mots Steubenville High alum Michael Nodianos offered up while watching Jane Doe's assault was, "Her puss is about as dry as the sun right now." Watching the "dead girl" suffer various violations, he correctly gathered that she was not an enthusiastic participant—but whether that extended to a lack of lubrication is another matter. The fact is, we (mercifully) have no idea about that, and it's completely irrelevant to whether she was raped—which is a question of *consent*, not physiological minutiae.

But this belief that the female body serves as its own polygraph, confirming or contradicting whatever the female mouth is claiming about consent, is equally pernicious and pervasive. Victims are still suspected of lying if their vulvas aren't visibly shredded after a rape.

In 2008, California superior court judge Derek Johnson told the court at a convicted rapist's sentencing, "I'm not a gynecologist, but I can tell you something. If someone doesn't want to have sexual intercourse, the body shuts down. The body will not permit that to happen unless a lot of damage is inflicted, and we heard nothing about that in this case. That tells me that the victim in this case, although she wasn't necessarily willing, she didn't put up a fight."[12]

Setting aside the fact that "not necessarily willing" is in fact the definition of nonconsent, no kidding that he's not a gynecologist!

On the other hand, Representative Phil Gingrey of Marietta, Georgia, is one (just like Ron Paul and John Willke), and that didn't stop him from backing up Akin's bad science. During a Smyrna Area Chamber of Commerce meeting, Dr. Gingrey opined, "In a situation of rape, a legitimate rape, a woman's body has a way of shutting down so the pregnancy would not occur. [Akin's] partly right on that."

Moments later, by way of explaining how Akin was also partly wrong, Gingrey directly contradicted himself: "But the fact that a woman may have already ovulated 12 hours before she is raped, you're not going to prevent a pregnancy there by a woman's body shutting anything down because the horse has already left the barn, so to speak."[13]

In other words, it's a biological fact that a woman can become pregnant from a rape considered "legitimate" by disgusting old men—or by any other intercourse that happens at the right time in her cycle. But let's not let the actual biological facts stand in the way of a good story.

It's not hard to see why this falsehood is so seductive. If every vagina could intuit the difference between consensual and nonconsensual sex, then we might have more ways of distinguishing rape from nonrape that don't require listening to a woman's own account of what happened.

Nebulous vagina magic isn't quite as reliable as, say, noses that grow whenever women lie, but it's *something* to help reasonable people know who's a real victim and who's just "crying rape." And that's such a useful concept, the fact that it's imaginary hardly seems reason enough to abandon it.

"Crime Has Consequences"

When we refuse to acknowledge that a victim's testimony is legitimate evidence—perhaps not enough to send someone to prison on its own, but a good reason to suspect a crime has really occurred—we treat victims like criminals. If we believe that any given police report of rape stands a good chance of being false, when we know only a small minority actually are, we establish a habit of treating women as complicit in crimes committed against them.

Washington state's John Koster, who ran for Congress in 2012, gave us a perfect example of how this works. When asked about abortion exceptions for rape or incest, he replied:

> Incest is so rare, I mean, it's so rare. But, uh, the rape thing—You know, I know a woman who was raped and kept her child, gave it up for adoption. She doesn't regret it. In fact, she's a—she's a big pro-life proponent. But, on the rape thing, it's like, how does—how does putting more violence onto a woman's body and taking the life of an innocent child that's not—that's a consequence of this crime, how does that make it better? You know what I mean?[14]

The interviewer then says, "Yeah, but she has to live with the consequence of that crime," to which Koster replies, "Well, you know. Crime has consequences."

Crime has consequences. *Crime has consequences.* That's what you say to a teenager who got busted for shoplifting, not to a victim of a violent assault.

Seriously, imagine he was talking about anything but rape there. "Don't feel safe in your own home since it was burglarized? Well, you know. Crime has consequences." "Haven't been able to sleep since you were mugged at gunpoint? Crime has consequences." "In terrible pain since someone beat the shit out of you? Crime has consequences." "Dead now, because someone murdered you? Crime has consequences, young lady. You probably should have thought of that."

It's not some kind of slip or gaffe. All of this hedging about "the rape thing" goes back to the wrongheaded and dangerous belief that an enormous number of women who report rape are, in fact, guilty of a crime—not just the "sin" of premarital sex but the actual crime of filing a false report. People like this presume that there's a fifty-fifty chance (at least) that any woman who goes to police and says, "I was raped," is herself breaking the law—so all alleged victims must be investigated thoroughly on suspicion of that crime.

Combine that with a strong religious belief that (a) premarital sex warrants punishment and (b) a woman's highest purpose is motherhood, and of course it makes sense to tell a pregnant rape victim, "Well, you know. Crime has consequences." She probably did something wrong anyway, and her only problem is that now she has to do what she was put on earth to do.

In that worldview, genuine rape is so rare, it's "small ball" (Republican political strategist Ron Christie), and talking about it is "an unfortunate distraction from the issues that matter" (Texas senator Ted Cruz). But women "crying rape" because they're embarrassed to admit they had sex, or because they're angry at a man they had consensual sex with (and downright evil enough to have him investigated for rape as revenge), well, that stuff happens all the time. Because: Women. You know how they are.

Crime has consequences. So do elections, fortunately—Koster did not win the seat he ran for. But he gave us a classic example of how the Republican party in the twenty-first century thinks about women. We're moral and emotional children, prone to lying, cruelty, and acting without thinking. We have casual sex, then casually terminate the resulting pregnancies, because we just don't quite understand where babies come from. (And if we're feeling cranky, we might even accuse the fathers of our aborted fetuses of raping us, just to watch them squirm.)

To be fair, it's not clear that women in the Republican Party understand the biological basics of reproduction, either. During a June 2013 debate on a proposed, highly restrictive abortion ban, Texas representative Jodie Laubenberg—a cosponsor of the bill—said she opposed exceptions for rape or incest because emergency rooms typically offer "what's called rape kits where a woman can get cleaned out, basically like a D and C."[15]

A D and C—dilation of the cervix and curettage, or scraping, of the uterus—is one kind of abortion procedure, but it has precisely nothing to do with a rape kit, the colloquial name for evidence collected in a medical setting after a sexual assault. In her attempts to clarify the statement later, Laubenberg said she momentarily confused "rape kit" with emergency contraception sometimes offered to rape victims in emergency rooms, but that, too, has nothing to do with a D and C. The "morning-after pill" is a high dose of estrogen taken within a few days of unprotected intercourse, which interferes with ovulation.

These are your elected officials, ladies and gentlemen. They literally do not know how babies are made (or aren't made, as the case may be), but they're sure rape victims can't get pregnant, abortion is precisely equivalent to murder, emergency room doctors can "clean women out," and half the world's population are lying, scheming jezebels.

Again, there's a reason why I went so far into the weeds of abortion here. Let's not get so distracted by Laubenberg's staggering ignorance that we forget her actual position: because emergency contraception is available at hospitals, no rape or incest exception is necessary in a law about when and how people may access abortion.

The implication is obvious: "legitimate" rape victims immediately seek medical attention. If a woman never went to the hospital, how do we know she was *really* raped when she comes waltzing in, looking for the abortion care she's supposedly had a constitutional right to since 1973? How do we know she's not just *saying* she was raped because she regrets having sex?

Oh, look. There we are again.

Spousal Rape and Parental Rights

It's bad enough that so many legislators believe women should be forced to bear the children of rape, but wait—it gets worse! In most states, the rapist can then assert his parental rights.

Only nineteen states have any laws attempting to prevent a victim having to share custody with her rapist, and according to *Mother Jones* reporters Dana Liebelson and Sydney Brownstone, among those:

13 require proof of conviction in order to waive the rapist's parental rights. Two more states have provisions on the issue that only apply if the victim is a minor or, in one of those cases, a stepchild or adopted child of the rapist. Another three states don't have laws that deal with custody of a rapist's child specifically, but do restrict the parental rights of a father or mother who sexually abused the other parent.[16]

If your first thought is, "But realistically, what rapist would want to be a daddy?" you're forgetting that most rapists know their victims, and plenty of them are spouses or domestic partners. There is a clear correlation between intimate partner violence in heterosexual couples and unintended pregnancy, for starters. In a study published in a 2010 issue of the journal *Contraception*, the researchers write:

> One specific element of abusive men's control that may, in part, explain the association is overt pregnancy coercion and direct interference with contraception. Some males use verbal demands, threats and physical violence to pressure their female partners to become pregnant. Reproductive control may also take the form of direct acts that ensure a woman cannot use contraception—birth control sabotage—including flushing birth control pills down the toilet, intentional breaking of condoms, and removing contraceptive rings or patches.[17]

In a survey of 1,278 women who sought services at one of five California family planning clinics, these researchers found that 53 percent had been victims of intimate partner violence, and among those, 19 percent had experienced pregnancy coercion, and 15 percent, birth control sabotage. And 40 percent reported at least one unintended pregnancy.

So we know that some abusive men will go to great lengths to get their partners pregnant (thus making it that much harder for the women to leave). We know that some of those use "threats and physical violence" to get the pregnancy they're after. Thanks to the CDC's 2010 National Intimate Partner and Sexual Violence Survey, we know that more than one in three abused female respondents "experienced multiple forms of rape, stalking, or physical violence," and that over the course of a lifetime, nearly one in ten women in the United States will be raped by an intimate partner.[18]

In light of all that, does it seem so far-fetched that a man would rape a woman *and* want to raise a child that resulted from his crime? That he'd want to control her with a lifelong tie and rub her face in what he's managed to get away with? Would it surprise you if a rapist saw fatherhood primarily as an opportunity to raise the emotional stakes, to create a bargaining chip even more precious to his victim than her own life? Or if he just got off on the idea of controlling *two* people?

It sure shouldn't. But again, rape myths cloud our ability to consider scenarios like this. Spousal rape has only been illegal in all fifty states since 1993, because it took that long to convince enough legislators that it really happens, and it's really a crime.

Seventeenth-century English jurist Matthew Hale—famous for his oft-invoked warning that "rape is an accusation easily to be made and hard to be proved, and harder to be defended by the party accused"—also wrote, "The husband cannot be guilty of a rape committed by himself upon his lawful wife, for by their mutual matrimonial consent and contract, the wife hath given up herself in this kind unto her husband, which she cannot retract."[19]

Until the late twentieth century, when feminist agitation for the reform of rape laws finally began to penetrate our nation's collective thick skull, Hale's three-hundred-year-old notions remained the standard. The marriage contract automatically included sex on demand, regardless of the wife's feelings at any given time. The idea of consenting to unlimited future sex, without restrictions, should strike any reasonable person as absurd; consent can only be freely given if the opportunity to withdraw it exists. But when you consider how long Hale's pronouncements held sway in US and British courts, you begin to see why so many of us have ass-backward ideas about what it means.

The unfortunate result of that widespread ignorance is not only that we still imagine "real" rapists jumping out of the bushes, or hiding in dark alleys, but that we still regard the crime as especially repugnant because it involves dirty, shameful genitals and can rob a "pure" woman of her virtue. A lot of lawmakers were still stuck on that point well into the twenty-first century. "Rape, ladies and gentlemen, is not today what rape was," said Tennessee state senator Douglas Henry in 2008. "Rape, when I was learning these things, was the violation of a chaste woman, against her will, by some party not her spouse. Today it's simply, 'Let's don't go forward with this act.'"[20]

Yes, exactly! Human beings have a right to say, "Let's don't go forward with this act," and have their wishes respected, even if they're not "chaste," and even if they're married to the person who does want to go forward with the act in question. That's both what the law says in every state of the union and what any sensible person would call a simple truth—an iteration of the golden fucking rule. But not Douglas Henry.

And not South Dakota state senator Bill Napoli, who, when asked to describe a scenario in which allowing someone to terminate a pregnancy would be a valid option, said, "A real-life description to me would be a rape victim, brutally raped, savaged. The girl was a virgin. She was religious. She planned on saving her virginity until she was married. She was brutalized and raped, sodomized as bad as you can possibly make it, and is impregnated. I mean, that girl could be so messed up, physically and psychologically, that carrying that child could very well threaten her life." [21]

But if she wasn't a virgin? Wasn't religious? Didn't plan on saving herself? If she wasn't "brutalized and raped, sodomized *as bad as you can possibly make it*"? (I shudder to think what that even means.) Well, then, I guess one can only conclude she was asking for it.

The Power of the Vote

Impeachment might have a certain appeal, but as I said in chapter 6, using your vote in every election is the number one thing you can do to keep ignorant clowns out of office. Campaign for their opponents. Support leaders who prioritize women's health and safety—and recognize that those who want government control of female fertility do *not* prioritize women's health and safety.

The thinking behind the admonition "If she doesn't want to get pregnant, she shouldn't spread her legs" is exactly what drives people to blame rape victims for wearing provocative clothing, drinking heavily, or having any sexual history at all. The common denominator is a woman who wants to be sexual on her own terms without being punished for it, who wants the power to say both yes and no as freely as a man can.

That's pretty much all of us, if you had any doubt: 95 percent of American women have had premarital sex by the age of forty-four. Even by age twenty, three-quarters of Americans have had sex, while only 12 percent have married.[22] Additionally, 99 percent of sexually active women between fifteen and forty-four have at some point used contraception. The average woman hopes to have only two children in that whole adult lifetime of having sex.[23]

So in case you hadn't already figured this out via common sense, the data is conclusive: women desire sex, seek it out, and have it, even when they don't want to become pregnant. If you're a grown man who somehow still doesn't grasp this concept, ask yourself two questions:

1. Have I ever felt the urge to have sex for fun, without causing massive, potentially life-threatening changes to my body, followed by parenthood?
2. If at some point I didn't feel like having sex with someone, would I want that person to respect my opinion on the matter and cease trying to have sex with me?

If you answered yes to both questions, congratulations! You know exactly what it's like to be a grown woman. Nevertheless, an amazing amount of political energy is still—in the twenty-first century—spent propping up the fiction that women need male supervision to make decisions about their sexual activity and fertility.

"Recent rollbacks of women's political rights—especially reproductive rights—stem directly from the belief that women shouldn't have control over their own bodies," writes feminist author Jessica Valenti in *The Purity Myth: How America's Obsession with Virginity Is Hurting Young Women*. "More and more, policy that affects women's bodies and rights is being formulated with the myth of sexual purity in mind."[24]

Enough is enough. Whether we're talking about access to legal abortion or the definition of "legitimate rape," the fundamental question is: Who gets to decide when, where, and why a woman has sex?

There is only one correct answer, and any politician who needs more than two seconds to come up with it does not deserve your vote.

PART III

THE CULTURE OF RAPE

CHAPTER 8

Virgins, Vamps, and the View from Nowhere

I n her 1992 book *Virgins and Vamps: How the Press Covers Sex Crimes*, Helen Benedict writes of "eight factors that lead the public, and the press, to blame the victim for a rape and to push her into the role of 'vamp.'"[1] Not surprisingly, they dovetail with the basic rape myths we've already discussed.

The eight factors are:

1. The victim knowing the assailant.
2. The lack of a weapon.
3. The victim and perpetrator being of the same race.
4. The victim and perpetrator being of the same class.
5. The victim and perpetrator being of the same ethnic background.
6. The victim being young.
7. The victim being perceived as pretty.
8. The victim "in any way deviat[ing] from the traditional female sex role of being at home with family and children."[2]

Regarding items 3, 4, and 5, Benedict explains what you probably already guessed: the more privileged the victim, and the less privileged the assailant, the more likely it is that the media will take an accusation of rape seriously. If you must be raped, you should try to be an upper-class white woman attacked by a poor person of color, because that's your best chance of being perceived as credible.

Says Benedict, "If prejudices to do with ethnicity or nationality can be called in to slur the assailant, the victim will benefit."[3] Similarly, the less sexualized you are, the more likely you are to be believed, so you should try to be an older woman who's never been considered much of a looker.

Virgin or Vamp is old enough that in writing about the Central Park Five case, Benedict operates on the assumption that the right men were convicted. Nevertheless, after reading a great deal of more recent reporting on sexual assault and rape charges while writing this book, I can confirm that not too much has changed in the last twenty-three years.

There Are Worse Things Than Being Kidnapped by a Pedophile

If the most blameworthy sexual violence victim by current Western standards is, say, an attractive, poor, twenty-something trans woman of color, employed as a sex worker and raped by a police officer, then what would a blameless victim look like? Perhaps a freckle-faced, eleven-year-old California girl abducted by strangers on her way to school? Or a young white boy the same age, taken while riding his bicycle in rural Missouri? If kids like that were held and repeatedly raped by violent criminals for *years on end*, we couldn't possibly blame them, could we?

Have I taught you nothing? Of course we could!

Shawn Hornbeck, the young boy, spent four and a half years living in a one-bedroom apartment with his rapist and captor; he was rescued in 2007 as a result of the search for a younger boy the criminal had recently taken. And when Jaycee Lee Dugard, the California fifth grader, was found in 2009, she'd been a prisoner of convicted sex offender Phillip Garrido and his wife, Nancy, for eighteen years and had two children by Garrido.

The first—and second, third, fourth, and gazillionth—question each one of them was asked in subsequent interviews was, "Why didn't you try to escape?"

In each case, the abused child had some contact with other people, some theoretical opportunity to get away, and that was enough to set folks a-judgin'. Everything we know about Stockholm Syndrome, brainwashing, and abuse—to wit, that a controlling, manipulative person can convince someone else to feel completely, helplessly dependent on them—didn't curb some people's need to blame the victim.

Fox News's reliably odious Bill O'Reilly, for instance, didn't "buy the Stockholm Syndrome thing" with regard to Shawn Hornbeck and suggested on his show, *The O'Reilly Factor*, that the boy didn't try to escape because "there was an element here that this kid liked about this circumstances."[4]

Go ahead and take a second to let that sink in.

O'Reilly's logic, if you can call it that, dictates that spending four and a half years in a one-bedroom apartment with a man who regularly rapes you, never seeing your family or friends, and fearing for your life might not be such a bad deal for a kid because, hey, no homework!

"The situation here for this kid looks to me to be a lot more fun than what he had under his old parents," he told Fox legal expert Greta van Susteren. (His "old parents"! As if *the man who abducted him and at least one other boy* was just Hornbeck's new daddy.) "He didn't have to go to school. He could run around and do whatever he wanted."[5]

Being kidnapped by a pedophile: it's basically like summer camp that never ends, if you ask Bill O'Reilly.

The following day, after reader mail made it clear that O'Reilly had gone over the top even for a champion victim blamer like himself, he offered this clarification:

> I actually hope I'm wrong about Shawn Hornbeck. I hope he did not make a conscious decision to accept his captivity because Devlin made things easy for him. No school, play all day long.[6]

(Play. All. Day. Long. You cannot make this shit up.)

> But to just chalk this up to brainwashing and walk away is turning away from the true danger of child molesters and abductors. All American children must be taught survival skills, must be prepared to face crisis situations. That is the lesson of the Shawn Hornbeck story.[7]

You know, I actually hope I'm wrong about Bill O'Reilly. I mean, I have no training in psychology, so I'm not qualified to diagnose anyone with, like, a personality disorder. I hope he *does* have an ounce of conscience, a soupçon of human empathy deep inside him, a scintilla of warm blood hidden in some wee capillary.

But to just chalk this up to gross attention-mongering and walk away is to turn away from the true danger of rape culture. All American children must be taught that if someone hurts them, it is not their fault; must be prepared to understand as adults that criminals, not victims, are the ones responsible for their crimes. That is the lesson of the Bill O'Reilly story.

In all seriousness, we should listen to Elizabeth Smart on this subject. Smart, who was abducted from her home at age fourteen and held for nine months before being rescued, told NBC News in a 2013 interview, "It is wrong for any person to ever judge someone in any situation saying, 'Well, why didn't you try to run? Why didn't you scream? Why didn't you try to do something?' That is so wrong and, frankly, offensive to even ask that question."[8]

Smart, a religious virgin from a stable, two-parent family when she was taken, is the kind of victim the media can usually muster a great deal of sympathy for, but even she is asked "frequently" why she didn't take the first opportunity to demand help. As with Dugard and Hornbeck, the element of the story that makes it so horrific—sustained captivity—is also the one that makes some people question whether these kidnapped children brought at least part of their ordeals upon themselves.

Journalists who harp on this point may believe they're only asking what's on everyone's mind, but in fact, they're keeping an absurd, offensive question at the foreground of a story that should be about a child who's been the victim of multiple terrible crimes. Demanding that young people kidnapped as children and held captive for months or years justify their inability to escape is the apex of victim blaming, and it's grotesque.

"Personal Responsibility"

I could give you examples from Fox News all day long, but I'll limit myself to one more before I turn my attention to what the Fox folks would call "the liberal media."

In September 2014, Forbes.com columnist Bill Frezza was fired after writing a doozy of a victim-blaming article, "Drunk Female Guests Are the Gravest Threat to Fraternities." It was basically just what you'd expect from the title—an aging frat bro railing against "a world that no longer believes in personal responsibility" and "*new standards being promulgated on campus,*" wherein students are expected not to rape each other, even while drunk.[9]

"In our age of sexual equality," wrote Frezza, "why drunk female students are almost never characterized as irresponsible jerks is a question I leave to the feminists."[10]

Ooh, ooh, I can answer that one! But first, let's hear what the panelists on Fox News's *Outnumbered*, a show that pits one hapless man against four women, had to say.

"Where's the personal responsibility for both sides?" asks Andrea Tantaros. "Really! If we say personal responsibility for women, the feminists go berserk!" Adopting a mocking tone, she continues, "They're like, 'No, we should be able to wear whatever we want, and drink as much as we want, and pass out in the streets.'"[11]

Well, yes, actually, we should be able to do all that. Passing out in the street is never the ideal outcome of a night on the town, and I hope anyone doing that will get a stern but loving talking-to from people who care about their well-being. But there is no Bad Personal Choices threshold past which someone deserves to be raped, let alone one past which rape is not a criminal act. In your haste to denigrate women who carry themselves like some kind of *adults*, choosing their own clothing and deciding how much to drink without supervision, please try not to forget that.

Cohost Kirsten Powers then takes the baton:

> It makes the drunk girl completely clean no matter what happens—and again, we have to say it because some cuckoo person is going to start blogging how we are supporting women getting raped, which we do not support. And she is not guilty or any of those things, but the point is that the drunk woman is—she's just not held accountable for anything. The drunk guy, however, is supposed to make all these amazingly perfect decisions, and not make any mistakes.[12]

No one steps in to remind these women that we are talking about holding fraternity members accountable for *raping people*, not for drinking too much and acting like dummies. Which brings us back to Frezza's question, echoed by Tantaros: Where's the personal responsibility? Why aren't female students who get wasted characterized as irresponsible jerks?

Answer: They are! By every feminist I know! (At least, the women who *act* like irresponsible jerks are. Some people just get drunk quietly and listen to sad music or write fan fiction; I have no beef with them.)

When it came out that the newly crowned Miss America 2015 had been kicked out of her sorority for abusive hazing practices, I read about it first on feminist blogs. When it felt as if the whole world was discussing Ray Rice, Adrian Peterson, and the NFL's domestic violence program at the start of the 2014 football season, Erin Gloria Ryan at Jezebel.com was one of the loudest voices asking why women's soccer champ Hope Solo, accused of drunkenly attacking her seventeen-year-old nephew, didn't receive the same level of scrutiny. (Granted, other feminist writers called that a false equivalency, but contrary to popular opinion, disagreement is allowed within feminism.)

Here is my official position as a feminist: If you get drunk and treat people shabbily, you're an irresponsible jerk. If you get drunk and commit crimes, you're an irresponsible jerk and a criminal. These things are true irrespective of gender.

The reason feminists "go berserk" when people like Frezza, Tantaros, and Powers talk about young women's "personal responsibility" vis-à-vis frat parties and rape is simple: *rape is a crime.* No one, of any gender, is legally allowed to rape someone else while drunk—just as no one's allowed to drive a car, beat someone up, steal money, destroy property, or commit fraud while drunk. It is everyone's responsibility to remain on the side of *not* committing crimes while drinking. Women and men are held to exactly the same standard, in that respect.

But no, victims are not typically held to the same standard as criminals. Our legal system does not (technically) require victims to make only impeccable life decisions or else forfeit their right to protection under the law. If a frat boy gets plastered, wanders into the street, and gets hit by a drunk driver, the driver is the criminal. If a businessman overindulges at happy hour and insults an equally loaded person who decides to punch said businessman in the face, the punch thrower is the criminal. If two people drink the exact same amount of alcohol and do the exact same amount of the exact same drug, and then one murders the other, the killer is the criminal, and the dead person is the victim. See how this works?

Likewise, if two people get equally fucked up, and then one rapes the other, *the rapist is the criminal*. Even if the person who got raped was flirting, even if she went into a bedroom with the rapist, even if her friends told her she should probably go to bed an hour before it happened, and she told them to piss off and ordered shots. The person who got raped is the victim. Period.

This principle is neither unfair nor gendered; it's common fucking sense, and we understand that when it comes to any crime other than rape. But rape myths, combined with a feigned objectivity New York University media scholar Jay Rosen calls "the View from Nowhere," create a media atmosphere in which every remark about rape must be "balanced" by its most extreme possible counterpart. Fox News may have "trolling liberals" in its mission statement, but mainstream and even expressly left-wing outlets sometimes seem afraid that if they take any obvious position on rape—including "it's bad"—without airing a counterargument, they'll be accused of an ethical lapse.

In a post at his blog PressThink, Rosen writes about the difference between the View from Nowhere and a more functional definition of "objectivity":

> If objectivity means trying to ground truth claims in verifiable facts, I am definitely for that. If it means there's a "hard" reality out there that exists beyond any of our descriptions of it, sign me up. If objectivity is the requirement to acknowledge what is, regardless of whether we want it to be that way, then I want journalists who can be objective in that sense. Don't you?[13]

Yes, absolutely!

But the View from Nowhere, which tries "to secure a kind of universal legitimacy" by pretending there's no pesky human being filtering the objective facts, is fatally flawed. It's what makes reporters go to two polarized sources for opinions, instead of applying their own reason and judgment to determine where the truth most likely lies. In reporting on rape cases, it's what inclines journalists to treat claims by victims and alleged criminals with equal skepticism, affecting a detached, all-seeing stance, which in turn fuels the myth that a large number of rape reports are likely false. It's what makes the Andrea Tantaroses of the world say things like, "Where's the personal responsibility for both sides?" when the two sides in question are rapist and victim.

"Gray" Matters

In a 2007 *Cosmopolitan* article, "A New Kind of Date Rape," author Laura Sessions Stepp coined the term "gray rape" to describe "sex that falls somewhere between consent and denial." Despite the headline, there's nothing new about her subject: in 1994, Katie Roiphe published *The Morning After: Fear, Sex, and Feminism*, an entire book arguing that people throw around the term "rape" too casually, especially to describe regrettable but consensual drunken hookups. That book, in turn, was a reaction to the work of feminists looking to name an experience that was far from new, but rarely discussed; Robin Warshaw's contemporary classic, *I Never Called It Rape*, had sparked mainstream awareness of "date rape" only six years earlier.

Stepp sees no need to acknowledge that every example she uses to bolster her argument is a clear case of nonconsent. "Alicia" told her date "flat-out that she didn't want to proceed to sex" and told him to stop before he "ignored her and entered her anyway." "Laura" was in college when she got drunk and made out with a guy who then stripped off her pants and entered her, despite the fact that she said no. A twenty-year-old Naval Academy student woke up to a football player having sex with her. Remind me where the "gray" is here?

But because the women in question felt guilt, confusion, and self-doubt—as a great many victims do—Stepp freely categorizes their experiences as something other than violent crimes. And she doesn't stop at reducing these violations to lesser charges; she invents a quasi-legal term that incorporates the worst of both worlds—"rape" because it is, and "gray" because few will believe it's that simple. The "gray" in "gray rape" is an imaginary fog of questions about what consent means and whether you really need it *every* time.

Repackaging rape victims' tendency toward self-recrimination as a mitigating—or at least muddying—factor simultaneously contributes to and reflects a culture in which women are afraid no one will believe them if they report a rape. Stepp (and umpteen commentators since) have tried to blame "hookup culture," binge drinking, the decline of religious values, popular music, teenage hormones, poor communication, and bad parenting for sexual violence. In other words, they've put the onus for rape on anything except rapists.

Believers in "gray rape" encourage victims of all genders, but especially young women, to consider what they might have done to provoke their attackers and whether there's any possibility that those nice people just didn't realize what they were doing could be characterized as a crime. They conflate being sexually inexperienced or awkward with being unable to tell the difference between consent and nonconsent, calling every report of rape into question and handily obscuring the motives of people for whom nonconsent is the whole point.

Great Men Don't Rape-Rape

It was absolutely shocking, in the wake of Roman Polanski's arrest, to see how many mainstream journalists tried to brush off the statutory rape he committed by pointing out that people said his thirteen-year-old victim looked closer to twenty, that her mother practically forced the girl on him, and that she doesn't want to talk about it anymore, so out of respect for the survivor, we should neither prosecute Polanski nor call him a rapist.

There was a celebrity petition, framing the arrest as unjust persecution of a gentle old man, signed by so many people that if I wanted to boycott them all, I would have to forgo movie watching for several generations. Directors Pedro Almodovar, Martin Scorsese, David Lynch, Jonathan Demme, Wim Wenders, and, perhaps not surprisingly, Woody Allen all signed. The star power on that list was no accident; a spokesperson for producer Harvey Weinstein told CNN, "We are calling every filmmaker we can to help fix this terrible situation."[14]

The "terrible situation" of a fugitive rapist being arrested after thirty years of freedom, but okay.

At that point, 138 Hollywood figures had already signed the petition. The people who merely added their names to a list are bad enough, but I still can't watch Jack Nicholson, in whose home the rape took place, or his then-girlfriend Anjelica Huston, without thinking, "You were there. *You were right there.*"

Not to be outdone by the film industry, journalists made a nauseating show of their dedication to the cinematic arts and open-mindedness about a little long-ago child rape. Take the *Washington Post*'s Anne Applebaum—wife of Polish foreign minister and Polanski supporter Radoslaw Sikorski—who blamed the director's "original, panicky decision to flee" on "an understandable fear of irrational punishment," owing to his childhood in communist Poland and the loss of his mother in the Holocaust.

Setting aside that criminal punishment for raping a child and fleeing the country prior to sentencing would, in fact, be rational, what of the three decades he had to rethink that decision? Applebaum doesn't say. Although she acknowledges that he "did commit a crime"—at least two, by my count, but that's a start—she actually tries to defend him with the most maddening possible argument: "There is evidence that Polanski did not know her real age."[15]

Okay, first, although Polanski only pled guilty to unlawful sex with a minor, let's not forget that he gave this child champagne and Quaaludes, *and*, on top of that, she testified that she did not consent to having sex with him. Either one would be considered evidence of rape regardless of the victim's age, so her youth is really just the icing on the cake.

Still, that a grown person with a platform in one of the nation's most venerable newspapers would stoop to "She looked older!" to defend a friend who, at forty-six years old, drugged and raped a thirteen-year-old, should tell you what kind of culture we're living in. One that starts with *r* and rhymes with "grape."

Listen, if you can't think of a way to determine a young female human being's age, apart from looking at her and guessing, here's a tip: atop all that nubile flesh, you will find a head, containing a brain and a mouth that is very probably capable of answering questions. I promise, it is not considered rude to ask a lady her age until she is much, much older. Go for it.

"But what if she lies?" you will inevitably wonder, if you're the kind of person who needs to entertain this hypothetical in the first place. Well, again, it's a matter of asking yourself two questions:

1. Are you over eighteen?
2. Is there even the tiniest bit of doubt in your mind that this person is at least as old as you?

If you answered yes to both of those questions, do not have sex with this person. Go find a willing partner who is definitely at least as old as you are, or jerk off, or maybe just go have a nap or watch some TV. What you do next is not my business, as long as you *do not have sex with a person who might not be old enough to legally consent.* Follow this one simple rule, and you will never accidentally rape a child. Easy peasy.

If only Polanski had asked himself those questions in 1977, his supporters wouldn't have had to embarrass themselves all over the international media in 2009. Joan Z. Shore, for example—a former Paris correspondent for CBS News—wouldn't have found herself publishing this ridiculous statement in the Huffington Post: "The 13-year-old model 'seduced' by Polanski had been thrust onto him by her mother, who wanted her in the movies."[16] As though being pimped out by her own mother, if true, made the girl *less* of a victim?

Likewise, actress Debra Winger wouldn't have had to publicly accuse Swiss authorities of philistinism, twisting the arrest into an appalling blow against artistic freedom.[17] And poor old Whoopi wouldn't have to deal with the likes of me beating the "rape-rape" thing right into the ground.

Also, a thirteen-year-old wouldn't have been raped. There's that.

There are numerous examples of men taking up for Polanski in the wake of his arrest, but it's worth noting that so many women came to the director's defense. The problem with rape culture is that it doesn't pick and choose who gets the message that adolescents who look like adults are asking for it, or that it's possible for a thirteen-year-old to consent to sex with a man more than three times her age, let alone "seduce" him. It doesn't address the memo claiming an identifiable difference between "rape" and "rape-rape" to anyone in particular. It doesn't specify that only men should identify with a Great Man™ and Artistic Genius™ who happened to have a little lapse in judgment, so many years ago.

It suffuses the environment we all live in, encouraging women to mistrust and blame each other, and to always prioritize men's feelings and needs above our own.

The Media's Groping Problem

In May 2011, when news broke that action hero and former California governor Arnold Schwarzenegger was getting divorced, in part because he'd fathered a child with a household employee, Conor Friedersdorf of the *Atlantic* wrote, "I've yet to encounter anyone surprised by the news. It's because we remember. Eight years ago, on the eve of the special election that won him the statehouse, the *Los Angeles Times* published a scathing story about his groping problem."[18]

That article, by James Rainey, explained that "eventually, a total of 16 women, 11 of them giving their names, described physical humiliations suffered at the hands of [Schwarzenegger]."[19] Those "humiliations" alleged numerous instances of uninvited, unwanted touching, which ran the gamut from inappropriate to illegal.

Obviously, this bombshell didn't stop Californians from electing Schwarzenegger anyway. But support for the new governor went beyond indifference to his alleged crimes, or forgiveness for them; a number of Californians got angry at the *L.A. Times* for reporting on the accusations. Not at Schwarzenegger for jeopardizing his future political career by repeatedly taking liberties with women he encountered, but at the journalists who brought it to the public's attention.

"Some accused the paper of a politically motivated attack, meant to hurt Schwarzenegger and prop up the struggling Davis," wrote Rainey. "They complained with particular vehemence about the timing of the story, published five days before the recall vote. At least 10,000 subscribers cancelled the paper, according to executives who were with the paper at the time."

Of course. To a true lover of American-style democracy, the only thing worse than a governor who allegedly commits sexual assault is a free press that reports on it. Makes perfect sense.

The Schwarzenegger "love child" story came to light not long after then-head of the International Monetary Fund, Dominique Strauss-Kahn, was accused of raping a West African hotel maid. DSK and his defenders—including French blowhard Bernard-Henri Lévy, already famous in the United States for his florid, ass-kissing defense of convicted rapist Roman Polanski—kept insisting that Strauss-Kahn had probably just worked his suave old European guy magic on Nafissatou Diallo that day.

"The Strauss-Kahn I know, who has been my friend for 20 years and who will remain my friend, bears no resemblance to this monster, this caveman, this insatiable and malevolent beast now being described nearly everywhere," Lévy vomited in the *Daily Beast*. "Charming, seductive, yes, certainly; a friend to women and, first of all, to his own woman, naturally, but this brutal and violent individual, this wild animal, this primate, obviously no, it's absurd."[20]

Charming. Seductive. A friend to women. *Obviously*. In France, according to several reports, Strauss-Kahn is nicknamed "the Great Seducer."[21]

Sure, there were only eight minutes between Diallo entering and leaving Strauss-Kahn's room, but that's plenty of time for a sixty-something master lady-killer to:

- proposition a strange woman thirty years his junior (and just trying to do her job)
- achieve an enthusiastic "Sure, let's bone right now!"
- follow through on that
- kick her back out the door.

If you think that scenario sounds not just implausible but basically impossible, you are obviously not the Great Seducer. QED.

Accordingly, the American media spent a great deal of time airing out its inferiority complex by wondering whether French social mores weren't more sex-positive and ultimately better for men and women alike. It's all about respecting cultural differences, you see! Here in the uptight, puritanical United States, you can go to prison for shaking a lady's hand, but in Europe, sticking your dick in someone's mouth is just a friendly way to say howdy! Let the Great Seducer seduce.

The problem is whether Strauss-Kahn is indeed "the Great Seducer" has very little to do with whether he might also be "the great rapist," because rape is not actually seduction gone pear-shaped. Similarly, any consensual affairs Schwarzenegger had over the years have very little to do with his "groping problem," which would probably be better described as "a problem with giving a tiny rat's ass about consent."

That's not to say these things are entirely unrelated, mind you. There are certainly points of overlap between being a cad and being a criminal: an overblown sense of entitlement, an apparent lack of empathy for anyone you might hurt, an erection. But cheating on your wife is not a gateway drug to sexual assault. They are two different things, one of them a crime. (If you're a journalist, please take a moment now to repeat that to yourself a few times.)

And then please consider this: A man who's known for grabbing women's breasts and asses without their consent (a crime) is not just some slightly pathetic, lovesick fool until the day someone accuses him of non-consensual penetration. He was actually already a sexual predator.

Do you see the difference? One guy treats women rather shabbily, and he should be ashamed of himself. The other guy treats women like inanimate objects that he is entitled to do whatever he wants to, and he should be ashamed of himself and also held legally responsible for his crimes.

But when you have a man who is known for both cheating repeatedly and taking a handful of another human being whenever he sees fit, the reporting inevitably becomes a horrifying clusterfuck of conflation, rationalization, and misinformation. So having sex with someone other than your wife becomes the moral equivalent of sticking your hand down someone's pants without her consent—both filed under the rubric of "sexual indiscretions" or "regrettable peccadilloes"—while rape remains this whole other thing that only monsters far outside the general population would ever do.

After that, of course people start saying it's ridiculous to assume that just because someone would cheat on his wife, he's probably also capable of rape. Because *that is actually true*: those things are not directly related.

It's somewhat less ridiculous, however, to assume that just because someone would commit nonpenetrative sexual assaults, he might also be capable of committing penetrative ones. What's genuinely ridiculous is the rush to minimize—or glamorize—a public figure's known "groping problem" when he's accused of something a bit farther along the nonconsensual continuum. *Sure, everyone knew the lion liked to chase gazelles and pin them down and bat them around a bit for fun, but he would never eat one! That's just not in his nature.*

If you're still confused, ask yourself this simple question: How the hell did a habit of grabbing fistfuls of boob become the hallmark of a "great seducer"?

"Sex by Surprise"

I said the liberal and progressive media would get their due in this chapter, and their response to the 2010 sexual assault and rape allegations against WikiLeaks founder Julian Assange offers volumes of suitable material. Please forgive me for dwelling on this subject a little longer than others, but it contains so many examples of the ways in which media figures min-imize the gravity of serious accusations and smear alleged victims who come forward.

At this writing, Assange remains in hiding at the Ecuadorian embassy in London, where he moved after a British court decided that Sweden, where the alleged assaults took place, had the right to extradite him. Two different women reported being violated by Assange, in addition to hav-ing consensual sex with him. One, known in the press as Miss A, told police that, after she agreed to sex, Assange balked at her insistence that he use a condom, pinning her arms and trying to put his naked penis inside her while she physically resisted. In other words, she says that instead of accepting her perfectly reasonable condition for consensual sex, Assange made a deliberate choice to push forward in a manner she expressly did not consent to. Later, he agreed to wear a condom, but it somehow ended up with a tear in it, and Miss A expressed suspicion that he deliberately destroyed it.

The other woman who reported that Assange violated her, known as Miss W, told police that, among other things, she woke up to find his penis inside her. And although he has not been tried—or even formally charged—at this writing, Assange's own defense has acknowledged pub-licly that, yes, he really did put his dick in a sleeping woman.

"They fell asleep and she woke up by his penetrating her," said attor-ney Ben Emmerson at the July 2011 extradition hearing. "She may have been upset, but she clearly consented to its continuation and that is a cen-tral consideration."[22]

A central consideration in *what*? How harshly he's punished for the rape you just described?

Clare Montgomery, the barrister representing Swedish authorities at that hearing, called Emmerson out for "effectively winding the law on consent back to the 19th century," adding, "At best, the words 'I let him' amount to submission, not free consent."[23] Exactly! But as we've already discussed at length, it's amazing how many people aren't clear on the simple fact that sleeping people cannot freely consent to sex.

After a European arrest warrant was issued for Assange in December 2010, much of the original coverage downplayed the seriousness of that allegation, imputing that the whole case was a politically motivated witch hunt, based on some vague misunderstanding over a condom. And when you tried to trace that rumor back to its origin, you inevitably arrived at one of three articles:

1. "The WikiLeaks Sex Files: How Two One-Night Stands Sparked a Worldwide Hunt for Julian Assange," by Richard Pendlebury in the *Daily Mail*, a famously sensationalistic British tabloid. Pendlebury insinuates that Assange was the victim of a "honeytrap" by the US government and declares that "Sweden's complex rape laws are central to the story."

2. "Assange Besieged," a barely readable but widely circulated screed by Israel Shamir and Paul Bennett in the muckraking magazine *Counter-Punch*. Claiming that Assange stands accused merely of (1) not calling after a one-night stand, (2) asking a woman for bus fare, (3) having unprotected sex, and (4) sleeping with two women in the same week, the authors also go on about one victim's "anti-Castro, pro-CIA streak," her "favorite sport of male-bashing," and her expertise in "sexual harassment and the male 'master suppression techniques.'" (Whatever those are.)

3. A now-deleted AOL News article by Dana Kennedy, which itself relied heavily on Pendlebury's piece and a Swedish tabloid. Kennedy's article introduced the twin claims, which evinced cockroach-like tenacity in subsequent coverage, that there is a Swedish law against "sex by surprise" and that the warrant for Assange's arrest "apparently stems from a condom malfunction."[24] Both of those nuggets came from a lawyer for Assange, which did not give anyone inclined to believe them pause.

Now let's take look at some of the damage those three articles wrought.

"Anatomy of a Smear"

At Gizmodo (a high-traffic tech blog owned by Gawker Media), Jesus Diaz picked up the "sex by surprise" claim and ran with it:

> According to Swedish law, a woman can denounce a man if he
> doesn't use a condom after he has been requested to wear it, even
> if the sex is completely consensual, like apparently was the case here.
> They call this offense "sex by surprise." It could get him condemned
> to a maximum fine of 5,000 Swedish kronor ($715), but no jail time.[25]

Diaz cites no source, apart from the lawyer's claim, and you will not
be surprised to learn that nothing of the sort appears in the Swedish criminal code. The rest of his post is a recap of Pendlebury's article, building to
this geyser of righteous indignation:

> While you can say Assange is a douchebag for not putting a con-
> dom on and continuing after the woman requested he use a condom,
> there was *no* rape accusation in both cases.... Perhaps Fox and most
> of the media out there is going with the "Assange wanted for rape"
> line because "Assange wanted for broken condom and not using a
> condom in morning sex" doesn't have quite the same ring to it.[26]

Note the dig at Fox there. If you've read this far, you're well aware
that I'm no fan of the conservative network and wouldn't trust one of
their news reports unless I were an eyewitness, but in this case, that's not
even the point. Diaz is reminding you that the American right is eager
to drum up anti-Assange sentiment because of his technically illegal but
widely praised work with WikiLeaks, where he published classified documents that detailed abuses of government power.

Honestly, Diaz is probably right about that. I'm sure conservative
reporters relished the chance to knock down a hero of the left—just as
I'm sure the US government was delighted to see Assange brought low
and more than willing to cooperate with international efforts to put him
in prison for any reason. But unlike many journalists of the left, I never
believed my government was behind a "honeytrap" operation to frame
Assange for rape or that the obvious political motivation for pursuing him
aggressively meant he was necessarily innocent.

To my mind, there is no reason to believe that these two propositions
are mutually exclusive: Julian Assange may have committed the sex crimes

of which he's been accused, *and* he probably wouldn't have been prose-cuted if various world powers weren't champing at the bit to take him down. I don't have enough information to prove either conclusively, but theoretically, there's no reason why both couldn't be true simultaneously.

But based on a few weak sources—combined with the seductive image of Assange as a high-tech Robin Hood, taking power from shady government officials and giving it to the people—a whole bunch of civil liberties–loving journalists produced work that was terribly disappointing to anti-rape activists.

In a post called "Anatomy of a Smear," Kit Eaton at *Fast Company* accused the *New York Times*, among others, of participating in a "smear campaign" against Assange for reporting, accurately, that he was charged with "rape, sexual molestation, and unlawful coercion."[27]

The paper of record was wrong, according to Eaton, because Assange was *actually* "facing arrest for violating a Swedish law about sex without condoms, rather than a mainstream interpretation of 'rape.'"

> Assange's former lawyer yesterday "confirmed" the charges were to do with sexual misconduct concerning sex without condoms. Assange's current lawyer then revealed Swedish prosectors [sic] had told him they were not seeking Assange for "rape" at all, instead the alleged crime is "sex by surprise," which carries a penalty of a fine, although the details of the allegations haven't been revealed yet.[28]

That Eaton's sole source for that paragraph was Kennedy's AOL News article (elsewhere, he draws on Pendlebury's *Daily Mail* piece) is almost beside the point. More troubling even than the widespread reli-ance on that one article is the ease with which Eaton, and so many others, accepted the word of *defense lawyers* as gospel truth.

Defense lawyers! Their entire job is to make people think their clients aren't guilty. And a journalist's job is to investigate such claims, not regur-gitate an accused criminal's preferred talking points.

After reading Kennedy's article, Pulitzer Prize–winning reporter David Cay Johnston, in a letter to journalism watchdog Jim Romenesko, wrote: "The first rule of journalism—check it out—seems to have been forgotten by every journalist in the world writing about the Swedish 'rape' charges against Julian Assange."[29]

Hear, hear! Finally, someone is talking sense about fact-checking and exercising healthy skepticism. I can't wait to hear what else he has to say.

Except, wait a minute, what's up with those quotes around "rape"?

"The exception," Johnston continues, "is Dana Kennedy of AOL."

Oh, brother.

He continues:

Our best news organizations—The NYTimes, WashPost, WSJ, LATimes, USA Today, AP, ABC, CBS, NBC, NPR, PBS and Reuters—all used "rape" as the crime at issue with little to no nuance, clips at Google News show. None, as best I can tell, reported that the crime in question is condom slippage.[30]

Yep, it's totally bizarre how none of those venerable institutions reported an easily debunked claim that came straight from the accused's defense.

Kevin Drum, writing for the progressive publication *Mother Jones*, tried to exercise a bit more skepticism and restraint in a blog post about Pendlebury's piece, cautioning that it contains "loaded language" best ignored. Nevertheless, he said, Pendlebury "does lay out the basic narrative fairly well."[31]

Really? Pendlebury's narrative begins with the premise that "there remains a huge question mark over the evidence," plays up the "radical" and "militant" feminist background of one victim, and questions whether either one behaved like a "real" victim. (Both women saw Assange socially after the alleged assaults. This is actually quite common in cases where the perpetrator is known to the victim—I talked to my own rapist at a couple of parties before I dropped out of the college we both went to—but will invariably be used to cast doubt on the victim's testimony that the same man violated her.)

Pendlebury uses the phrase "made love" to describe an alleged assault, dwells on reports of one victim "boasting to friends about her flirtation" with Assange, and claims that "there is scant evidence—in the public domain at least—of rape, sexual molestation or unlawful coercion."

(Enough for prosecutors to issue an international arrest warrant and send him into hiding, but who's counting?) He ends with the words, "the allegations simply don't ring true." And all of this information, I remind you, comes from anonymous sources.

In my book (specifically, this one), that's not "laying out the basics fairly well," so much as "torturing the basics to bolster a preconceived conclusion that the accused is innocent."

So, what did Pendlebury get right, in Drum's estimation?

> Basically, it involves consensual sex that allegedly turned unconsensual because (in one case) a condom broke and (in the other case) Assange refused to wear a condom in the first place—both of which are crimes in Sweden under the circumstances Assange is charged with (i.e., forcibly continuing with intercourse despite the withdrawal of consent).[32]

Consensual sex turned "unconsensual"! Forcible intercourse, following the withdrawal of consent! In other words, *rape*. Why does Drum—along with half the liberal and progressive commentators on the matter, in late 2010—seem to think these things are only crimes in Sweden?

Getting the Reporting Right

It doesn't take a crack investigative reporter to locate suggested best practices for reporting on sexual violence. Here are some tips from articles and reports that appear within the first two pages of a simple web search.

"Get the language right. Rape or assault is not 'sex.' A pattern of abuse is not an 'affair.' Rape or sexual assault is in no way associated with normal sexual activity; trafficking in women is not to be confused with prostitution."[33]—Dart Center for Journalism and Trauma Tip Sheet

"Be careful about details that could imply you are *blaming victims*. Describing what a girl was wearing, or how she made a choice, can be perceived as assigning blame."[34]—Kelly McBride, The Poynter Institute

"If the victim you are reporting about comes from a marginalized community—if they are queer, trans, poor, disabled, an immigrant, a person of color or a sex worker—take extra care that the pernicious stereotypes that surround that community do not impact your piece."[35]—Jessica Valenti, *The Nation*

"Tell the whole story. Sometimes media identify specific incidents and focus on the tragic aspects of it, but reporters do well to understand that abuse might be part of a long-standing social problem, armed conflict, or part of a community history."[36]—Chicago Task Force on Violence Against Women and Girls

"In the interest of balance, journalists may use language that unwittingly implies that the victim was an equal actor. In fact, in order to portray sexual violence accurately, it is important to use language that puts the burden of action on the reported perpetrator."[37]—Reporting on Sexual Violence: A Media Packet for Maine Journalists

To these, I would add: Don't write about people you admire being accused of sexual assault or rape, if you can't even entertain the possibility that they really did it.

Just as Roman Polanski's fans and colleagues rushed to minimize his crimes because they couldn't reconcile the gentle old artistic genius with the confessed child rapist and longtime fugitive, Assange's defenders apparently wanted to believe in anything that would explain the charges away. Whether it was a conspiracy involving the CIA, a bizarre Swedish law that criminalized unprotected sex, or good old, reliable lying bitches, *some* other explanation had to be true. And as long as a lot of other people were saying the same thing—even if it all originated with the same few questionable sources—it really felt as if Assange *must* be the unfortunate victim of a political vendetta (plus maybe lying bitches).

Of course, it's possible that's actually true; as with Roethlisberger's alleged rapes, my position is that regardless of whether they happened, this response to reports of serious sex crimes was shameful and dangerous. It's understandable that people who admire Assange's work and idolize the man himself would hold fast to the possibility that these women are lying and he's been set up. But for journalists, prioritizing a childish desire to protect your heroes over a clear-eyed appraisal of the available evidence is unforgivable. When you find yourself arguing, "All of our most respected news sources say X, but I suspect they're lazy and wrong, based on this one piece that quotes the accused's defense lawyer saying Y," it's probably time to take a deep breath and admit you can't write about this subject with integrity.

That's not to say that covering the news requires perfect objectivity; I'm not even a big believer in the categorically *imperfect* version many journalists still aspire to. Like Jay Rosen, I much prefer transparency to pseudo-objectivity, and I hope he's correct that the industry is shifting in that direction. For journalists and laypeople alike, I believe it's better to be up front about your biases than try—inevitably in vain—to conceal them. And when confronted with the inescapable fact that you fucked up, apologizing goes a long way.

Finally, it never hurts to fact-check, even after you've heard something repeated a lot. For instance, if you've only heard a translation of something crucial to your story, you'd do well to find a native speaker to walk you through the nuances of the original wording. Imagine if AOL's Dana Kennedy had asked someone like Linnéa, a Swedish feminist living in the United Kingdom, for a little help with the phrase "sex by surprise." As Linnéa explained on her blog, Feminism and Tea, in December 2010, "överraskningssex, as it would be translated in Swedish, is slang for rape."[38]

CHAPTER 9

Pop Rape

It's been a long time since I saw the 2006 action movie *Crank*, in which Jason Statham plays a man who will die if his heart rate drops to a normal level, but I still vividly recall the scene in which Statham's character grabs his girlfriend (Amy Smart) in the middle of Los Angeles's Chinatown and demands sex, right there, right then.

Smart's character doesn't know that her boyfriend believes he will literally die if she won't acquiesce, so her perfectly logical response to a request for midday street sex is no. And instead of, say, doing jumping jacks while explaining his predicament, Statham's character just forces himself on her.

If you Google "*Crank* rape scene," you'll find what I'm talking about, but not under that name. Instead, it's labeled "Amy Smart has sex in public" and captioned: "You either hate this scene or love it but I think it's a very hot scene and if I were in Statham's shoes, I would have done the same thing. Enjoy this awesome clip of Amy Smart getting some lovin' in 'Crank.'"

Here's what happens in that clip, after Smart's character first says no. She struggles with Statham, and they both fall to the ground. She tries to crawl away, screaming, "Get off me! No!" as he clings to her ankles. Finally, she screams "Stop it!" and smacks him in the face. That actually does slow him down a little, but then she feels guilty and goes to him, apologizing as she caresses his face, which gives him a chance to grab and kiss her. She's

still struggling and screaming "NO!" as he flips her on her back and pene-
trates her.

Cut to a shot of a Chinese lantern, while some tinkly music plays. Cut
back to Smart's character, pinned on the ground by her boyfriend, who
just stuck his dick in her after she screamed, fought, tried to get away, and
begged him repeatedly to stop.

"Fuck it. Take me right here," she says, moaning with pleasure, as
though he was waiting for permission. See? All that screaming and trying
to get away wasn't because she didn't want to have sex on a public street
with her coked-up boyfriend! It was just foreplay.

Reframing consent as a gray area that's always open to interpretation
affords plausible deniability to pop culture makers who present criminal assaults as normal sexual behavior. In the 2009 comedy *Observe and
Report*, Seth Rogen's character jams his penis into a passed-out, vomit-
covered Anna Faris—but when he pauses moments later, her character
wakes up and slurs, "Did I tell you to stop, motherfucker?" Just as in
Crank, retroactive consent is meant to relieve the audience's tension, reassuring us that no matter what she said or did before, *she wanted it*.

When the extended trailer featuring that scene was released, it didn't
go unnoticed by people with strong opinions about feminism, comedy,
or both. On the excellent blog Sociological Images, Occidental College
sociologist Lisa Wade wrote:

> Discussion on the internet is centered around two questions: (1)
> Is this rape? and (2) Is this funny?… If the trailer doesn't convince
> you that we live in a rape culture, then the fact that we are actually
> debating the answers to questions (1) and (2) certainly should.[1]

And if you have any doubt that the people behind this know exactly
what they're doing, Rogen cleared that up in a now-deleted YouTube
interview, transcribed by Amanda Hess at the *Washington City Paper*:

> When we're having sex and she's unconscious like you can literally
> feel the audience thinking, like, how the fuck are they going to make
> this okay? Like, what can possibly be said or done that I'm not going

to walk out of the movie theater in the next thirty seconds?... And then she says, like, the one thing that makes it all okay.[2]

Nope, sorry. That really doesn't make it all okay. Playing a rape scene for laughs doesn't turn it into something other than a rape scene. All it does is add more normalized imagery of sexual violence to the cultural stew.

"Why Didn't You Just Say 'Bad Date'?"

In a 2008 episode of *Mad Men*, secretary Joan Holloway (Christina Hendricks) gets a visit from her fiancé, Greg, at the end of a workday. Joan's already uncomfortable when he lures her into her boss's office, but when he pushes her down on the floor, her protests shift from a lighthearted "Not in here," to a more emphatic, "No, I mean it," and then finally to "Stop, Greg, no!" She physically struggles, but eventually resigns herself to lying still until he's finished, while the man she loves clamps one hand across her face.

As writer and attorney Michelle Dean wrote in a blog post after the episode aired, "Joan's rape was not a particularly 'hard case,' as lawyers like to say—in the middle of it HER FIANCE IS HOLDING HER FACE DOWN."[3]

Nevertheless, Hendricks told *New York* magazine that fans didn't always interpret the scene as depicting a crime. "What's astounding is when people say things like, 'Well, you know that episode where Joan *sort of* got raped?' Or they say *rape* and use quotation marks with their fingers," says Hendricks. "I'm like, 'What is that you are doing? Joan got raped!' It illustrates how similar people are today [to the 1960s], because we're still questioning whether it's a rape. It's almost like, 'Why didn't you just say *bad date?*'"[4]

The enlightened, twenty-first-century reader is supposed to recognize the phrase "bad date" as a shameful remnant of our past, like the overt sexism, racism, homophobia, child neglect, office drinking, and cigarette smoking that are so jarring to younger *Mad Men* viewers. It's hard to say how long that term has been shorthand for "prefeminist conception of acquaintance rape," but the first time I heard it used thusly was in an episode of the early-'90s drama *Sisters*, in which one main character, Georgie, dramatically reveals that she was raped as a teenager. "Back then," she says tearfully, "we just called it a bad date." (I'm paraphrasing from a twenty-year-old memory, but the internet confirms that there was such a scene in the October 30, 1993, episode.)

Georgie never considered what happened to her rape until her college-age niece became the victim of a similar crime; it's clear to the viewer that she simply had no framework for understanding the violation she suffered. At least, it was clear to *this* viewer, in 1993, that the scene was meant to convey that point. If *Sisters* aired today, there would almost certainly be commenters all over the internet arguing that flashback-Georgie didn't fight hard enough, that the scene was ambiguous, and if she didn't call it rape for all those years, how can anyone say it was? If the internet wasn't convinced that Joan Holloway was raped, there's no reason to assume today's fans would agree that Georgie was.

Before you say we've come too far for that, let me remind you that contemporary pop culture is still in the business of openly painting rape victims as sluts who deserved what they got. In the spring of 2013, Tyler Perry's *Temptation: Confessions of a Marriage Counselor* was released to more than two thousand screens, earning $21.6 million on its opening weekend. *Temptation*'s title character, Judith, is clearly attracted to one of her clients but repeatedly resists his advances, up to and including telling him to stop, saying no, and physically fighting him once it becomes clear that he doesn't intend to respect her wishes. The rapist's response: "You can say you resisted."

When he's finished, Judith says she never wants to see him again, and there's no indication that she changed her mind about whether she wanted to have sex. The logical conclusion is that she was raped. That's not how the story plays out, though. On her blog, the writer Carolyn Edgar describes what happens next:

> Harley demands to know if Judith's husband is better in bed than he—and instead of saying, "Of course, since he's not a rapist"— Judith flashes back to what passes for steamy lovemaking in a Tyler Perry movie. We're then made to understand that Judith did indeed consent, or at least, gave in.[5]

As far as the movie's concerned, there's no meaningful difference.

"It would have been easy to include any detail that shows the audience ... there was consent involved," wrote Nico Lang at the *Frisky*, in a post straightforwardly titled "Tyler Perry Has a Rape Problem in *Temptation*."[6] Instead, after that experience, Judith begins dating the man who raped her.

What's more, says Lang, "Perry insists on punishing her in increasingly over-the-top ways (for forsaking Jesus or something)." Oh, right, did I mention that Harley is the devil incarnate? Like, literally? *Temptation*, as its title suggests, is a Christian fable about what happens when a career woman cheats on her husband—with a rapist.

"Notably," says Edgar, "Perry screened this film for 100 pastors prior to its release. They gave him their blessings. That fact may be more troubling than the film itself."[7]

What About Free Speech?

In May 2013, feminist writer Lindy West faced off with comedian Jim Norton on the sadly now-canceled *Totally Biased with W. Kamau Bell*. It's worth looking up the clip to watch it, but their conversation basically boiled down to "Censorship is bad" (Norton) versus "Censorship is bad, but I'm not censoring you—I'm calling you a jerk" (West).

Predictably, that nuance was lost on much of the audience. Less than a week later, West wrote a post at Jezebel titled "If Comedy Has No Lady Problems, Why Am I Getting So Many Rape Threats?" The centerpiece was a video of the author reading some of her recent emails and Twitter replies in a chilling, unbroken monotone:

> Jim should rape this bitch and teach her a lesson no need for you to worry about rape uggo Jabba has nothing to worry about not even a prison escapee would rape her Jim raped her in this one I disagree with her point of view because she's a fat ugly cunt fat ugly angry no man in her life this is the conclusion that big bitch is bitter that no one wants to rape her do some laps lardy holy shit her stomachs were touching the floor let's cut the bullshit that broad doesn't have to worry about rape norton raped this bitch in debate[8]

The video continues, but you get the idea. To wit, Lindy West is fat (she is and will tell you so herself) and ugly (subjective, but I personally think she's gorgeous), so (a) her views are meaningless, and (b) she needn't fear rape. In fact, she probably wishes she could get raped.

Never mind that one can't actually wish for something that's defined by not wanting it.

Also, according to these geniuses, West lost the debate badly—that is, she got totally raped, har har!

I'm not even going to comment on the frequent use of "rape" to mean "triumph over a foe," and all that implies about gender relations in the twenty-first century. I'm just going to let Dane Cook—a comic I usually find deeply unpleasant—speak for me, for the first and last time.

In his "Isolated Incident" comedy special, Cook says:

> People throw the word "raped" around too casually. Have you ever played video games online and listened to the way people talk to each other? "Oh dude, you just shot me in the back, dude, you raped me!"
>
> I'm pretty sure if I sat down with a woman who's been through that horrific situation, and I said, "Can you describe what this was like, going through this?" she's not gonna look at me and go, "Have you ever played Halo?"

That's a rape joke that makes me laugh, for the record. The butt of the joke isn't a person who's been raped, but people who casually trivialize a serious crime to exaggerate their own petty grievances. It works because it points to something recognizably true and recognizably absurd.

But the responses to West's appearance on *Totally Biased* illustrate the problem with big-name comics making weak *nonjokes* about rape: they have loads of fans who are breathtakingly ignorant about sexual violence, free speech, and, most important, comedy. Those fans think being criticized is the same as being censored and that someone calling out their heroes for being unnecessarily cruel and *unfunny* is an enemy of laughter.

Of course, if they did a search on West's name and "rape jokes," they would find a piece she wrote for Jezebel after the Tosh incident, in which she offers this disclaimer for those confused about the definition of "censorship":

In case this isn't perfectly clear yet: You can say whatever you want.
You can say whatever you want. You can say whatever you want.
You can say whatever you want. You can say whatever you want.[9]

The catch is, other people can also say whatever they want—such
as, "Wow, you sure sound like an asshole." Those who endeavor not to
be regarded as assholes often spend time *thinking* before we speak. Even
before we joke.

In fact, you know who spends more time thinking about the jokes they
make than anybody else? People who get paid to tell jokes. For the most
part, Daniel Tosh and Jim Norton do not stand up on stage and impro-
vise—unless forced to by hecklers, for instance, and even those responses
are frequently practiced. They usually stand up on stage and perform material that has been written down, edited, rehearsed, tried out on audiences,
and refined according to that feedback. They can charge you to hear them
tell jokes because they've spent a great deal of time thinking about the
nature of comedy and revising their work to achieve maximum funny.

And *that's* what makes it so galling when these men go out there
with jokes that make light of rape victims, as opposed to rapists or rape culture. Their defenders—and, shamefully, some of the professionals—try to
pretend the controversy is about whether certain kinds of jokes should be
banned, or whether offensive humor is ever okay, or whether feminists just
need to lighten up. In reality, though, what we're talking about is the art
of comedy. Invoking Lenny Bruce or George Carlin to defend your sense
of humor only works if you understand the difference between making
pointed cultural observations and being a bully.

Or, as West puts it, "The key—unless you want to be called a garbage-
flavored dick on the internet by me and other humans with souls and
brains—is to be a responsible person when you construct your jokes."[10]

You can say whatever you want. But you'll have to own it.

Life Imitates Art, and Vice Versa

The same goes for artists in other media: think about what you're doing,
take responsibility, and try not to make society noticeably worse. Like, for

example, don't describe a woman's body as something you "enjoyed" without her knowledge. That's actually called rape.

In early 2013, Rick Ross rapped the line, "Put Molly [ecstasy] all in her champagne, she ain't even know it / Took her home and enjoyed that, she ain't even know it," on the Rocko song "U.O.E.N.O." After being called out for it by every feminist on the internet and not a few mainstream media outlets, Ross tried to clear up his views.

"I don't condone rape," he tweeted, as though it should have been obvious. "Apologies for the lyric interpreted as rape."[11] Interpreted! Oh, did you perceive something rapey in that line about drugging a woman and using her body while she's passed out? I'm so sorry you feel that way.

Finally, Ross said, "Apologies to my many business partners, who would never promote violence against women." That one, I believe he meant from the bottom of his heart. Only after he lost a lucrative deal with Reebok did he release a statement that actually went to the core of the matter:

> To every woman that has felt the sting of abuse, I apologize. I recognize that as an artist I have a voice and with that, the power of influence. To the young men who listen to my music, please know that using a substance to rob a woman of her right to make a choice is not only a crime, it's wrong and I do not encourage it.[12]

Ross's advice came too late for his contemporary CeeLo Green, who later that year would be charged with a felony for slipping ecstasy to an unsuspecting woman. She also reported that he sexually assaulted her, but Los Angeles prosecutors declined to file a charge of rape of an intoxicated person[13] (sigh), and in August 2014, Green pled no contest to the drug charge.

In the days following his sentencing—probation and community service—Green didn't just thank his lucky stars and move on. He took to Twitter, as you do.

In reference to the victim's claim that she woke up naked in bed with him, with no memory of what went before, Green wrote, "People who have really been raped REMEMBER!!! When someone brakes on [sic] a home there is broken glass where is your plausible proof that anyone was raped."[14]

As if that weren't enough, he continued: "If someone is passed out they're not even WITH you consciously! so WITH Implies consent."[15]

L.A. Times blogger August Brown accurately called the latter "a statement as rhetorically confusing as it is offensive."[16]

CeeLo's people must have gotten to him shortly thereafter, because the tweets were soon deleted, followed by his whole Twitter account. He then issued an apology that implied perhaps he wasn't even the one who wrote them: "I truly and deeply apologize for the comments attributed to me on Twitter. Those comments were idiotic, untrue and not what I believe."[17]

The damage was done, though. Almost immediately, TBS canceled Green's reality series, *The Good Life*. In the weeks that followed, several concert venues and music festivals dropped his upcoming bookings. Earlier in 2014, Green had already quit NBC's *The Voice*, a competitive reality show on which he'd been a coach to promising young singers for four seasons. There was speculation at the time that NBC pressured him to leave because of the pending case.[18]

The swift, public declamation of both CeeLo's remarks and "U.O.E.N.O." was heartening to see, but it's still depressing as hell to think that two successful grown men in the public eye in 2013 apparently didn't know enough to *shut up about* drugging and assaulting women (a strategy that may have worked for Bill Cosby for decades) let alone not to do it. These are men who are paid millions to be, in part, savvy about projecting certain images and winning the favor of large audiences—how could they not realize how they were coming across?

Unless they did. Only a few years earlier, Ross and Green collaborated on the song "Tears of Joy," which included the charming lyric "Life is just a pussy race / Snatch a bitch take her back to your place." The album that song was on, Ross's *Teflon Don*, debuted at number 2 on the Billboard 200 and was chosen as one of *Rolling Stone*'s top 30 albums that year. So maybe they knew exactly what they were doing.

Cleaning Out Hip-Hop's Closet

In her early-nineties essay "Seduced by Violence No More," black feminist scholar bell hooks says "it should not surprise or shock" that rape culture "has found its most powerful contemporary voice in misogynist rap music."

Black males, who are utterly disenfranchised in most every arena of life in the United States, often find that the assertion of sexist domination is their only expressive access to that patriarchal power they are told all men should possess as their gendered birthright.[19]

In other words, our society teaches all men they're entitled to money, power, and women's bodies, while systematically denying black men access to the first two. The legacy of slavery and Jim Crow laws, entrenched institutional racism and present-day bigotry all conspire to block African American men from many of the paths to wealth and cultural authority that are open to white men. (When not describing life as a "pussy race," the lyrics to "Tears of Joy" even address this theme: "Yesterday I read my horoscope / Tell me, lord, will I be poor and broke? / Tell me, lord, will I be dealing dope?")

It's understandable, then, that some black men would default to the third great American symbol of masculine importance: controlling women. As hooks puts it, "The 'it's-a-dick-thing' version of masculinity that black male pop icons like Spike Lee and Eddie Murphy promote is a call for real black men to be sexist and proud of it, to rape and assault black women and brag about it."[20] Her examples of cultural leaders may sound outdated today, but as Ross's contribution to "U.O.E.N.O." demonstrates, the point is not.

Acknowledging this reality does not excuse misogyny in hip-hop by any means, but it does complicate it. It's also important to note, as hooks does, that mainstream media most often amplifies the ugliest voices—stoking racist stereotypes like the practically unkillable myth of black men's intrinsic sexual aggression—while ignoring those who use their art to promote positive messages. And in the twenty years since she wrote "Seduced by Violence No More," at least one significant change has come to the hip-hop industry: a whole lot more women are now contributing their own experiences.

In 2012, twenty-one-year-old rapper Angel Haze released "Cleaning Out My Closet," a devastating account of childhood sexual abuse. Using language every bit as graphic and disturbing as the worst antiwoman lyrics, she turns that familiar vulgarity on its head:

My heart was pumping it was thumping with like tons of my fear
Imagine being seven and seeing cum in your underwear
I know it's nasty but sometimes I'd even bleed from my butt
Disgusting right? Now let that feeling ring through your guts

Interestingly, Haze told British newspaper the *Telegraph* in 2013 that one of her musical influences was her fellow Detroiter Eminem, a white rapper often criticized for his exceedingly misogynistic lyrics. (Jackson Katz spends the better part of a chapter in *The Macho Paradox* arguing that "the very appeal of Eminem's music depends on widespread acceptance of violence against women as a cultural norm."[21]) The young artist, who spent her childhood in a cult and much of her teens alternating between homeless shelters and friends' couches, says of the controversial musician, "He was so angsty and I was so angry. It was like catharsis to listen to him."[22]

That's one good reason to avoid blanket condemnation of certain genres and artists, however problematic: you never know who might be inspired in a positive direction by something offensive. Still, a young woman being fearlessly, heartbreakingly honest about the sexual violence she's experienced is a welcome alternative to "Life is just a pussy race." Haze's fans, of all genders, think so, too.

"I got so many people messaging me, more boys than girls actually, who have had the same experience," she told the *Telegraph*. "It really helped me and I think it helped them too."[23] As for men who want to "rescue" her after hearing all that she's suffered, Haze scoffs, "It's so annoying. You can't save someone who does not need saving."[24]

Writing about "Cleaning Out My Closet" in the *Atlantic*, American studies scholar Michael P. Jeffries argues that hip-hop's "well-documented and inexcusable problems with sexism," have made it a genre "ripe for reformers. Moreover, as one of the dominant, storytelling-driven art forms consumed and made by young people, rap provides a way for survivors and allies to testify, argue, and change hearts and minds."[25]

Indeed. People like Rick Ross, CeeLo Green, and Eminem (among many others) may have built careers on misogynistic posturing, but they'll soon be replaced by a whole new generation.

Especially Heinous

Back on the depressing side of the fence, even pop culture that focuses squarely on sex crimes can't seem to resist perpetuating rape myths. NBC's *Law & Order: Special Victims Unit* focuses exclusively on "sexually based offenses," usually involving women or children. But an analysis of the first five seasons by feminist scholars Lisa Cuklanz and Sujata Moorti found that the show largely squanders its unique opportunity to subvert harmful stereotypes.

> The storylines on SVU thematize and elaborate key elements of feminist understandings of sexual violence. However, paradoxically, this feminist take on the subject of rape is not carried through in SVU's treatment of women. Some of the storylines condemn aspects of feminine behavior and character, including empathy and intuition. Female characters seldom can or do form bonds with each other. Female criminals are manipulative and use relationships to harm others; numerous storylines explore narratives of moral depravity and extreme violence on the part of women.[26]

At this writing, *SVU* has just begun its sixteenth season. Viewers can't seem to get enough of manipulative women and their moral depravity.

The comedian John Mulaney has a terrific line about the character played by Ice-T on *SVU*: "What's so great about him is that he's been with the SVU for, like, eleven years, and he still treats every case like it's his first, in terms of *total confusion*."[27]

It's not even just Ice-T's character, Tutuola (although yeah, it's frequently him). When it comes to cases where a female victim's credibility is in question, a funny thing happens: suddenly, all three of the male detectives—Stabler, Munch, and Tutuola, for most of the series—act as if they've never met a genuine rape victim with a complicated story before, leaving only Mariska Hargitay's Olivia Benson* to stand up for the woman.

---

* Despite my criticism of the show's writing, I should note that Hargitay credits it with raising her own awareness about sexual and domestic violence. In 2004, she founded the Joyful Heart Foundation, which has raised over $15 million for programs that help victims directly and draw national attention to issues like rape kit backlogs in police departments.

Take, for instance, the unsubtly named 2010 episode "Gray." Early on, the four *experienced sex crimes detectives* are standing around discussing a young college woman's report of being raped while she was extremely drunk.

"What if Chuck was drunk, too?" asks Tutuola. "How was he to know she wasn't sober enough to consent?"

Benson brings up the obvious analogy of drunk driving: the law expects us all not to commit crimes, even when booze has sent our judgment out the window. Instead of conceding the point, though, Munch and Tutuola shift into full-on, tag-team victim blaming.

> **Munch:** Come on, Liv. What does the girl expect? She gets bombed, goes up to a guy's apartment—what's she gonna do, play Scrabble?
>
> **Tutuola:** It's getting to the point where a guy needs a permission slip to get past first base.

On behalf of all of us, Benson looks at the two of them like they're the world's biggest assholes.

Watching this recently, along with several episodes featuring similar exchanges between Benson and at least one of the dudes, I kept coming back to Mulaney's bit: "It's like, 'You work in the *sex crimes division.* You're gonna have to get used to that.'"[28]

In the Season 2 episode "Closure," Benson is once again both the sole woman and the sole voice of reason, discussing a student acquaintance rape victim with Stabler, Tutuola, and Captain Donald Cragen:

> **Tutuola:** Word on campus is, she was practicing for her oral exams.
>
> **Stabler:** Witnesses said she came on to Joe.
>
> **Tutuola:** A lap dance sends a pretty strong signal.
>
> **Benson:** She was drunk.
>
> **Stabler:** So was he.
>
> **Benson:** So that excuses it?
>
> **Stabler:** No, but her behavior's open to interpretation.
>
> **Tutuola:** She might have played it out and woke up with a case of buyer's remorse.

Benson: So now we're blaming the victim?

Cragen: Nobody is blaming her, but we all know how hard it is to get an indictment on he-said/she-said, even without any ambiguities.

Actually, Cragen, I count at least two people blaming her. And they're detectives in the *sex crimes unit*.

I understand that the writers are only trying to present common reactions to claims of rape, but putting such remarks in the mouths of law enforcement characters is rape culture in action. You'd think a show that begins each episode with the invocation "In the criminal justice system, sexually based offenses are considered especially heinous" would present a criminal justice system in which sexist, slut-shaming bullshit like "She was practicing for her oral exams" and "What's she gonna do, play Scrabble?" would only come from the sleaziest defense attorneys.

But then, these fictional characters work for the same NYPD that in real life produced Kenneth Moreno and Franklin L. Mata, who kept returning to the apartment of an intoxicated woman they were meant to see safely home. Maybe it's just verisimilitude.

The Golden Age of Rape TV

In a 2007 essay titled "Television Viewing and Rape Myth Acceptance Among College Women," communications scholars Lee Ann Kahlor and Dan Morrison write:

Relatively little research documents the presence of rape myths in television programming. However, the available data indicate that myths are fairly prevalent when the topic of rape is broached in programming. For example, Brinson analyzed 26 prime-time television storylines that contained references to rape, and... found that 42% of the storylines suggested that the victim wanted to be raped, 38% of the storylines suggested the victim lied about the assault, and 46% of the storylines suggested that the victim had "asked for it" in the way she dressed or acted (male and female characters were equally likely to make this accusation). On the other hand, only 38%

of the storylines contained any opposition to the myth that the victim had asked for it.[29]

Not surprising, yet totally appalling.

Granted, Brinson's study is from 1992, a rather long time ago, and
Kahlor and Morrison note that subsequent research shows TV depictions
of sexual violence becoming more nuanced and less victim-blamey overall.
But those depictions have also become far more common. We've come a
long way since Edith Bunker fended off a rapist with birthday cake, in a
1977 "very special episode" of *All in the Family*, but the increased prevalence of rape stories in popular culture has a down side.

The 2013–2014 television season brought an unprecedented amount
of rape to the small screen. *SVU*'s Benson—already written as a survivor
of attempted sexual assault, not to mention the child of a rapist father—
was kidnapped and tortured for days by a serial killer, who was just about
to rape her when she broke free and beat the shit out of him. FX's *The
Americans*, ITV/PBS's *Downton Abbey*, HBO's *Game of Thrones*, Net-
flix's *House of Cards*, and ABC's *Scandal* all showed major female characters being raped, in the present or in flashbacks. In spring 2013, *New
York*'s Margaret Lyons wrote that of 135 scripted dramas on the air, 109
had featured a rape or a murder in the previous season.[30]

The problem with this sudden rapeapalooza is not only the desensitization to violence but the fact that—as anyone who's ever sat through
a *Law & Order: Special Victims Unit* marathon could tell you—one can
only tell so many stories about sex crimes before being tempted to write
twists involving devious "victims" and innocent "perpetrators." After a
few sensitive and moving portrayals of sexual violence, writers inevitably
feel an urge to find a fresh angle, and that's one place where things can go
seriously wrong.

Even in stories where the good guys stay good and bad guys stay bad,
fictional rape is sometimes used to provide little more than cheap shock
value. "For all the dramatic and social good rape as a theme can bring to television," writes feminist media critic and sex expert Jaclyn Friedman in the
American Prospect, "rape as a plot device is manipulative and damaging."[31]

Friedman calls the rape on *Downton Abbey* a "clumsy" and "cynical"
effort to create drama between two married characters whose storyline

had gone stale. The result is that, as the season unfolds, viewers see the victim's husband struggling with the aftermath of her rape more than she does. The violation of her body is written as a catalyst for *his* personal growth. Ew.

By contrast, Friedman applauds the ABC drama *Private Practice* for a multi-episode arc that explored a survivor's perspective thoroughly and realistically:

> We see Charlotte at first not wanting to tell anyone, not wanting to report, not wanting to get help. We see the other main characters each trying to find their way to let her know they were there for her. Charlotte gets to make some tentative strides and then have new outbursts and struggles, because healing is never linear.[32]

Washington Post culture blogger Alyssa Rosenberg says the current crop of scripted dramas—*Downton Abbey* notwithstanding—are similarly raising the bar for thoughtful, realistic depictions of sexual violence. While older television plotlines often focused on male detectives solving the crimes,

> the new breed of prestige drama has upended that convention. These shows are interested in survivors, who are often among the central characters rather than extras. The attackers are not abstract monsters but respected members of society. The male leads are often complicit in the violence or are unacceptably oblivious to the female characters' experiences. And no one gets rescued; no one gets a day in court. The drama is less about the process of killing, jailing or confronting a rapist, and more about how these women's lives have been inflected by their rapes, often years into the future.[33]

Healing isn't linear, support and justice aren't guaranteed, cops aren't always sympathetic, rapists aren't monsters, and there is no such thing as "what a *real* victim would behave like." If more television writers recognized these truths, the medium could go a long way toward countering our pervasive ignorance about rape. But even that might not undo all of the cultural damage TV inflicts on us.

When Kahlor and Morrison measured the "rape myth acceptance" levels and television viewing habits of a group of college women, they found a significant correlation between watching TV and buying into victim-blaming rhetoric. Not just watching *SVU* or *Mad Men* or *Sisters* or soap operas in which victims marry their rapists, mind you, but "*general, daily television use*" (emphasis theirs). That link "is particularly problematic from a health communication perspective; it suggests that television use has the potential to erase, over time, the already limited effects that rape education campaigns have on audiences."[34]

Well, that's just great.

Refusing to Be Passive Consumers

Relax. I'm not about to tell you to stop watching TV—or seeing Seth Rogen or Jason Statham or Tyler Perry movies, or listening to misogynistic hip-hop. I'm not especially interested in censoring entertainment media, either. (When an Eminem might inspire an Angel Haze, who would ever be qualified to determine what stays and what goes?) I am keen on *criticizing* it, in hopes that people will stop writing and producing stereotypical bullshit of their own volition, because they realize it's wrong, harmful, and above all, not entertaining.

But while we're wishing and waiting, the least we can do is connect some dots. A culture that thinks Joan Holloway was only "sort of" raped is also a culture that believes a victim must be bruised and torn apart to be believed. A culture where "Took her home and enjoyed that, she ain't even know it" is something a grown man would sing in public without a second thought is also one where a jury can listen to police officers describe going back to a drunk woman's house three times to "snuggle" and think, "Yeah, that sounds reasonable." The entertainment we consume both reflects and reifies the rape myths we cherish. We owe it to ourselves to take it seriously and expect better.

In late 2012, the British Board of Film Classification said it would take a harder line against movie scenes that glorify torture or imply that victims enjoy being raped. BBFC director David Cooke told the *Hollywood Reporter* that the new policy was a response to public concern about "young men with little experience, and more vulnerable viewers, accessing sadistic and sexually violent content, which could serve to normalize rape and other forms of violence and offer a distorted view of women."[35] (The concerned British public sounds shockingly feminist!)

That response arrived at the BBFC via old-fashioned market research, but we live in an age of unprecedented communication between entertainment creators and consumers. We can tweet at musicians and film directors, comment in TV forums that showrunners read, and ask our favorite actors "anything" when they visit Reddit, "the front page of the internet." Bloggers can get press credentials and land interviews with celebrities. The walls that used to surround the entertainment industry have grown porous, and fans increasingly feel entitled to demand media that doesn't insult their intelligence or humanity.

When a consensual sex scene from one of George R. R. Martin's popular fantasy novels was rewritten as a rape scene on *Game of Thrones*, the HBO TV show based on them, the fan response was swift and thorough. The entire internet seemed to cry at once, "What the *hell* was that?"

Longtime television blogger Alan Sepinwall interviewed the episode's director, Alex Graves, who claimed it wasn't a rape because the victim (Cersei) and perpetrator (Jaime) are so attracted to each other, she *eventually* wanted it. "Well, it becomes consensual by the end," said Graves, "because anything for them ultimately results in a turn-on, especially a power struggle."[36]

At *New York* magazine's culture blog, Vulture, Denise Martin asked Graves how the show runners decided to play it that way and why they changed the book's version so drastically. "There wasn't a lot of talk about it, to be honest," says the director.[37]

The interviewer explains that there's been "a lot of chatter about it online," and reminds Graves that the scene in question "ends with Cersei saying, 'It's not right, it's not right,' and Jaime on top of her saying, 'I don't care. I don't care.'" Is he quite sure, she seems to be asking, that he wants to stick with "It's eventually consensual" as his final answer?

Yep!

> It's my cut of the scene. The consensual part of it was that she wraps her legs around him, and she's holding on to the table, clearly not to escape but to get some grounding in what's going on. And

also, the other thing that I think is clear before they hit the ground is she starts to make out with him. The big things to us that were so important, and that hopefully were not missed, is that before he rips her undergarment, she's way into kissing him back. She's kissing him aplenty.[38]

Oh. Okay. Here's a thought, though: If you have to explain in detail where the "consent" was for your mystified viewers, it's possible you didn't shoot the scene you thought you shot. It's possible—likely, even—that what you shot was a rape scene.

A year or two ago, I would probably have been outraged and depressed to see that rationalization coming from someone who has the power to shape an extremely successful show. I'd have seen it as evidence that nothing has changed since *Crank* in 2006, or *Observe and Report* in 2009: Men who get paid to tell stories still believe that a victim's sudden shift from terror (or unconsciousness) to consent can magically purify the forgoing rape scene. Men who get paid to tell stories still believe that a woman screaming no and trying to wriggle out from under an assailant might plausibly get turned on by the "power struggle." *Plus ça change, plus c'est la* fucking barf.

But something *has* changed recently: the men who get paid to tell stories like that are being held accountable for it now.

"The reaction I've seen on Twitter, in emails and on other blogs suggests nobody is agreeing with Graves' interpretation of the scene and are viewing it as rape, plain and simple," writes Sepinwall in an update to his post about the episode.[39] Elsewhere on *New York*'s culture blog, Margaret Lyons says:

> If there's a point at which we're supposed to believe this is anything other than nonconsensual sex, I don't know what it could be. It is absolutely not "consensual by the end"—plus, the idea that a rape could be "consensual by the end" is grotesque and dangerous. It plays into the worst *she said no, but she* meant *yes* pernicious lies of rape culture.[40]

Sing it, Margaret!

At feminist-flavored geek and pop culture site the *Mary Sue*, Rebecca Pahle is concerned about her ability to enjoy the show the same way going forward. "Did you have to make it so whenever, throughout the rest of the show, Jaime has good character moments, you're asking us to cheer for a rapist? To sympathize with a rapist?"[41] she wonders. Amanda Marcotte at *Slate* expresses the same disappointment:

> Graves' inability to see what he's put out there compromises Jaime's character and, frankly, makes a joke of a very serious, very violent act. (Graves calls it a "turn on," as if "sexy rape" is a thing. It is not.) Prior to this rape, Jaime was a morally ambiguous character whose bad behavior, while deplorable, at least was motivated in ways that the audience could understand. Now he just comes across as another terrible man who abuses women because he can.[42]

I could go on, citing similar responses from outlets large and small, but you get the picture. Even if we're still stuck watching "*ultimately consensual*" rapes, we have more power to push back than ever before. Whether Alex Graves ever reconsiders his interpretation of that particular scene is immaterial, because tomorrow's directors are growing up among plugged-in audiences that are savvy, vocal, and fed up.

CHAPTER 10

Trolls, Gamers, and the New Misogyny

The word "troll" as applied to an internet shit-disturber arose in the 1990s but changed in the first years of this century, according to Whitney Phillips, a scholar of digital culture and author of the book *This Is Why We Can't Have Nice Things: Mapping the Relationship Between Online Trolling and Mainstream Culture*. Writing in the *Daily Dot*, an online publication in which she curated a 2013 series on antisocial online behavior, Phillips explains that in the very early days of the twenty-first century, "a distinctive subculture began to cohere around the term 'troll,' complete with a shared set of values, aesthetic, and language."[1]

At that point, some people—usually men and usually white—began proudly self-identifying as "trolls" and building a troll community centered on the /b/ board at 4chan.org, an unmoderated forum for anonymous users that over the years has spawned beloved memes (lolcats), amusing troll-lite trends (Rickrolling), a loosely connected, occasionally righteous group of hacktivists (Anonymous), and unfathomable amounts of misogynistic garbage.

4chan was created in 2003 by fifteen-year-old Christopher "moot" Poole, and at first consisted only of an /a/ board for discussion of anime and a /b/ board for everything else.[2] Although there are many others now (4chan is almost old-fashioned and quaint by modern troll standards),

Vox's Dylan Matthews writes that "/b/ remains the most popular and the epicenter of the culture that has come to be associated with the site." In September 2014, 4chan told potential advertisers it received twenty million unique visitors a month, and based on traffic, analytics site Alexa rated it the 461st most popular website in the United States.[3]

In a long piece for the *Atlantic*, Phillips explains what 4chan's emergent trolling subculture was all about:

> Trolling as described by self-identifying trolls is a game, one only the trolls can initiate and only the troll can win. Pulling from a seemingly endless nest of self-referential memes, and steeped in a distinctive shared language, subcultural trolling is predicated on the amassment of lulz, an aggressive form of laughter derived from eliciting strong emotional reactions from the chosen target(s). In order to amass the greatest number of lulz possible, trolls engage in the most outrageous and offensive behaviors possible—all the better to troll you with.[4]

"In cases where lulz aren't explicitly cited," she adds, "the go-to explanation is that they're 'just screwing around' and their only goal is to 'rile people up.'"[5]

The True Nature of "Lulz"

If you don't spend a lot of time on the internet, you might take that explanation to mean troll behavior is basically harmless, meaningless, stupid fun. You would be wrong. The key words are "eliciting strong emotions from the chosen targets," an exceedingly generous understatement.

"RIP trolling," for instance, is what these guys call harassing grieving people for "lulz." Trolls routinely deface memorial pages for dead children and teens with graphic violent imagery and remarks that make light of the tragedies. They especially like to torment the friends and relatives of people who commit suicide. After actor Robin Williams died in 2014, trolls sent his grown daughter Photoshopped images of dead bodies via Twitter, along with comments like, "look at what he did to himself because of you."

Lindy West, who experienced so much harassment after speaking out about the damage cheap rape jokes can do, was also a victim of "RIP trolling" when a troll assumed the voice of her deceased father on Twitter. Even the few lines of information on his Twitter profile were designed to wound her. In a 2015 piece for National Public Radio's *This American Life*, West explained, "The little bio on Twitter read 'embarrassed father of an idiot—other two kids are fine, though.' His location—dirt hole in Seattle."[6]

What kind of person does something like that? West actually got to find out. After she wrote publicly about how hurtful this particular troll was, he emailed her to apologize, saying, "When you included it in your latest *Jezebel* article, it finally hit me. There is a living, breathing human being who's reading this shit. I'm attacking someone who never harmed me in any way and for no reason whatsoever."[7]

West went on to interview her troll for *This American Life*, and I highly recommend looking that episode up in its archives when you get a chance. What he revealed about his motives was essentially what any reasonable adult had already guessed: he trolled because he was unhappy with his own life and resentful of people like West, who present a confident and contented face to the world. But I'm still stuck on that admission from his original email: until West wrote about how terrible the troll made her feel, he simply hadn't recognized her humanity.

That's a problem of the internet age, to be sure, but it's also a function of a culture in which men are taught to see women as passive objects to collect and discard as it suits them. Combine those two things, and you end up with a lot of men who are really angry at women who speak publicly without asking permission.

One of the first high-profile victims of antifeminist trolling was tech writer Kathy Sierra, who in 2007 made international news after posting on her blog: "I have canceled all speaking engagements. I am afraid to leave my yard, I will never feel the same. I will never be the same."[8] Her withdrawal from public life was in response to an ongoing campaign of harassment originating within the /b/ troll subculture and described by Greg Sandoval in the *Verge* in 2013:

Some visitors to Sierra's blog called "open season" on the now 57-year-old.

Hundreds of commenters on her blog made rape and death threats. "I hope someone slits your throat," wrote one person. People posted photoshopped images of her with a pair of panties choking her, or a noose near her head.[9]

What had Sierra done to deserve all this? Trick question: no one deserves that. But there are a few leading explanations for the intense focus on her.

One of a relatively few well-known and respected women in the tech industry at the time, Sierra wrote, taught, and spoke about coding and design with earned authority. Some number of her harassers seemed merely to want to cut her down to size—seems that some men can't stand it when women thrive in male-dominated fields.

More specifically, Sierra had spoken out in favor of moderating online comments, that is, creating and enforcing standards of civil discourse on websites that increasingly represent people's workspaces, and banning those who deliberately antagonize authors or fellow commenters.

Today, every rational person who's spent more than ten minutes on the internet is in favor of comment moderation, and some are even calling for the end of comments altogether. But in 2007, many website owners and news organizations still believed in the ideal of a constructive wide-open conversation. Failing that, they believed that the unconstructive kind brought in valuable page views for no extra money. Such broad support for unmoderated comments offered cover to trolls who knew that decent moderation would bring the end of lulz and thus resisted it with everything they had.

Trolls "dropped docs," or doxxed, Sierra, publicly revealing her home address and Social Security number. They invented lies about her past, including, as Sandoval explains, "false statements about her being a battered wife and a former prostitute."[10] And once doxxed, Sierra was suddenly open to real-world abuses ranging from identity theft to some troll making good on those threats to rape and kill her.

That's how bad self-identified trolls were in 2007. In 2013, Sierra gave her first interview since those dark days, telling Sandoval, "What happened to me pales in comparison to what's happening to women online today."[11]

"Creepshots," "Jailbait," and the Front Page of the Internet

4chan's /b/ is also where an anonymous user first dumped dozens of nude celebrity photos in the summer of 2014, before they began appearing in too many places to count.

Some of the women targeted claimed the pictures were fake (and like most nude celebrity photos, some undoubtedly were), but others acknowledged them as both real and stolen. The media, infuriatingly, kept referring to them as "leaked photos"—implying that they were deliberately, if quietly, released by the subjects—instead of highlighting the theft. But one actor whose pictures made the rounds, Mary Elizabeth Winstead, tweeted about the violation:

> To those of you looking at photos I took with my husband years ago in the privacy of our home, hope you feel great about yourselves. Knowing those photos were deleted long ago, I can only imagine the creepy effort that went into this. Feeling for everyone who got hacked.[12]

Although /b/ was ground zero, those pictures and the voyeuristic shits looking for them quickly converged on the website Reddit in a thread—eventually, a series of threads—called "The Fappening." ("Fap," if you are lucky enough not to know this, is internet slang for masturbation.) Eventually, Reddit authorities banned the stolen celebrity photos, but, at this writing, they still allow "subreddits" devoted to naked pictures posted without the consent of nonfamous subjects. "Revenge porn"—private photos released by spurned exes—is alive and well there, among other places.

Reddit, which calls itself "the front page of the internet," is essentially a giant message board covering countless subjects, including things like feminism, antirape activism, and the terrible behavior of trolls. But owing to its patchy moderation practices and 64 percent male user base,[13] Reddit can also start to feel like the world's largest meeting of the He-Man Woman-Hater's Club. Men's rights activists and "pick-up artists" (both of whom I'll get to momentarily) thrive there, and for years it was the primary stomping ground of a middle-aged Texan programmer named Michael Brutsch, who, under the name "Violentacrez," was one of the most notorious trolls on the web.

In 2012, reporter Adrien Chen revealed "Violentacrez" as Brutsch in a long article for Gawker that explored the programmer's trolling history and how Reddit culture welcomes vile antisocial behavior. Writes Chen:

> If you are capable of being offended, Brutsch has almost certainly done something that would offend you, then did his best to rub your face in it. His specialty is distributing images of scantily-clad underage girls, but as Violentacrez he also issued an unending fountain of racism, porn, gore, misogyny, incest, and exotic abominations yet unnamed, all on the sprawling online community Reddit. At the time I called Brutsch, his latest project was moderating a new section of Reddit where users posted covert photos they had taken of women in public, usually close-ups of their asses or breasts, for a voyeuristic sexual thrill. It was called "Creepshots."[14]

Brutsch's taste for "exotic abominations" was directly related to the power he came to wield at Reddit. Because the troll vehemently defended his right to enjoy the most debased "not safe for work" (NSFW) content on Reddit, yet could be counted on to report anything gallopingly illegal, Reddit administrators eventually decided to use him as an unpaid moderator for the whole NSFW side. Says Chen: "It was easier to outsource the policing of questionable content to Violentacrez than to dirty their hands themselves, or ostracize him and risk even worse things happening without their knowledge."[15]

And so Brutsch was the guy in charge of the most offensive subreddits going, even when he wasn't the one starting them. "Creepshots" wasn't his creation, but he was the brains behind "Jailbait," where people could share photos of teenaged girls, often lifted from their public social media profiles. As moderator, he removed actual child porn but encouraged—and posted—bikini shots of underage girls for the fapping pleasure of dirty old men. He also started, moderated, and contributed to sections called "Choke a Bitch," "Beating Women," and "Rapebait," among others.

Public outcry eventually led to both "Jailbait" and "Creepshots" being banned, the latter after a substitute high school teacher in Georgia was found to have posted pictures he surreptitiously took of students. But Brutsch, who started some of the most over-the-top threads purely to tweak those who expressed outrage about offensive content, was regarded by many as a heroic defender of free speech.

Like the trolls who tormented Kathy Sierra when she advocated moderating comments, Brutsch's fans seem to believe their constitutional right to freedom of speech means the right to speak—and post images—anywhere, at any time, no matter who owns the space, who else is speaking, or who might get hurt. No matter how many times these people are reminded that being told to knock it off by private website owners is not quite on a par with being imprisoned for speaking out against an oppressive government, they continue to act as though democracy owes them a soapbox on every corner.

That overwhelming sense of entitlement helps form a picture of who trolls are, even while most of them remain anonymous. Says Phillips:

> I have every reason to believe that the majority of trolls on the English-speaking web are, like Violentacrez, white, male and somewhat privileged. Not because I have personally counted all the trolls on the English-speaking web, but because trolls perform these characteristics. They enact gendered dominance ("your resistance only makes my penis harder," a popular trolling refrain, speaks volumes). They universalize their own assumptions and ethical imperatives (for example the assertion that nothing on the Internet should be taken seriously). They have enough free time to sink hours and hours into their online exploits, and have access to the necessary technologies to do so. I am entirely comfortable asserting these basic symbolic demographics.[16]

Me, too. And the same applies to a group that overlaps heavily with these bozos: men's rights activists.

MRAs, PUAS, and the New Misogyny

By 2013, trolls organizing on 4chan had graduated from simply trying to shock and frighten any successful woman to deliberately fomenting discord within the feminist movement. Picking up on (sincere and accurate) criticism by feminists of color that the movement consistently buries their voices and concerns, trolls started "Operation Lollipop," a long con in which participants impersonating women of color picked fights with white feminists. The immediate "lulz" came whenever someone took them seriously as social justice activists, and the overarching plan was to get feminists too busy yelling at each other to do any activism. (Silly trolls. Feminists are *always* busy yelling at each other, but we manage to get plenty done anyway.)

Many activists on Twitter noticed something off about the troll accounts—notably that several sounded a lot like racists affecting a stereotypical version of African American vernacular English, because that's exactly what they were—and eventually, Operation Lollipop participants took their "social justice warrior" (more on this term later) caricatures too far over the top. When they tried to launch the hashtag "#endfathersday" to expose feminists' supposed hatred of men, they exposed themselves, once and for all, as a bunch of lying jackasses.

At that point, an African American activist who goes by Sassycrass on Twitter started collecting examples of their absurdity under the hashtag "#yourslipisshowing." Looking at her tweets, you see that these trolls' language choices easily gave them away; when they weren't butchering AAVE, they were clumsily mimicking social justice lingo. Anyone with a tiny bit of skepticism and a passing familiarity with either argot should have spotted the mocking undertones immediately. In both cases, the seams showed because, as Sassycrass put it, "They CANNOT disguise their contempt for us. It ALWAYS comes through."[17]

Eventually, Twitter's social justice community, led by the women of color "Operation Lollipop" targeted, identified over two hundred troll accounts devoted to provoking discord among women's rights activists. Just as it was no surprise that the campaign was conceived on 4chan, it was utterly predictable that many of the people behind it identified as men's rights activists and pick-up artists.[18]

The guiding principle of men's rights activism, as it's currently practiced, is that feminism is evil and must be abolished. Self-identified MRAs will tell you they're all about *real* equality, with a focus on bringing the unacknowledged suffering of men to light—which, if it were true, would make them natural allies of feminists. But as David Futrelle, who runs the MRA-watchdog blog We Hunted the Mammoth, explains it:

Unlike the original Men's Movement, which was inspired by and heavily influenced by feminism, the self-described Men's Rights Movement is largely a reactionary movement; with few exceptions, Men's Rights Activists (or MRAs) are pretty rabidly antifeminist, and many are frankly and sometimes proudly misogynistic.[19]

Futrelle also follows the online pick-up artist (PUA) community, which promises lonely men who feel entitled to women's bodies a strategy for gaining access to them—besides using soap and trying not to come off as a flaming asshole. The guys who frequent PUA sites (and shell out for books and classes by PUA gurus) don't want relationships with the type of women they could attract by being kind and decent, and taking a genuine interest in another person's feelings. They just want to have sex with "10s," and the PUA lifestyle promises them that the key to getting that lies in manipulation, persistence, and deliberate cruelty.

George Sodini, who murdered four women and injured nine others before killing himself at a Pennsylvania gym in 2009, had taken a workshop with PUA guru R. Don Steele. Sodini left behind a diary loaded with rage about his rejection by women he felt entitled to.[20]

Elliot Rodger, who killed seven people and himself in Isla Vista, California, in 2014, left behind videos and a manifesto in which he explained his motive. The short version: "I don't know why you girls aren't attracted to me, but I will punish you all for it.... You are animals and I will slaughter you like animals. And I will be a god."[21]

Elliott Rodger used to post on PUAHate message boards, which are not, as you might think, gathering spots for reasonable people who find the PUA "game" odious. They're for men like George Sodini, who feel betrayed because it didn't work for them. These guys are perfectly on board with the part where pick-up artists objectify and degrade women, while reinforcing the message that men are fully entitled to use women's bodies as they see fit. They just don't like the part where they still can't get laid.

That tells you pretty much everything you need to know about the kind of man who's attracted to the PUA community.

PUAs often object to being lumped in with MRAs, whom they see as embittered "beta" males—in other words, losers. I lump them together here both because that amuses me and because the two groups produce equally large amounts of antiwoman propaganda under the guise of help-ing hapless men. Futrelle calls this "The New Misogyny."

> These aren't your traditional misogynists—the social conservatives and religious fundamentalists who make up much of the far right. These are guys, mostly, who range in age from their teens to their fifties, who have embraced misogyny as an ideology, as a sort of sym-bolic solution to the frustrations in their lives—whether financial, social, or sexual.[22]

Many also openly embrace violence against girls and women. *The New Hate* author Arthur Goldwag, writing for the Southern Poverty Law Center—i.e., the organization that tracks hate groups in America—describes MRAs' online output:

> There are literally hundreds of websites, blogs and forums devoted to attacking virtually all women (or, at least, Westernized ones)—the so-called "manosphere," which now also includes a tribute page for Tom Ball ("He Died For Our Children"). While some of them voice legitimate and sometimes disturbing complaints about the treatment of men, what is most remarkable is the misogynistic tone that pervades so many. Women are routinely maligned as sluts, gold-diggers, temptresses and worse; overly sympathetic men are dubbed 'manginas'; and police and other officials are called their armed enablers.[23]

Ball, who committed suicide by self-immolation, became an MRA, and specifically a fathers' rights activist, after losing custody of his daughter, twenty-five years before his death. Goldwag paraphrases the final words he sent to the *Keene Sentinel* before lighting himself ablaze: "All he had done, he said, was smack his 4-year-old daughter and bloody her mouth after she licked his hand as he was putting her to bed. Feminist-crafted anti-domestic violence legislation did the rest."[24]

This is the first thing to remember about MRAs: many of them got involved with men's and father's rights after being accused of domestic violence and handled accordingly by the justice system. Obviously, false accusations and even false convictions happen, as I discussed at length in Chapter 4. It is certainly within the realm of possibility that an unsuspecting man could have children with a woman so hateful that she'd lie and say he was violent toward her or their children in order to punish him.

Far more *likely*, though, is that any given MRA who tells a sob story about his abuse by the courts actually got there the same way Ball did: by abusing another person.

The second thing to remember, which Futrelle told me in an interview, is this: "They don't do anything other than yell and complain. The one form of activism they do is harassing individual women."

Much of that harassment takes place on the internet, where intrepid MRAs evince seemingly limitless energy for leaving comments explaining that women are lying, cheating, vengeful beasts, that the point of feminism is to destroy all men, and that anyone who disagrees is an obvious misandrist. (The word "misandry," meaning hatred and fear of men, is an MRA calling card. The fact that some women speak about misogyny—the hatred and fear of women, codified in many worldwide religions and not a few laws—is itself evidence of our misandry, according to these guys.) But sometimes, their hatred spills over into the real world.

In November 2012, author and longtime MRA guru Warren Farrell gave a talk at my alma mater, the University of Toronto, sponsored by a "men's issues awareness" group on campus. If you're not familiar with Farrell, he's the author of *The Myth of Male Power* and such bon mots as "A man being sued after a woman has more sex than intended is like Lay's being sued after someone has more potato chips than intended," and "We have forgotten that before we began calling this date rape and date fraud, we called it exciting." ("Date fraud" is an MRA term for when a woman goes home with a man yet refuses to have sex. Naturally, they're trying to promote a false equivalency between that and rape.)

About one hundred antisexist protesters stood outside the building where Farrell was to speak, holding signs and chanting everything from "Women hold up half the sky!" and "No hate speech on campus!" to the more straightforward "Fuck Warren Farrell!" There was some blocking of doors, some shoving, and one arrest (which did not result in any charges). It was all pretty sedate, as these things go, but as far as some of the most vocal MRAs are concerned, it was their Waterloo.

Their loudest complaint is that the protestors blocked doors, which I concede they should not have done. The real problem, though, is that in MRA World—just like Troll World, not that the two are mutually exclusive—criticism is tantamount to censorship, and yelling is a violation of fundamental freedoms. (Except, of course, when they're doing it.) Because people turned out to voice their displeasure at the university offering a platform to Farrell, you see, a number of young men were deprived of their right to listen to a virulent misogynist without anyone calling them "fucking scum" for it.

Paul Elam, proprietor of the top MRA blog A Voice for Men, vowed revenge on a woman seen as a ringleader in a video of the protest. In a letter to the University of Toronto Student Union, he threatened:

> We are beginning with the activist bullying and piling hatred and lies on a student for attempting to hear Dr. Farrell's talk. We have her image and know her general location. We will identify her and profile her activity and name for public view.
>
> We will not stop there, or just with her. And while we will not publish our complete intent, we are dogged in our efforts.[25]

A screenshot of the woman in question appears in the same post, with the Nazi-esque caption, "Seeking this undesirable's identity." Inevitably, they found it.

Once A Voice for Men published the young protestor's identity, comments on her YouTube videos soon included garbage like the following, screen-captured by Futrelle and published on We Hunted the Mammoth:

> "Someone needs to rape that bitch at the end."—Jeff V
> "The 'you are fucking scum' bitch should be raped."—Sockcutter
> "These dumb whores could use a Max Hardcore throatfuck session, cures any feminism guaranteed."—Styrbjorne Stark[26]

Futrelle notes that A Voice for Men's writers and readers make a habit of this behavior, and it helps to explain why the men's rights movement is sometimes referred to as the "abusers' lobby."

The "activism" of the site and its followers, insofar as it consists of anything more than self-promotion, often mirrors the actions of abusers—AVFM is known for harassing individuals, usually women, and exposing (or threatening to expose) personal information that could be used to stalk and harm them, in an attempt to intimidate them and other feminists and shut them up. Indeed, the site on several occasions has offered $1000 "bounties" on the personal information of its foes.[27]

MRAs also took part in some real-world "activism" in western Canada in the summer of 2013. Three years earlier, a sexual assault awareness campaign called "Don't Be That Guy" kicked off with posters in major cities that combined striking images with slogans like "Just because she isn't saying no... doesn't mean she is saying yes" and "It's not sex... when he changes his mind." So naturally, three years later, a group calling itself Men's Rights Edmonton created "Don't Be That Girl" posters.

You can probably guess the slogans. "Just because you regret a one-night stand... doesn't mean it wasn't consensual." "Just because you regret your life choices... doesn't mean it was rape." "Lying about sexual assault = a crime." Men's Rights Edmonton spokesperson Karen Straughan (yep, there are female MRAs) told CBC News that the original campaign—which aimed to shift our usual view of sexual assault prevention as the victim's sole responsibility—"frames all men as potential sexual predators."[28]

As Mary Elizabeth Williams wrote at *Salon*:

> I'm almost too bored by the spectacular, lazy stupidity on display here to comment. I'll just say this—nobody thinks all men are potential rapists. Talking about rape isn't the same as accusing anybody of rape. And when there's a public awareness campaign to address the kind of thinking that leads to guys deciding that an unconscious female is fair game to sexually assault, a campaign that seems to have successfully reduced crime, that is a good thing.[29]

Futrelle, who has an astonishing tolerance for combing through MRA bullshit, pointed out that Men's Rights Edmonton has strong ties to the blog A Voice for Men, where founder Elam has written about women who hang out in bars and accept freely offered drinks from men: "In the most severe and emphatic terms possible the answer is NO, THEY ARE NOT ASKING TO GET RAPED. They are freaking begging for it. Damn near demanding it."

Also, because Elam lives in a fantasy world where imaginary rapes are successfully prosecuted all the time, he's promised to do his part to right the balance: "Should I be called to sit on a jury for a rape trial, I vow publicly to vote not guilty, even in the face of overwhelming evidence that the charges are true."[30]

Much as he might insist on a meaningful distinction between the two groups, the most popular MRA on the internet sounds an awful lot like the most popular PUA when he talks about rape. Daryush Valizadeh, known online as Roosh V,* owns top PUA blog Return of Kings, where, in early 2015, he proposed "that we make the violent taking of a woman not punishable by law when done off public grounds." In other words, the only kind of rape he thinks should be illegal is, in his words, "a maniacal alley rape."[31]

There's your "manosphere," folks: a safe haven for harassers, abusers, and rapists.

Gamers Versus Women

Video game culture, traditionally a bastion of adolescent masculinity, sometimes seems hell-bent on becoming a similar festival of misogyny, despite the number of women who play and love games—and who would love to see the industry dial back its rampant sexism.

In the early summer of 2012, media critic Anita Sarkeesian, creator of a video series called Feminist Frequency, asked the public for help funding a series called Tropes vs. Women in Video Games. On the Kickstarter page that hosted her call for donations, Sarkeesian identified herself as a "gamer" and explained:

> I love playing video games but I'm regularly disappointed in the limited and limiting ways women are represented. This video project

---

* Disclosure: Roosh V once named me one of the "9 Ugliest Feminists on the Internet." I found that so delightful, I made it my Twitter bio for a while.

will explore, analyze and deconstruct some of the most common tropes and stereotypes of female characters in games. The series will highlight the larger recurring patterns and conventions used within the gaming industry rather than just focusing on the worst offenders. I'm going to need your help to make it happen![32]

She set a goal of $6,000, enough to help her produce a five-video series on the top 5 sexist roles for female characters in video games: "The Damsel in Distress," "The Fighting F#@k Toy," "The Sexy Sidekick," "The Sexy Villainess," and "Background Decoration." Within a day, she'd reached the goal. Before the limited funding period came to an end, she'd raised $158,922.

The extraordinary response was largely a vote of confidence and support from women and men appalled by what happened in between: Sarkeesian became the target of a coordinated harassment campaign, much like the one that caused Kathy Sierra to fear leaving her house. In an update to the Kickstarter page soon after the launch, Sarkeesian wrote:

> The intimidation and harassment effort has included a torrent of misogyny and hate speech on my YouTube video, repeated vandalizing of the Wikipedia page about me, organized efforts to flag my YouTube videos as "terrorism," as well as many threatening messages sent through Twitter, Facebook, Kickstarter, email and my own website. These messages and comments have included everything from the typical sandwich and kitchen "jokes" to threats of violence, death, sexual assault and rape. All that plus an organized attempt to report this project to Kickstarter and get it banned or defunded.[33]

At her own blog, she shared screengrabs of some of the comments to her YouTube page. Some highlights:

"She needs a good dicking, good luck finding it though."
"You are a fucking hypocrite slut" (because she identifies as feminist but wears makeup and "huge slut earrings").
"LESBIANS: THE GAME is all this bitch wants."

"fuck you feminist fucks you already have equality."

"Looking like you are, I can understand where the hate for sexy
    female characters comes from, but please, scamming people
    won't solve a thing you useless cunt."

"what a stuck up bitch. I hope all them people who gave her money
    get raped and die of cancer."[34]

In the Kickstarter update, Sarkeesian noted the irony that all of this
vitriol came before anyone had even seen a video. "It's very telling," she
wrote, "that there is this much backlash against the mere idea of this series
being made."[35]

Once she actually started posting entries to the Tropes vs. Women
series, her detractors lost their minds. The insults and violent imagery
were relentless over the next two years, leading up to August 2014, when
Sarkeesian received a series of threats so frightening she contacted police
and left her home.

A Twitter user calling himself "Kevin Dobson" rapidly sprayed
threats at her, including "I'm going to rape your cunt with a pole," "I'll
drink your blood out of your cunt after I rip it open," and "I'm going to
go to your apartment and rape you to death. After I'm done, I'll ram a tire
iron up your cunt."[36] Horrifyingly, that last tweet included Sarkeesian's
home address. Another tweet from "Kevin Dobson" threatened to kill her
parents and included their address.

A few weeks later, Sarkeesian told gaming website Kotaku that in
March 2014, the Game Developers Choice Awards received a bomb
threat because she was due to receive recognition there.[37] Meanwhile, a
couple of young men, Jordan Owen and Davis Aurini, started their own
crowdfunding campaign to produce a documentary called "The Sarkeesian
Effect," which would critique both the critic herself and other "Social Justice Warriors," defined thusly:

"Social Justice Warrior" (SJW) came about as a pejorative term to
refer to a person who berates other internet users over matters of
political correctness, but has since evolved to refer to a specific movement within tech and gaming culture that is based around professional victimhood, intimidation, and the proliferation of falsehoods.[38]

People who criticize video games that feature mostly naked women as objects, playthings, and victims, you see, are part of a dangerous, mendacious movement that threatens the very heart of gamer culture.

And for that they deserve to be raped and killed.

In a long post that also touches on 4chan trolls and the "psychopathic" pursuit of lulz, Andrew Todd, gaming editor of *Badass Digest*—himself a man who loves games!—offers this explanation of aggrieved male gamers:

> Central to the self-centred psychology of these people is that they see themselves as the targets of a grand conspiracy of feminist, progressive journalists and game developers that seeks to destroy their ability to . . . something. They have no actual issue. It's all perceived persecution at the hands of political correctness. These "theories" are so narcissistic, so devoid of substance, that the only way to explain them is through delusion.[39]

Like MRAs, the gamers who rail against Sarkeesian—and anyone else who takes the video game industry to task for its dehumanizing imagery and persistent lack of diversity—envision themselves as activists for a cause they can never quite articulate. Perhaps recognizing that branding issue, in 2014 they began to rally, ironically, beneath the banner of "ethics in gaming journalism."

The feminist versus gamer conflict that came to be known as Gamergate erupted after an ex-boyfriend of game developer Zoe Quinn posted a hateful screed accusing her of sleeping with a journalist who reviewed her work. A frenzy of the usual misogynist vitriol followed, with Quinn and another developer, Brianna Wu, becoming prime targets alongside (still, always) Sarkeesian. "It's about ethics in journalism!" became young, male gamers' new battle cry, even though the original claim about Quinn was untrue, and most sincere crusaders for "ethics" in any discipline won't publicize the home addresses of people receiving rape and death threats.

It's hard to explain Gamergate to someone who didn't watch it unfold—and even I didn't watch too closely, partly because I'm not a gamer and partly because my stomach can only take so much. You'll have to trust me that if you haven't heard of it before, (a) you're lucky, but (b) it really is a big deal. *Law & Order: SVU* even did a Gamergate episode in early 2015 (and, predictably, made an utter hash of it). It sounds so silly, on paper—and it *is* silly, in terms of Gamergaters' professed motivation for terrorizing women. But make no mistake, a form of terrorism is what they're practicing.

The Gamergaters' object is to make women feel unsafe in their own homes and public spaces, as well as the games industry in general. They use intimidation and threats of violence to control the behavior not only of specific women they dislike and disagree with, but of all women with any interest in playing or designing games. Quinn and Wu have, like Sierra and Sarkeesian, been forced to leave their houses and pull out of events in the wake of relentless harassment and credible threats. Watching that, any young woman who loves gaming has to be wondering whether it's worth risking her health and safety to pursue a career developing them.

"During the reign of terror of Gamergate, I have had hundreds of conversations with other women," Wu wrote in February 2015. "We're exhausted, we're terrified we'll be next, we're all thinking of quitting."[40] To continue doing the job she loves is to risk her life; it can only be a matter of time before a new Elliot Rodger or George Sodini, after marinating in the sexist hatred at Gamergater sites, goes beyond simply threatening and actually murders someone in the name of "ethics in journalism."

What is a woman in that industry—or considering going into it— supposed to do? Find another career, just to be safe? Keep her head down and her mouth shut to avoid stoking the murderous rage of angry young men? What constitutes a "reasonable precaution" in the face of death and rape threats inspired by *your very existence*?

Wu's description of the compromise she's struck says it all: "I'm doing everything I can to save my life, except be silent."[41]

It's Time We All Became Proud Social Justice Warriors

In a *Daily Beast* article called "Your Princess Is in Another Castle: Misogyny, Entitlement, and Nerds," self-described nerd Arthur Chu connects the dots between the object of many games—saving the princess, who becomes your prize—and a society that treats women as objects for the taking.

The overall problem is one of a culture where instead of seeing women as, you know, people, protagonists of their own stories just like we are of ours, men are taught that women are things to "earn," to "win." That if we try hard enough and persist long enough, we'll get the girl in the end. Like life is a video game and women, like money and status, are just part of the reward we get for doing well.[42]

So-called Social Justice Warriors who insist that women have thoughts, feelings, and desires of our own are a threat to that culture of male entitlement and female passivity. In their eyes, we are shrill, hysterical hordes advancing in the name of "political correctness," which seems to mean mass castration and/or the destruction of all joy. The enemy is at the gates, and true defenders of gamer culture are ready to harass and abuse us all into submission—hell, rape and kill us, if they have to—until the war is won.

"'Social Justice Warrior' is a term whose pejorative use perplexes me," writes Andrew Todd, "because aside from the source of its invention, it sounds like a really badass thing to be. I'd much rather label myself a Social Justice Warrior than a warrior for . . . whatever it is that these people are warriors for."[43]

What these people are warriors for is a bunch of granfalloons.

"Granfalloon" is a word Kurt Vonnegut coined for his novel *Cat's Cradle* to describe "a proud and meaningless association of human beings."[44] For example, enjoying your coworkers, paycheck, and office is lovely (if rare), but the company itself—unless it's a family business or the realization of your own entrepreneurial dreams—is a granfalloon. No matter how many team-building exercises you're forced to complete, your connection to the other people who work for the same employer doesn't signify anything especially important. "Company pride" is an illusion that benefits your corporate overlords, who hope to boost morale without improving anybody's working conditions or paychecks.

Similarly, a group identity built around a hobby—whether it's knitting, golf, gaming, trolling, or posting porn online—is a granfalloon. The hobby itself neither confers nor implies any particular qualities on the part of its members; individuals of different tastes, faiths, political views, and work ethics can all participate without conflict, because this thing they do together actually says nothing about how they see themselves or the world.

After students at Pennsylvania State University rioted in response to the firing of Joe Paterno—who, as head coach of the school's football team, protected Jerry Sandusky as he molested boys for years—feminist writer Jess Zimmerman identified sports teams and fandom as such "proud and meaningless associations":

> What happens when your vision is clouded by a granfalloon? Well, as long as someone is playing by the rules of the group, you become inclined to ignore even major transgressions against outsiders. This illusory kinship overshadows your real kinship with other members of human society—which, despite having a lot of different norms and mores, as we all learned in 7th-grade social studies, has worked out a few basic common principles of compassion and decency such as "no raping children."[45]

Jerry Sandusky and, to a lesser extent, Joe Paterno violated the rules of human society. But they were leaders of the Penn State Nittany Lions, a granfalloon, and role models in some of our most beloved abstract sources of illusory kinship, like school spirit, teamwork, and athletics. We're trained to see those concepts themselves as valuable and important, even though schools, teams, and athletes vary wildly in their praiseworthiness. So when outsiders began to criticize Sandusky and Paterno, other true believers in those ultimately meaningless categories went to the mat for their perceived kin, instead of for humanity.

The same is true of young men who feel their self-concept threatened by a woman who critiques video games and of trolls who amp up their cruelty in response to being shamed. People they see as outsiders—Social Justice Warriors—threaten the meaningless pride such boys and men take in belonging to a category like "Enjoys Playing Video Games" or "Says Shitty Things to Make Other Guys Laugh." So gamers and trolls will fight to protect the granfalloon, and never mind the expense to the rest of us.

I should note that the category of Social Justice Warriors itself has the potential to be a granfalloon; people come to activism from countless different backgrounds, and like any other groups of human beings, activist circles inevitably contain some number of manipulators, liars, and attention-mongers. There is always the risk of valuing a particular group— be it a nonprofit organization, a certain publication, or your own Twitter disciples—more than the cause it's meant to work for.

But "people who care about advancing social justice and actively try to make that happen" is a meaningful group identity. It suggests common goals and a willingness to join forces for a purpose—unlike, say, men's rights activism, which suggests nothing more concrete than "I have serious issues with women."

Let the trolls, MRAs, PUAs, and raging gamers say what they will—a Social Justice Warrior *is* a really badass thing to be. We're the ones work-ing to make our society a place where everyone has the opportunity to live freely and without fear.

CHAPTER 11

Reasons for Hope

For as much as I complain about how little has changed in the decades since feminists first began a national conversation about rape, there are some noteworthy differences between the twenty-first century and the 1970s or even the '90s.

I've avoided loading down this book with detailed stories of individual rapes, for instance, because I feel those testimonies can easily be found elsewhere these days. That wasn't the case when Susan Brownmiller was writing *Against Our Will* or when Robin Warshaw was interviewing survivors for *I Never Called It Rape*. Women simply sharing their experiences was radical and revolutionary for a long time. Now it seems that new venues are appearing every day for survivors to open up about what they've endured. More and more, people are disclosing what used to be seen as shameful secrets, refusing to carry the burden of self-blame. I feel comfortable leaving that focus to them and to other writers on rape culture.

But I've referred to my own 1992 rape throughout this book, without going into detail, and that feels like a bit of a cheat. Plus, it just so happens that one of the worst things that ever happened to me is a good way to introduce all of the recent changes that give me hope for our culture—hope that one day, after some more time and collective effort, we'll be able to say, "'Rape culture' is a ridiculous overstatement," and mean it.

My Story

I was seventeen. It was my first week at college on an idyllic New England campus with fewer than five hundred students. It was one of those schools with no grades and little structure, where creative nerds went in hopes of productively expressing all the resentment we'd built up over years of traditional education. Our dorms were white colonial houses with green shutters, set alongside an expansive lawn, and on the weekends, we took turns hosting house parties that looked a lot like stereotypical Greek keggers, except for most of us being too artsy and historically unpopular to acknowledge the resemblance.

I was wearing a tight dress, borrowed from a "friend," although I hadn't been there long enough to have any real friends. I was, in a general sense, interested in meeting guys and maybe even having sex, although I never had before. I was drinking a lot—for the third or fourth time in my life. Punch, probably vodka-based. For a long time, I told myself and anyone else who had to hear this story that it was Everclear—Everclear punch was a thing in the '90s, if you weren't there—because grain alcohol would explain how I got so drunk, so fast. But being seventeen years old, nine hundred miles from home, and desperate to be liked would also explain it pretty well.

He approached me on the dance floor with a drink. We danced. I liked that part. He went and got me more drinks, because he was over twenty-one, and I liked that part, too.

At some point, we went outside. I don't know where I thought we were headed—could I have been naïve enough to think he was just walking me home?—but I know I stopped right there on the lawn between two dorms and kissed him. I liked that part, too, not so much because of the kiss itself, which was sloppy and awkward, but because going to parties and kissing boys on the way home implied that yes, college life was indeed going to kick high school's ass.

The part I liked lasted a very short time before he pulled me down on the ground. Before I'd even adjusted to being on a different plane, he pulled my underwear off and put his penis inside me.

I said "Stop," and wriggled around enough that his dick fell out. I slurred some other words at him, along the lines of "No, wait, please." And whatever I may have imagined before that moment, during my gym class self-defense unit or while walking through parking lots with a car key jutting out between two fingers, that was it. That was all the fight I had in me.

It's possible he didn't hear a no, specifically, or that my words were unintelligible. It's not possible he didn't know I was asking him to stop, or that he genuinely thought he had a willing partner at that point. Let's be clear about that.

When he finished, he stood up and walked away without a word. I felt around on the grass for my underpants and couldn't find them anywhere. There were a few other people milling around outside the doors of the house hosting the party, too far away to notice me. Otherwise, I was alone. I looked across the lawn at three white colonial houses with green shutters and wasn't completely sure which one I lived in. That's when I started sobbing.

My roommate woke up when I came in, still hysterical, and rushed to comfort me. She held me as I cried and told her I'd just had sex with a guy I didn't know, and my underwear was somewhere out on the lawn. The next morning, she marched me into our R.A.'s room, where I told the whole story and heard someone say for the first time, "Honey, that's called rape."

The R.A., the roommate, and I went to the hospital. I was only focused on preventing pregnancy and STDs, but the emergency room doctor—a man whose kindness and gentle manner I will never forget—explained what a rape kit entailed and asked if I wanted them to call the police and collect evidence. Two thoughts went through my head at that point: (1) I never got his name, and (2) if the police got involved, my parents would find out.

Even though several people had by then told me, "Honey, that's called rape," and I was starting to get it, I could only think about the fact that I'd gotten drunk out of my mind and had a penis inside me, two things my parents would surely disapprove of. Eventually, months later, I told them, and they were actually quite supportive; my mom even flew out that very weekend to visit. (Like the churlish teenager I still was, instead of being grateful, I mostly felt angry at her for making me miss one of the big, annual themed house parties.) But on the morning after, the thought of having to explain it to them was utterly terrifying, so I declined the rape kit. What was the point in collecting evidence against someone whose name I didn't even know, anyway?

I wasn't yet accustomed to living on a campus with fewer than five hundred people, which teaches you how few five hundred people really is. It didn't take a day before I spotted him in the dining hall and viscerally understood the phrase "My blood ran cold" for the first time. (There were so many firsts for me, just then. College freshmen have no idea how young they are.)

"That's him," I said to the friend I was with, although again, "friend" was a strong word for people I'd known less than two weeks. "That's the guy."

This particular young woman was a sophomore, and she recognized him, a senior. A "nontraditional" senior, in fact, that is, someone nearly a decade older than I was. There were a few of those around.

"Oh, no," she assured me. "That's _____. I know him. He would never do that."

And that was it, for several months. I never saw anyone else on campus I thought it might be, and I always felt a little weird around that guy, but again, it was a small campus. I occasionally even talked to him at parties. I hung out with people who considered him a good friend. I told myself he couldn't have been the guy who raped me—that must have been someone who didn't live on campus—because my not-yet-a-friend had sounded so sure, and people I liked really seemed to like him. Between the age and class difference, we didn't run into each other much, so it wasn't a big deal.

It went on like that until one day, I heard a rumor: That guy had raped somebody else.

And somebody else. And somebody else.

The person who told me that had no idea I'd once picked him out of a crowd as the guy who raped me—she was just sharing gossip about a mutual acquaintance. But that's what initiated Phase 2 of my rape story.

I sought out the people behind those rumors and learned he'd even been formally accused of rape through the school's channels before—by a student long since gone—and his "punishment" was writing her a letter of apology. (He'd also taken some time off, possibly not voluntarily, which explained his advanced age. Obviously, though, the college had welcomed him back.) I met another woman, a senior, who told me he'd raped her during a semester abroad, while she was sick in bed, loaded up on cough medicine with codeine. She wasn't willing to add her name to a complaint against him, but she offered to support me any other way she could.

It would be a very strange coincidence, I thought, if this guy who had a history of forcing himself on intoxicated woman, and whom I'd identified as my rapist less than twenty-four hours after the fact, was *not*, in fact, my rapist. I went back to the (now real) friend who'd originally told me, "He would never do that" and told her what I'd learned. She was aghast. She, too, offered to support me however she could, including testifying about that conversation in the dining hall and explaining that she'd steered me away from my gut reaction.

What happened to me is similar to a million other campus rape stories, but I want to note one thing that was different from many: I had loads of support. My friends, for the most part, never doubted me and certainly never blamed me. When I was still too afraid to tell my parents, yet unable to pay the hospital bill that came for my exam the morning after, my older sister stepped up to take care of the debt and keep my secret. That emergency room doctor was the best anyone could ever hope for in that situation. A pelvic exam is never pleasant under the best of circumstances, but I still recall how kindly he spoke to me, reaffirming that I'd been violated and I had a right to seek justice, without pressuring me to do anything I wasn't comfortable with. And the advantage of being at a tiny, emphasis-on-liberal liberal arts college is that I had access to many people who were informed about sexual violence and knew enough to help me heal instead of adding to my trauma.

It still got ugly from there. Not *worse*, given that point A was being raped, but it got ugly.

There was the other doctor, for instance, the one I saw on campus six months later for follow-up STD testing, whose disdain for sexually active young women was palpable. There were the mutual friends of my rapist and me, who had no idea how to treat either of us once I started telling people who it was. There were the nonmutual friends of his, who thought I was making it all up, and shot looks and comments to that effect in my direction. And then there was the hearing.

When I filed a complaint, it went to the school's sexual harassment committee—there was no sexual assault committee—which set a date to hear my argument and his. In addition to the friend who testified that I'd identified this person as my rapist, other friends of mine offered quasi-legal affidavits attesting, in essence, that I'd been really fucked up all year. The rape triggered depression and anxiety, which led me to skip a lot of classes and blow off a lot of homework. By this point, it was the end of the year, and I'd passed two out of six courses.

I told my story to the committee both in writing and in person. He told his story, separately. As far as I know, his argument was that he couldn't remember anything specific about the night in question, but he definitely had no recollection of anything I was talking about. This may even have been true. One of those mutual friends had said to me earlier, "Do I think he's the kind of guy who would rape somebody? No. Do I think he's a blackout drunk who does a lot of things he doesn't remember? Yes."

We were both thanked for our time and told to wait for a decision.

I went home for the summer, after telling the school I wouldn't be returning in the fall, even if they would have accepted me on academic probation. I didn't know where I'd go from there, but I knew I could never go back.

The decision came in the mail. The committee had concluded that yes, I was the victim of a rape, and it had seriously affected my studies. They would see that a note about personal difficulties was added to my transcript, a small mercy that would make it easier to convince another college to let me in later. They did not, however, believe that I had necessarily identified the correct suspect. The man I believed had raped me, who had already been through this whole process after another woman accused him, and who had reportedly raped at least one other student, would be allowed to graduate with his degree.

One member of the sexual harassment committee was a professor in his major department. He was the rapist's advisor. No one saw this as a problem.

I don't know where my rapist is now or if he's alive, for that matter. I've never even Googled his name; I'm occasionally curious, but when I think about typing it into a search bar, I'm stopped by the same superstitious dread I felt as a kid when someone pulled out a Ouija board at a party. I don't want to invite him back into my life like that, even in a way that can't possibly hurt me. So I assume he's probably pretty much as I last saw him: a messed-up alcoholic who can avoid hitting bottom indefinitely as long as he can get somebody to give him a pass at a crucial moment. He'd be pushing fifty now, so maybe that doesn't work as well as it used to. Maybe he's been sober for years. Maybe he's in prison for raping someone else.

You know what the worst—no, second worst—part for me is? More than twenty years later, I still haven't fully banished the thought that maybe I *was* wrong, and it *was* just a coincidence that the guy who made my blood run cold had been accused of raping other women. I mean, technically, it's *possible*—which is one reason why I haven't named him here. It's possible that I don't know who raped me and never will, which would mean I went through the humiliation of that hearing, and the socially miserable lead-up to it, for absolutely nothing.

But the worst part is, twenty years later, stories like that are still nauseatingly, shamefully common on college campuses. When people ask me about my rape, I usually describe it as "your typical After-School Special. Drunk at a party, first week of college, you know the rest." And they always do.

Rapists know it, too. My rape was a singular experience in my own life, but so many elements of it were positively *textbook*. Studies have shown that freshmen are especially vulnerable in the first few weeks after they arrive at school—some administrators call it the "Red Zone"—because they're likely to be inexperienced drinkers without a local support system, using alcohol to lessen social anxiety.[1] Predators exploit this, just as they exploit the fact that someone who flirts with a guy and leaves a party with him is unlikely to be believed when she says she was raped. (Again, my story varies from the typical one in that everyone believed me when I said I'd been raped—just not when I said I recognized my rapist a day later. It's fascinating how all of the usual bullshit about what you were drinking and what you were wearing and how much you *did* consent to falls away, if you give people another option to avoid believing a particular guy committed a particular rape.)

On the other hand, over the two years that I've been working on this book, I've seen changes I never imagined would come. And the difference in how people are responding to campus rapes, at both the institutional and the grassroots level, is one of several causes for genuine hope I'd like to leave you with.

Student Activists Demanding That Colleges and Universities Live Up to Their Responsibilities Under Title IX and the Clery Act

The federal law that would eventually be known as the Clery Act—technically the Jeanne Clery Disclosure of Campus Security Policy and Campus Crime Statistics Act—went into effect in 1991, a year before my rape. It's named after a nineteen-year-old woman who was raped and murdered by a fellow student in her dorm room at Lehigh University in 1986.

Only after their daughter was killed did Jeanne Clery's parents learn that the violent crime rate (including rape, robbery, and assault) at Lehigh had been unusually high in the preceding years; that most campus crimes nationwide were committed by other students; and that the school's security system was prone to abuses. (Clery's murderer, who lived off campus, entered her dorm through doors propped open by residents.)[2] They sued the university and used the resulting settlement money to found Security on Campus, a nonprofit dedicated to informing the public about campus crime, and began pressuring Congress to pass legislation requiring colleges and universities to improve security and report all crimes.

The act that eventually passed required colleges and universities receiving federal funding—that's most of them—to keep a public crime log, release an annual report of violent crimes on campus, and issue timely warnings to students about unsolved recent crimes, among other things. In 2013, President Obama signed the Violence Against Women Reauthorization Act, which amended the Clery Act to strengthen and expand those requirements. The following year, the Office of Postsecondary Education issued a "Dear Colleague Letter" (DCL) offering guidance on the matter:

> Notably, VAWA amended the Clery Act to require institutions to compile statistics for incidents of domestic violence, dating violence, sexual assault, and stalking and to include certain policies, procedures, and programs pertaining to these incidents in their annual security reports [ASRs]....
>
> For example, the statute requires institutions to specify in their ASRs the procedures that they will follow once an incident of domestic violence, dating violence, sexual assault, or stalking has been reported, including a statement of the standard of evidence

that will be used during any institutional conduct proceeding arising from such a report.[3]

A previous guidance document, the April 4, 2011, DCL from the
Department of Education's Office of Civil Rights, regarding schools'
responsibilities under Title IX of the Educational Amendments of 1972,
explained that colleges are to employ the standards of a civil court ("preponderance of the evidence") rather than a criminal court ("beyond a reasonable doubt") in determining whether a report of sexual harassment or
violence is actionable.

Prior to that, most of us thought of Title IX, which protects students
from sex-based discrimination, in terms of the positive impact it had on
girls' and women's school athletics. (There's even a manufacturer of women's activewear called Title Nine.) But the OCR's Dear Colleague Letter
reminded everyone that "sexual harassment of students, which includes
acts of sexual violence, is a form of sexual discrimination under Title IX."[4]
In a nutshell, the nineteen-page letter says this:

> If a school knows or reasonably should know about student-on-
> student harassment that creates a hostile environment, Title IX
> requires the school to take immediate action to eliminate the harass
> ment, prevent its recurrence, and address its effects.[5]

This document marked a historic shift in the government's approach
to sexual assault on campus, but that's not even my favorite thing about it.

My favorite thing is that two years later, survivor-activists Dana Bolger and Alexandra Brodsky got together and founded Know Your IX, an
information clearinghouse for students to learn about their legal rights
under Title IX and the Clery Act (more on that in a moment), and explore
resources for campus-based activism. Through their website (Know
YourIX.org), speaking engagements, and visibility in both social and mainstream media, these young activists have taken the message of the 2011
Dear Colleague Letter straight to the students who are meant to be protected by it.

Know Your IX is one of several survivor-activist networks, including
End Rape on Campus, founded by Annie Clark, Andrea Pino, and Sofie

Karasek, and SurvJustice, founded by Laura Dunn, that have been hard at work on behalf of student survivors over the last several years. (Pino and Clark are featured in the 2015 campus rape documentary *The Hunting Ground*, from the same team behind *The Invisible War*. The simple fact that such a film exists is also noteworthy progress.) In 2013, those activists launched a campaign called ED ACT NOW to pressure the federal government to enforce its own guidelines. The group noted that the Office of Civil Rights had, up to that point,

> never once sanctioned a college or university for sexual assault-related Title IX violations. Instead the agency quietly concludes investigations, asks universities to sign voluntary resolution agreements (VRAs)—essentially signed promises to do better next time—and issues no finding of violation. In the high stakes game of college rankings and university branding, schools get off scot-free: their reputations intact and with little incentive to make meaningful changes in the future.[6]

On July 15, 2013, dozens of ED ACT NOW activists traveled to Washington, DC, to deliver a petition with over one hundred thousand signatures, "calling on the OCR to conduct timely, transparent, coordinated, and proactive investigations; involve survivor-complainants in the process of arriving at any resolution to an investigation; and issue meaningful sanctions against non-compliant schools."[7] This led to meetings with officials from the Department of Education and Department of Justice, and the creation of a White House Task Force to Protect Students from Sexual Assault.

Just let those words sink in for a moment. *The White House Task Force to Protect Students from Sexual Assault*. That, I must admit, is something I never saw coming—neither in the aftermath of my rape in 1992, nor while I was writing the proposal for this book twenty years later.

Not Alone, the task force's first report, was issued in April 2014. It promotes bystander intervention (and specifically, engaging men in the fight); confidential consultation options for victims not ready to make a formal report; comprehensive sexual misconduct policies; trauma-informed training for school officials; better disciplinary systems; and partnerships with the community. And it promises increased transparency—including a website, NotAlone.gov, where students can directly file Title IX complaints—as well as improved enforcement.

Within a month of the report, the OCR issued its first two formal findings of noncompliance for sexual assault–related Title IX violations, to Tufts University and Virginia Military Institute. When this book went to press, eighty-five other colleges were under investigation for Title IX violations in their handling of sexual assault and rape cases.

Survivors did that. Students did that. The young people who are going to be running everything before we know it did that.

That gives me hope.

The Proliferation of Affirmative Consent Legislation and Policies

In the introduction to their 2008 anthology, *Yes Means Yes: Visions of Female Sexual Power and a World Without Rape*, Jaclyn Friedman and Jessica Valenti wrote:

> The goal of *Yes Means Yes* is to explore how creating a culture that values genuine female sexual pleasure can help stop rape, and how the cultures and systems that support rape in the United States rob us of our right to sexual power.[8]

Throughout the anthology (to which I was honored to contribute an essay), feminist and womanist writers argue for moving beyond the old battle cry of "No means no" and reconceptualizing sexual consent as something that must be given affirmatively—better yet, enthusiastically. In her essay "Offensive Feminism," feminist journalist and former attorney Jill Filipovic explained the concept as follows:

> Feminists insist that men are not animals. Instead, men are rational human beings fully capable of listening to their partners and understanding that sex isn't about pushing someone to do something they don't want to do. Plenty of men are able to grasp the idea that sex should be entered into joyfully and enthusiastically by both partners, and that an absence of "no" isn't enough—"yes" should be the baseline requirement.... If women have the ability to fully and

freely say yes, and if we established a model of enthusiastic consent instead of just "no means no," it would be a lot harder for men to get away with rape. It would be a lot harder to push the idea that there's a "gray area."[9]

In 2008, it was pretty much only feminists talking that way about consent—advancing the radical notion that it's incumbent upon men (and women) to ensure that their sexual partners actually want to have sex. But six years later, "Yes Means Yes" was beginning to be discussed seriously as a legal standard, not just a lofty ideal.

In September 2014, California governor Jerry Brown signed Senate Bill 967 into law, requiring colleges that receive state funding for financial aid "to adopt policies concerning sexual assault, domestic violence, dating violence, and stalking that include certain elements, including an affirmative consent standard in the determination of whether consent was given by a complainant."

That standard is described like so:

An affirmative consent standard in the determination of whether consent was given by both parties to sexual activity. "Affirmative consent" means affirmative, conscious, and voluntary agreement to engage in sexual activity. It is the responsibility of each person involved in the sexual activity to ensure that he or she has the affirmative consent of the other or others to engage in the sexual activity. Lack of protest or resistance does not mean consent, nor does silence mean consent. Affirmative consent must be ongoing throughout a sexual activity and can be revoked at any time. The existence of a dating relationship between the persons involved, or the fact of past sexual relations between them, should never by itself be assumed to be an indicator of consent.

Basically, if at any point, you're not completely sure your partner is into what you're doing, you need to stop doing it (if you're a student at a college that relies on state funding, and you don't want to risk getting thrown out). This is neither rocket science nor appalling government over-reach. This is being a decent human being.

Shortly after Bill 967 passed, writer, actor, and director Mindy Kaling's sitcom, *The Mindy Project*, aired an episode in which the necessary conflict between the show's two leads—who had entered a happy, loving relationship after two seasons of will-they-or-won't-they?—was all about issues of consent within a committed relationship. As the show opens on a shot of the bedroom door, we hear Mindy and Danny happily getting it on. Suddenly, Mindy yelps words to the effect of, "Danny! That doesn't go there!" followed by a clumsy separation and a bullshit apology: "I slipped."

Danny didn't slip, of course; a running joke throughout the show is that no man has ever "slipped" and ended up with his penis in the wrong hole. But over the course of the episode, these two people speak frankly about their sexual desires, sincerely apologize for lies and other relationship failures, and eventually come to a perfectly reasonable, grown-up agreement: if you want to try something drastically different in bed, *ask* first.

I thought the episode was groundbreaking not just because it was the first depiction of attempted anal sex on network prime time, but because I can't recall ever seeing adult partners on TV negotiate their sexual boundaries, in and out of bed, using *words*. And for my money, the episode is a perfect illustration of what "affirmative consent" is all about.

About one split second after his girlfriend said she isn't cool with what he is doing, Danny stops—not just the offensive act, even, but the whole sexual encounter. That's being a decent human being and taking responsibility for ensuring that "consent must be ongoing throughout a sexual activity." Mindy's lack of enthusiasm is portrayed as an instant boner killer, as it damn well should be.

Sure, in an ideal world, boyfriends would always ask before trying to penetrate a new orifice—and they definitely wouldn't try to cover it up with a weak lie after the fact. (In the show, Danny is duly shamed for that crap, by the way, and Mindy doesn't forgive him until he's apologized and they've agreed on how to handle things in the future so neither of them ever feels unsafe.) But to my mind, the episode sent exactly the right message about consent—it's not a black-and-white contract you sign before having sex, but an ongoing series of communications between sexual partners, whether that takes place during a single encounter or over several years.

Again, that fact should neither frighten nor confuse anyone who's had sex before. When you become sexually active, you quickly learn that sex as it's practiced in the real world nearly always demands small, quick renegotiations as you go along. Sometimes a long-term partner wants to try something new in bed, and sometimes even the old things hurt if you do them at the wrong angle. Sometimes the person on the bottom wants to be on top, or somebody's arm gets squished, or a head bashes into the headboard. Sometimes, an act that felt great when your partner started it actually makes you feel sore after a couple of minutes, and you need it to stop, even though you enthusiastically consented to the act before and loved what was happening up to that point.

Real people having real sex deal with this shit *all the time*. Practicing affirmative consent means being cognizant of how your partner's responding to everything that happens, doing everything you can to make sure you're both happy, and respecting the other person's boundaries even when they conflict with your immediate desires.

In other words, it's what decent people already do, without being told.

Far from making sex more confusing and unfounded rape accusations more likely, the affirmative consent model offers us all a measure of extra confidence that as long as we pay attention to our partners' responses, looking for active enthusiasm and making changes as the situation warrants it, we'll never accidentally stumble over the line between sex and rape—because that's really more like a wall that some people deliberately scale.

And if for some terrible reason we ever find ourselves falsely accused by a consensual sex partner, we'll be able to say honestly and assuredly that we received numerous indications of enthusiasm throughout the encounter—not just that we never heard a no or took a punch to the face.

Imagine, for instance, if Mindy reported Danny for putting his penis in her anus without consent—technically, she could argue that his attempt to "steal fifth base" was an assault. In that case, Danny could honestly tell investigators that prior to that moment, she was moaning, saying yes, telling him what he was doing felt good—and the second she told him what he was doing *didn't* feel good, he stopped. He was constantly aware of her level of engagement, and he respected the boundary she set. He should have asked first (and if they both wanted to have anal sex, they should have prepared better for it; that's not something to do on the fly, kids), but he was immediately responsive when she called time out.

That's a way better defense than "Well, she was lying still for most of it, not saying 'no' or throwing me off her, but when she did yell at me to stop, I stopped." It's also a description of way better sex. Who would want a partner who's not clearly expressing enthusiasm throughout the encounter? Someone who's looking for a victim, not a partner, that's who.

By mid-October 2014, bills similar to California's were under consideration in New York, New Jersey, and New Hampshire. The State University of New York had already transitioned to an affirmative consent standard at all of its campuses, and according to Inside Higher Ed, the whole Ivy League, save Harvard, had adopted a version of "Yes Means Yes" in their sexual assault policies.[10] The National Center for Higher Education Risk Management reported that eight hundred colleges and universities had done the same.

That gives me hope.

The Internet and Young People

In the last chapter, I discussed several ways in which the internet propagates rape culture, but I'd be remiss if I neglected to mention what an effective tool it can be in combating rape myths, connecting survivors, and providing information.

Besides the federal government's NotAlone.gov and other information clearinghouses like KnowYourIX.org and CleryCenter.org, local and national resources for violent crime victims are only a five-second Google search away. The Rape, Abuse & Incest National Network (RAINN) operates a National Sexual Assault Online Hotline, in addition to their telephone hotline and informative website, which help connect victims with local resources. Heather Corinna's Scarleteen, a marvelous website about sexual health for young people, offers a "bully-free zone" where teens can discuss assault and abuse (among many other topics), plus live chat and SMS services that enable them to ask direct questions of nonjudgmental adult educators. Information-wise, it's an amazing time to be young.

Trolls and bullies notwithstanding, the internet can also foster meaningful social connections. Just as important as the increased accessibility of organized services is the increased accessibility of other people who have endured similar experiences. On Tumblr and Twitter, on feminist, LGBTQI, and Social Justice Warrior blogs, survivors are telling their stories, exploding the myths that sexual violence is rare and being a victim is shameful. After I was raped in 1992, I went to my roommate, my RA, and the library for information and comfort. I met a few other women on campus who confided that they'd been victimized similarly but none of us had any idea how widespread the problem was. But if I were a college student today, I could find endless educational resources and connect with too many other survivors to count, without even leaving my bed. (I mean, leaving your bed is good, folks. I recommend it. But when you're lonely and depressed, the internet can be a lifesaver just as easily as it can make things worse.) This proliferation of voices sharing stories and demanding change has had a profound impact on the cultural conversation around rape and sexual assault, simply by (finally) growing too loud to be ignored.

After years of whispers about Bill Cosby allegedly drugging and raping women, the comedian Hannibal Buress mentioned it during a 2014 stage show, and thanks to social media, the open secret finally became an open discourse. Twitter wouldn't shut up about it, which meant online journalists found it newsworthy, which soon led to coverage from "old" media, and all the while, more and more women felt emboldened to report their own abuse at the beloved entertainer's hands. What had languished for decades as a rumor about some number of anonymous women—save a few who'd filed civil suits that went largely ignored—became, in the space of a few months, a front-page news story about dozens of women with concrete allegations, many of them choosing to make their full names public.

Comedians Amy Poehler and Tina Fey, hosting the seventy-first Golden Globe Awards, boldly joked at Cosby's expense before an audience of nineteen million viewers. Referring to the fairy tale musical *Into the Woods*, Poehler described the trials of the female protagonists: "Cinderella runs from her prince, Rapunzel is thrown from a tower for her prince, and Sleeping Beauty just thought she was getting coffee with Bill Cosby."

Fey and Poehler followed up that expertly crafted rape joke (see?) with marble-mouthed impressions of Cosby's Jell-O Pudding ads, the kind every half-assed comic has had in their repertoire since the mid-1980s—only their version of the avuncular dessert-maker mumbled cheerfully about spiking the pudding. The Golden Globes audience was visibly shocked and uncomfortable, which was at least partially the point. As Spencer Kornhaber wrote in the *Atlantic*, that second gag was

> an attempt to redefine Cosby's public persona permanently. Right after Robert DeNiro with "you talkin' to me?," Cosby's one of the most commonly impersonated figures in American culture. People who tuned in last night will probably find it harder to do or see someone do that impersonation now without thinking about rape. That's a significant development for anyone who thinks that public figures should be held to account when there's strong evidence they've used their fame to take advantage of others.[11]

A few weeks later, during the *Saturday Night Live* fortieth anniversary special in early 2015, Kenan Thompson impersonated Cosby in a *Celebrity Jeopardy* sketch that reinforced this new definition of the older comic's public image while highlighting how fast the change had happened. Thompson's Cosby appeared in a "Video Daily Double" about cocktail mixing, which was almost immediately cut off by Will Ferrell's horrified Alex Trebek: "Oh, oh, dear God, no! I'm very sorry! We filmed that in June!"

I must admit, I've felt a bit like Fake Trebek while writing this book. Every time I finished writing up one high-profile case or aspect of the emerging national conversation on sexual violence, some new development would demand a rewrite. (Like, for instance, the news that more than twenty-five women had accused Bill Cosby of rape or assault.) I know that by the time you read this, scores of new stories will have broken, which is frustrating for me as an author, but incredibly heartening for me as a human being. In the nineties, it seemed that we all went through a brief phase of fretting about date rape, then promptly forgot all we'd learned, but in the 2010s, it feels more as if a dam has finally burst. It feels as if maybe, finally, this conversation won't taper off until sexual violence does.

That gives me hope. So does the generation that's keeping it going.

In September 2014, Columbia University student Emma Sulkowicz began a long-term performance piece that would serve as her senior art thesis: carrying a fifty-pound, extra-large twin mattress everywhere she went on campus, until the school imposed some punishment on a fellow student who, she reported, had raped her two years before. Sulkowicz didn't approach any authorities until—like me, twenty years earlier—she heard another woman complain of abuse by the same man. (Two other people reporting he sexually assaulted them came forward after Sulkowicz did.) After a university hearing, Sulkowicz was told—like me, twenty years earlier, albeit for different reasons—that there was not enough evidence to warrant punishing him.[12]

It's the same basic story as countless other campus rapes—and the reason why organizations like Know Your IX exist. But Sulkowicz made sure hers was different. She refused to accept Columbia's decision quietly and devised a way to ensure the school couldn't keep it hidden. *Mattress Project (Carry That Weight)*, as she titled her performance piece, quickly captured national headlines. The image of a young victim lugging around a replica of her own crime scene, reifying the burden of being a woman in a rape culture, was irresistible.

And that, in turn, led to the image I want to leave you with. On October 29, 2014, Columbia students deposited twenty-eight mattresses at the door of university president Lee Bollinger, one to represent each complaint in the Title IX case pending against their school. At 130 other universities on that same day—organized via social media and the website CarryingTheWeightTogether.com—students held mattresses aloft like protest signs, expressing support for survivors and demanding that their institutions do better.

This being the internet age, photos of the protests soon made the rounds, and by about the fifth one I looked at, I was in tears. All of these young people—men, women, nonbinary—assembled to say, as publicly and visibly as possible, *Enough is enough.* I believe that's what—that's who—will move us from a rape culture to one that respects women's autonomy, takes sexual violence against any person seriously, and holds perpetrators accountable. As for the rest of us, the least we can do is try to keep their path forward clear.

Acknowledgments

If you're reading this with some expectation of seeing your own name, you probably deserve my utmost gratitude for your help in making this book come to life, and I offer it to you now. I hope you'll also see your actual name in the paragraphs that follow, but so many people offered support that meant a great deal to me as I worked on *Asking for It*, I know I'm going to forget a few.

My tenacious agent, Jacqueline Flynn, went above and beyond to connect me with Renee Sedliar at Da Capo, for which I am deeply grateful. Renee's wise edits and infinite patience made this book so much better, you guys, you don't even know. Claire Ivett also generously offered insight, and Beth Wright of Trio Bookworks gently corrected my stupid mistakes in punctuation and logic, among other things.

Thanks to Andi Zeisler, who did the first edit on much of the material in chapter 9, which appeared in the fall 2013 issue of *Bitch* under the title "Gray Matters." Portions of this book have also appeared in my column at *Dame*, so thanks are due to Kera Bolonik for both edits and permission. (For the record, I've also upcycled a few posts from my own various blogs, if you notice anything else that looks familiar.)

Several years ago, Jaclyn Friedman and Jessica Valenti asked me to contribute to *Yes Means Yes!: Female Sexual Power in a World Without Rape*, and they pretty much created a monster. Thanks for that, gals! Twanna Hines and David Futrelle sat down with me for interviews, and so many denizens of the feminist blogosphere influenced my work, directly and indirectly. The Gorgeous Ladies of Writing—Molly, Kelly, Wendy, and Claire—kept me sane(ish) through two and a half years of waking up to a Google Alert on "rape." My husband, Al, supported me in countless ways, as usual. I love that guy.

Finally, I want to thank all of the feminist and womanist writers who blazed the path for this book to exist. Notably, Susan Brownmiller, whose *Against Our Will* remains breathtakingly relevant; Emilie Buchwald, Pamela Fletcher, Martha Roth, and everyone who contributed to *Transforming a Rape Culture*; Jaclyn, Jessica, and my fellow contributors to *Yes Means Yes!*; Robin Warshaw, Peggy Reeves Sanday, so many more. Maybe even you. Thank you, thank you, thank you.

Notes

INTRODUCTION

1. Emilie Buchwald, Pamela Fletcher, and Martha Roth, eds., *Transforming a Rape Culture*, revised edition (Minneapolis: Milkweed Editions, 2005), xi.

2. "NISVS: An Overview of 2010 Summary Report Findings," National Intimate Partner and Sexual Violence Survey, 2010, cdc.gov/violenceprevention/pdf/cdc_nisvs _overview_insert_final-a.pdf.

3. Joseph A. Slobodzian, "Phila. Bar Slams Judge in Rape Case Teresa Carr Deni Had Its Support for a Third Term; Then She Reduced a Charge to Theft of a Prostitute's Services," *Philly*, Oct. 31, 2007, articles.philly.com/2007-10-31/news/25232857_1 _sexual-assault-charges-city-judge-gunpoint.

4. Eric Betz, "Victim Calls for Judge to Apologize," *Arizona Daily Sun*, Sept. 6, 2012.

CHAPTER 1: THE POWER OF MYTH

1. David Lisak, "Understanding the Predatory Nature of Sexual Violence," *Sexual Assault Report* 14, no. 4 (2011): 49–64.

2. Kashmir Hill, "Social Media Idiocy of the Day: Belvedere Vodka's Rape Joke," *Forbes*, March 23, 2012.

3. Hannah Frith and Celia Kitzinger, "Talk About Sexual Miscommunication," *Women's Studies International Forum* 20, no. 4 (1997): 517–528.

4. Kathryn Graham et al., "'Blurred Lines?' Sexual Aggression and Barroom Culture," *Alcoholism: Clinical and Experimental Research* 38 (2014): 1416–1424.

5. Ibid.

6. Ibid.

7. Meghan Daum, "Who Killed Antioch? Womyn." *Los Angeles Times*, June 30, 2007.

8. Susan Hansen, Rachel O'Byrne, and Mark Rapley, "Young Heterosexual Men's Use of the Miscommunication Model in Explaining Acquaintance Rape," *Sexuality Research and Social Policy* 7, no. 1 (2010): 45–49.

9. Cindy Horswell, "Prosecutor Calls Defendant in Gang Rape One of the 'Pack of Dogs,'" *Houston Chronicle*, Nov. 27, 2012.

10. Ibid.

11. James C. McKinley Jr., "Vicious Assault Shakes Texas Town," *New York Times*, March 8, 2011.

12. Ibid.

13. Juliet Macur and Nate Schweber, "Rape Case Unfolds on Web and Splits City," *New York Times*, Dec. 16, 2012.

14. Ibid.

15. Matthew Kaiser, "Some Rules About Consent Are 'Unfair to Male Students,'" *Time*, May 15, 2014.

16. Amy Grubb and Emily Turner. "Attribution of Blame in Rape Cases: A Review of the Impact of Rape Myth Acceptance, Gender Role Conformity and Substance Use on Victim Blaming," *Aggression and Violent Behavior* 17, no. 5 (2012): 443–452.

17. Diana L. Payne, Kimberly A. Lonsway, and Louise F. Fitzgerald, "Rape Myth Acceptance: Exploration of Its Structure and Its Measurement Using the Illinois Rape Myth Acceptance Scale," *Journal of Research in Personality* 33 (1999): 27–68.

18. Grubb and Turner, "Attribution of Blame in Rape Cases."

19. David Lisak, "Understanding the Predatory Nature of Sexual Violence," *Sexual Assault Report* 14, no. 4 (2011): 49–64.

20. Kimberly A. Lonsway, Joanne Archambault, and David Lisak, "False Reports: Moving Beyond the Issue to Successfully Investigate and Prosecute Non-Stranger Sexual Assault," *Voice* 3 (2009): 1–11.

CHAPTER 2: SIMPLE SAFETY TIPS FOR LADIES

1. Barbara Mikkelson, "Assaulted Tale (aka This Bird Won't Fly)," Snopes, July 11, 2011, snopes.com/crime/prevent/rape.asp.

2. Robert Jensen, "Rape Is All Too Normal," *Dallas Morning News*, Jan. 18, 2013.

3. Paul Walsh and Nicole Norfleet, "3rd Woman in Mpls. Sexually Assaulted Walking Alone at Night," *Star Tribune* (Minneapolis), Dec. 12, 2012.

4. Aaron Rupar, "MPD Releases Photos of Chicago Avenue Sexual Assault Suspect; Suspect Arrested [UPDATE]," Blotter, *City Pages*, Dec. 13, 2013.

5. Jackson Katz, "Violence Against Women—It's a Men's Issue," TEDxFiDiWomen, San Francisco, Nov. 30, 2012, ted.com/talks/jackson_katz_violence_against _women_it_s_a_men_s_issue.

6. *Rape and Sexual Assault: A Renewed Call to Action*, White House Council on Women and Girls and the Office of the Vice President, 2014.

7. Tara Murtha, "Why Men Should Be Taught Not to Rape—And What Rape Is," *RH Reality Check*, March 12, 2013, rhrealitycheck.org/article/2013/03/12/why -zerlina-maxwell-is-almost-right.

8. Ibid.

9. Sarah DeGue, *Preventing Sexual Violence on College Campuses: Lessons from Research and Practice*, White House Task Force to Protect Students from Sexual Assault, April 2014, notalone.gov/assets/evidence-based-strategies-for-the-prevention -of-sv-perpetration.pdf.

10. Ibid.

11. Ibid.

12. Katz, "Violence Against Women—It's a Men's Issue."

13. Thomas M. Millar, "Meet the Predators," Yes Means Yes! (blog), Nov. 12, 2009, yesmeansyesblog.wordpress.com/2009/11/12/meet-the-predators.

14. Erin G. Ryan, "Daniel Tosh Is Sorry He Told a Female Audience Member That She Should Get Hilariously Raped," *Jezebel*, July 10, 2012.

15. Lindy West, "How to Make a Rape Joke," *Jezebel*, July 12, 2012.

16. Jessica Valenti, *The Purity Myth: How America's Obsession with Virginity Is Hurting Young Women* (New York: Seal, 2009).

Chapter 3: Not-So-Innocent Bystanders

1. Spybug51, "Steubenville Rape Case—Michael Nodianos," YouTube, Jan. 10, 2013, youtube.com/watch?v=itBPdeNADlo.

2. Jackson Katz, *Macho Paradox: Why Some Men Hurt Women and How All Men Can Help* (Naperville, IL: Sourcebooks, 2006), Kindle.

3. Peggy Reeves Sanday, *Fraternity Gang Rape: Sex, Brotherhood, and Privilege on Campus* (New York: New York University Press, 1990), Kindle.

4. Bernard Lefkowitz, *Our Guys: The Glen Ridge Rape and the Secret Life of the Perfect Suburb* (Berkeley: University of California Press, 1997), Kindle.

5. Chris Staiti and Barry Bortnick, "In Colorado Town, Hazing Attack Leaves Victim an Outcast," Bloomberg, June 19, 2013.

6. Malaika Fraley, "'I Thought She Was Dead,' Officer Testifies in Richmond High Gang Rape Case," *Mercury News* (San Jose, CA), Nov. 15, 2010.

7. Cecilia Vega, "Richmond High School Rape Witness Describes Teen's Assault," ABC 7 San Francisco, Nov. 12, 2009.

8. Kevin Fagan, "Richmond Gang Rape Seen as Nearly Inevitable," *SFGate*, Nov. 1, 2009.

9. These were curated by the Tumblr site Helpful Comments at helpfulcomments.tumblr.com.

10. Jason Nark, "PLCB Pulls Date Rape Ads," *Philly*, December 8, 2011.

11. ControlTonight.com was shuttered at some point after the ads were pulled.

12. "One Student Pledge," Be the One, June 17, 2014, onestudent.org/be-the-one.

13. Jackson Katz, "What Men Can Do to Prevent Gender Violence," June 20, 2014, jacksonkatz.com/wmcd.html.

Chapter 4: The Problem of False Accusations

1. Kimberly A. Lonsway, Joanne Archambault, and David Lisak, "False Reports: Moving Beyond the Issue to Successfully Investigate and Prosecute Non-Stranger Sexual Assault," *Voice* 3, no. 1 (2009): 1–11.

2. David Lisak, Lori Gardinier, Sarah C. Nicksa, and Ashley M. Cote, "False Allegations of Sexual Assault: An Analysis of Ten Years of Reported Cases," *Violence Against Women* 16, no. 12 (2010): 1318–1334.

3. David Lisak, "False Allegations of Rape: A Critique of Kanin," *Sexual Assault Report* 11, no. 1 (2007): 1–2, 6, 9.

4. Committee to Review the Scientific Evidence on the Polygraph Board on Behavioral, Cognitive, and Sensory Sciences and Committee on National Statistics, Division of Behavioral and Social Sciences and Education, *The Polygraph and Lie Detection* (Washington, DC: National Academies, 2003), 212, 3.

5. *Lynching in America: Confronting the Legacy of Racial Terror*, Equal Justice Initiative, 2015, 10.

6. Zach Calef, "Englin Says University Will Charge Robb for False Rape Allegation," *Iowa State Daily*, Nov. 5, 2001.

7. Crimesider Staff, "Bonnie Sweeten, Mother Who Faked Kidnapping to Go to Disney World, Sentenced to 8 Years," *CBS News*, Jan. 27, 2012.

8. "Cops: McCain Worker Made Up Attack Story," *CBS News*, Oct. 24, 2008.

9. Cord Jefferson, "Accusing Black Men of False Crime Is Back in Style," *BET.com*, Feb. 18, 2011.

10. "'We, the Grand Jury': Text of Its Conclusions in the Tawana Brawley Case," *New York Times*, October 6, 1988.

11. Edwin Diamond, "The Sound Bites and the Fury," *New York Magazine*, July 18, 1988, 36–39.

12. Akiba Solomon, "Crystal Gail Mangum Isn't Innocent, but She's a Victim Just the Same," *Colorlines*, April 20, 2011, colorlines.com/archives/2011/04/crystal_gail _magnums_dark_twisted_past.html.

13. Ibid.

14. North Carolina State Bar v. Michael B. Nifong, Wake County, NC, Jan. 24, 2007.

15. Sydney H. Schanberg, "A Journey Through the Tangled Case of the Central Park Jogger," *Village Voice*, Nov. 19, 2002.

16. Sarah Burns, *The Central Park Five: A Chronicle of a City Wilding* (New York: Knopf, 2011), Kindle location 1147.

17. Patricia J. Williams, "Lessons from the Central Park Five," *Nation*, April 17, 2013.

18. Ibid.

19. Michele C. Black et al., *The National Intimate Partner and Sexual Violence Survey*, Centers for Disease Control and Prevention, 2010.

20. Lonsway, Archambault, and Lisak, "False Reports."

CHAPTER 5: TO SERVE AND PROTECT

1. "Ben Roethlisberger Lawsuit Settled," ESPN.go.com, Jan. 21, 2012.

2. Martha Bellisle, "Ben Roethlisberger Settles Lawsuit Alleging 2008 Rape," *USA Today*, Jan. 20, 2012.

3. "Ben Roethlisberger's Bad Play," *Smoking Gun*, April 15, 2010, thesmokinggun .com/documents/crime/ben-roethlisbergers-bad-play.

4. Some of Jane's sisters, in a face-palming detail you wouldn't believe if you saw it on *Law & Order: SVU*, were still wearing nametags that said "DTF"—"down to fuck"— from an earlier party. You'll note, however, that they did not say "DTBR," or "down to be raped."

5. "Ben Roethlisberger's Bad Play," *Smoking Gun*, April 15, 2010, thesmokinggun .com/file/ben-roethlisbergers-bad-play?page=4.

6. Amy Davidson, "Policing Roethlisberger," *New Yorker*, April 19, 2010.

7. Jonathan D. Silver and Dan Majors, "Roethlisberger Documents Give Details," *Pittsburgh Post-Gazette*, April 16, 2010.

8. Christian Boone, "New Details Emerge in Roethlisberger Case," *Atlanta Journal-Constitution*, June 9, 2010.

9. Davidson, "Policing Roethlisberger."

10. Amy Dellinger Page, "True Colors: Police Officers and Rape Myth Acceptance," *Feminist Criminology* 5, no. 4 (2011): 315–334.

11. Martin D. Schwartz, *National Institute of Justice Visiting Fellowship: Police Investigation of Rape—Roadblocks and Solutions*, National Criminal Justice Reference Service, US Department of Justice, Dec. 2010, ncjrs.gov/pdffiles1/nij/grants/232667.pdf.

12. Ibid.

13. Ibid.

14. Ibid.

15. Justin Fenton, "City Rape Statistics, Investigations Draw Concern," *Baltimore Sun*, June 27, 2010.

16. E. R. Quatrevaux, *A Performance Audit of the New Orleans Police Department's Uniform Crime Reporting of Forcible Rapes*, 2014.

17. Corey R. Yung, "How to Lie with Rape Statistics: America's Hidden Rape Crisis," *Iowa Law Review* 99, no. 3 (2014): 1197–1256.

18. Ibid.

19. Lolita Baldor, "Sex Is Major Reason Military Commanders Are Fired," *AP: The Big Story*, Jan. 20, 2013, bigstory.ap.org/article/sex-major-reason-military-commanders-are-fired.

20. "Pentagon Report on Sexual Assault in the Military in 2012," *New York Times*, May 7, 2013.

21. Jim Miklaszewski, Courtney Kube, and Tracy Connor, "Air Force's Sex-Abuse Prevention Honcho Charged with Sexual Battery," NBC News, May 6, 2013, usnews.nbcnews.com/_news/2013/05/06/18089279-air-forces-sex-abuse-prevention-honcho-charged-with-sexual-battery?lite.

22. Lolita C. Baldor, "Officer Defends Overturning Sexual-Assault Verdict," *AP: The Big Story*, April 10, 2013, bigstory.ap.org/article/apnewsbreak-officer-defends-overturning-verdict.

23. Ibid.

24. Anna Mulrine, "Fort Hood Prostitution Case Shows Military's Challenges with Sexual Assault," *Christian Science Monitor*, March 13, 2015.

25. Garance Franke-Ruta, "Ending the Culture of Impunity on Military Rape," *Atlantic*, May 9, 2013.

26. "Gillibrand Calls to Remove Military Sexual Assault Cases from Chain of Command," *PBS Newshour*, July 30, 2013, pbs.org/newshour/bb/politics-july-dec13-military_07–30.

27. James Taranto, "Sex, Lies and the War on Men," *Wall Street Journal*, June 19, 2013.

28. "The Section of Det. Thomas Woodmansee's Police Report That Deals with Patty's Confession," Truth in Justice, truthinjustice.org/29rape1.htm, accessed Aug. 8, 2014.

29. "Statement from Patty's Ophthalmologist," Truth in Justice, truthinjustice .org/29rape1.htm, accessed Aug. 8, 2014.

30. Bill Lueders, *Cry Rape: The True Story of One Woman's Harrowing Quest for Justice* (Madison, WI: Terrace Books, 2006).

31. "Section of Det. Thomas Woodmansee's Police Report."

32. Natalie Elliott, "I Was Raped and the Police Told Me I Made It Up," *Vice*, Jan. 9, 2013, vice.com/en_uk/read/i-was-rapedand-then-the-police-told-me-i-made-it-up.

33. Scott Shifrel, "Rape Victim's Truth: Sex Con Is Busted 7 Years After No One Believed Her," *New York Daily News*, March 19, 2004.

34. Dan Bilefsky, "In Court, Confronting Man with Story of a Rape and a Ruse," *New York Times*, Nov. 15, 2011.

35. Ralph Blumenthal, "The Dangerous Rise in Untested Rape Kits," *Marie Claire*, Aug. 10, 2010.

36. Armen Keteyian and Laura Strickler, "Exclusive: Rape in America: Justice Denied," *CBS News*, Nov. 9, 2009, cbsnews.com/news/exclusive-rape-in-america-justice-denied.

37. Erik Eckholm, "No Longer Ignored, Evidence Solves Rape Cases Years Later," *New York Times*, Aug. 2, 2014.

38. Joel Rubin, "LAPD Closes Backlog of Untested Rape Kits," *Los Angeles Times*, April 28, 2011.

39. Eckholm, "No Longer Ignored."

40. Debra Patterson and Rebecca Campbell, "Why Rape Survivors Participate in the Criminal Justice System," *Journal of Community Psychology* 38, no. 2 (2010): 191–205.

41. *Improving Police Response to Sexual Assault*, Human Rights Watch, 2013, hrw.org/sites/default/files/reports/improvingSAInvest_0.pdf.

42. Ibid.

43. Ibid.

44. Ibid.

45. Ibid.

Chapter 6: Unreasonable Doubts

1. *Rape and Sexual Assault: A Renewed Call to Action*, White House Council on Women and Girls, 2014.

2. Ibid.

3. Erin Alberty and Janelle Stecklein, "Study: Most Rape Cases in Salt Lake County Never Prosecuted," *Salt Lake Tribune*, Jan. 7, 2014.

4. Ibid.

5. Liesl Hansen, "BYU Professor Shines Light on Low Numbers of Sex Assault Prosecutions," *Digital Universe*, May 8, 2014, universe.byu.edu/2014/05/08/byu-professor -shines-light-on-low-numbers-of-sex-assault-prosecutions.

6. Alberty and Stecklein, "Most Rape Cases."

7. Bruce Frederick and Don Stemen, *The Anatomy of Discretion: An Analysis of Prosecutorial Decision Making* (New York: Vera Institute of Justice, 2012). Available at vera.org.

8. Ibid.

9. Diana L. Payne, Kimberly A. Lonsway, and Louise F. Fitzgerald, "Rape Myth Acceptance: Exploration of Its Structure and Its Measurement Using the Illinois Rape Myth Acceptance Scale," *Journal of Research in Personality* 33 (1999): 27–68.

10. Christina Cunliffe, Nina Burrowes, Sokratis Dinos, and Karen Hammond, *Do Rape Myths Affect Juror Decision Making?: A Systematic Review of the Literature*, BPP University College, Dec. 2012, bpp.com/carbon-content-1.0-SNAPSHOT/resources /ECMDocument?contentName=Rape_myths_Dec_2012.

11. *Rape and Sexual Assault*.

12. Scott Moxley, "Meet Jane Doe," *OC Weekly*, April 26, 2012.

13. Debbie Nathan and Michael Snedeker, *Satan's Silence: Ritual Abuse and the Making of a Modern American Witch Hunt* (1995; repr., Lincoln, NE: iUniverse, 2001), Kindle.

14. Ibid.

15. Chandra R. Thomas, "Why Is Genarlow Wilson in Prison?" *Atlanta* (Jan. 2006): 66.

16. Gina McCauley, "Genarlow Wilson: The Most Ungrateful and Entitled Child Rapist to Ever Graduate From Morehouse," What About Our Daughters?, May 20, 2013, whataboutourdaughters.com/waod/2013/5/20/genarlow-wilson-the-most -ungrateful-and-entitled-child-rapis.html.

17. Patrick Kirkland, *Confessions of a "Rape Cop" Juror* (New York: Gothamist, 2011), Kindle locations 208–210.

18. Ibid.

19. New York Penal Code Article 130, Sex Offenses.

20. Shamena Anwar, "A Jury Pool's Race Can Deny Justice," CNN, May 23, 2012, cnn.com/2012/05/23/opinion/anwar-bayer-hjalmarsson-jury-racism/index.html.

21. Kevin Shoesmith, "Five Years Jail for Bricklayer Lee Setford Who 'Lost Control' and Raped Drunken Woman at Beverley Home," *Hull Daily Mail* (London), July 2, 2014.

22. Ibid.

23. Thomas M. Millar, "Meet the Predators," Yes Means Yes! Nov. 12, 2009, yesmeans yesblog.wordpress.com/2009/11/12/meet-the-predators.

24. Eric Betz, "No Jail Time for Flagstaff Cop in Bar Groping," *Arizona Daily Sun*, Sept. 6, 2012.

25. Joe Nimmo, "Judge in Rape Trial Warning: 'Conviction Rates Will Not Improve Until Women Stop Drinking So Heavily,'" *Oxford Mail*, Aug. 26, 2014.

26. Ibid.

27. Dean G. Kilpatrick et al., *Drug-Facilitated, Incapacitated, and Forcible Rape: A National Study*, National Crime Victims Research and Treatment Center, 2007.

28. Nimmo, "Judge in Rape Trial Warning."

29. Jody Raphael, *Rape Is Rape: How Denial, Distortion, and Victim Blaming Are Fueling a Hidden Acquaintance Rape Crisis* (Chicago: Lawrence Hill Books, 2013), Kindle location 2911.

CHAPTER 7: THE POLITICS OF RAPE

1. Tara Culp-Ressler, "Surrounded by Men, Ohio Governor Signs Stringent Abortion Restrictions into Law," *ThinkProgress*, July 1, 2013, thinkprogress.org/health/2013 /07/01/2237701/ohio-budget-signed-into-law.

2. "Ron Paul Interview," *Piers Morgan Tonight*, CNN, Feb. 3, 2012.

3. Aviva Shen, "Linda McMahon Offers Ridiculous Excuse for Opposing Emergency Contraception in Cases of Rape," *ThinkProgress*, October 16, 2012, thinkprogress.org/election/2012/10/16/1018891/linda-mcmahon-flip-flops-on -morning-after-pill-for-rape-victims.

4. "Interview with Rick Santorum," *Piers Morgan Tonight*, CNN, Jan. 20, 2012.

5. Kevin Liptak and Gregory Wallace, "Obama on Rape Comments: They 'Don't Make Any Sense,'" CNN, Oct. 25, 2012, cnn.com/2012/10/25/politics/indiana-mourdock -senate-rape.

6. Episode 15, season 13, *The View*, ABC, Sept. 28, 2009.

7. Julie Carr Smyth, "Ohio Doctor Helps Perpetuate Rape Pregnancy Ideas," *AP: The Big Story*, Aug. 24, 2012, bigstory.ap.org/article/ohio-doctor-helps-perpetuate -rape-pregnancy-ideas.

8. Kim Geiger, "Todd Akin Not Alone in Adhering to Bogus Rape Theory," *Los Angeles Times*, Aug. 20, 2012.

9. American College of Obstetricians and Gynecologists, "Statement on Rape and Pregnancy," Aug. 20, 2012, acog.org/About-ACOG/News-Room/News-Releases/2012 /Statement-on-Rape-and-Pregnancy.

10. Meredith L. Chivers and J. Michael Bailey, "A Sex Difference in Features That Elicit Genital Response," *Biological Psychology* 70, no. 2 (2005): 115–120.

11. Natalie Angier, "A Scientific Reckoning of the Sex Drive," *New York Times*, April 10, 2007.

12. Christopher Goffard, "California Judicial Panel Admonishes O.C. Judge for Rape Comments," *Los Angeles Times*, Dec. 14, 2012.

13. "Gingrey Defense of Akin's Rape Comments Misses the Mark," PolitiFact, Jan. 16, 2013, politifact.com/georgia/statements/2013/jan/16/phil-gingrey/gingrey -defense-akins-rape-comments-misses-mark.

14. Emily Heffter, "Koster Draws Fire over Comments About Abortion, 'the Rape Thing,'" *Seattle Times*, Oct. 31, 2012.

15. Sue Owen and W. Gardner Selby, "UPDATED: Jodie Laubenberg Says Texas Rape Kit Is Like Dilation and Curettage Procedure," PolitiFact, June 24, 2013, politifact.com/texas/statements/2013/jun/24/jodie-laubenberg/jodie-laubenberg -says-texas-rape-kit-dilation-and-.

16. Dana Liebelson and Sydney Brownstone, "Imagine You Were Raped. Got Pregnant. Then Your Rapist Sought Custody," *Mother Jones*, Aug. 24, 2012.

17. Elizabeth Miller et al., "Pregnancy Coercion, Intimate Partner Violence and Unintended Pregnancy," *Contraception* 81, no. 4 (2010): 316–322.

18. Michele C. Black et al., *National Intimate Partner and Sexual Violence Survey 2010 Summary Report*, Centers for Disease Control and Prevention, National Center for Injury Prevention and Control, Division of Violence Prevention, 2011.

19. "New Laws Recognizing Marital Rape as Crime," *New York Times*, Dec. 28, 1984.

20. Amanda Terkel, "TN State Senator: 'Rape Just Isn't What It Used to Be,'" *Think Progress*, Feb. 14, 2008.

21. Fred De Sam Lazaro, "Bill Napoli Interview, " *PBS Newshour*, March 3, 2006.

22. Lawrence B. Finer, "Trends in Premarital Sex in the United States, 1954–2003," *Public Health Reports* 122, no. 1 (2007): 73–78. Jessica Valenti, *The Purity Myth: How America's Obsession with Virginity Is Hurting Young Women* (New York: Seal, 2009), 58.

23. Kimberly Daniels, William D. Mosher, and Jo Jones, "Contraceptive Methods Women Have Ever Used: United States, 1982–2010," *National Health Statistics Reports*, no. 62 (2013).

24. Valenti, *Purity Myth*, 123.

CHAPTER 8: VIRGINS, VAMPS, AND THE VIEW FROM NOWHERE

1. Helen Benedict, *Virgin or Vamp: How the Press Covers Sex Crimes* (New York: Oxford UP, 1992), 19.

2. Ibid.

3. Ibid.

4. Ben Armbruster, "O'Reilly: Abducted Child 'Liked His Circumstances,' Had 'a Lot More Fun' Than Usual," Media Matters for America, Jan. 17, 2007, mediamatters .org/research/2007/01/17/oreilly-abducted-child-liked-his-circumstances/137753.

5. Ibid.

6. Ibid.

7. Ibid.

8. Tracy Jarrett, "'I Was Broken Beyond Repair': Elizabeth Smart Recalls Kidnapping Ordeal," *NBC News*, Oct. 5, 2015, nbcnews.com/news/other/i-was-broken-beyond -repair-elizabeth-smart-recalls-kidnapping-ordeal-f8C11336267.

9. Erin G. Ryan, "Frat Alumni President Blames 'Drunk Female Guests' for Ruin- ing Fun," *Jezebel*, Sept. 24, 2014, jezebel.com/frat-alumni-president-blames-drunk -female-guests-for-ru-1638524129/all.

10. Ibid.

11. David Edwards, "Fox Hosts Blame Drunk Girls for Frat Rapes: 'These Guys, What Are They Supposed to Do?,'" *Raw Story*, Sept. 25, 2014, rawstory.com/rs/2014/09 /fox-hosts-blame-drunk-girls-for-frat-rapes-these-guys-what-are-they-supposed-to-do.

12. Ibid.

13. Jay Rosen, "The View from Nowhere: Questions and Answers," PressThink, Nov. 10, 2011, pressthink.org/2010/11/the-view-from-nowhere-questions-and-answers.

14. "Filmmakers Demand Polanski's Release," CNN, Sept. 29, 2009, cnn.com/2009 /SHOWBIZ/Movies/09/29/polanski.filmmakers.protest.

15. Anne Applebaum, "The Outrageous Arrest of Roman Polanski," *Washington Post*, Sept. 27, 2009.

16. Joan Z. Shore, "Polanski's Arrest: Shame on the Swiss," *Huffington Post*, Sept. 27, 2009, huffingtonpost.com/joan-z-shore/polanskis-arrest-shame-on_b_301134.html.

17. Mark Graham, "Roman Polanski Update: Victim Wants Charges Dismissed,

Debra Winger Thinks It's One Big Instance of 'Philistine Collusion,'" *Vulture*, Sept. 29, 2009, vulture.com/2009/09/polanski_roundup.html.

18. Conor Friedersdorf, "Schwarzenegger Fathered Child with Household Staffer, Hid It as Governor," *Atlantic*, May 17, 2011.

19. James Rainey, "On the Media: Schwarzenegger-Shriver Split Recalls Earlier News Reports," *Los Angeles Times*, May 11, 2011.

20. Bernard-Henri Lévy, "Bernard-Henri Lévy Defends Accused IMF Director," *Daily Beast*, May 15, 2011.

21. Katie Nelson, "Dominique Strauss-Kahn, Busted for Sexual Assault, 'Won't Get Away with It,' Brother of Accuser Says," *New York Daily News*, May 17, 2011.

22. Paul Owen and Robert Booth, "Julian Assange Extradition Appeal Hearing," *Guardian* (London), July 12, 2011.

23. Ibid.

24. David C. Johnston, "Letters: AOLer Kennedy's Assange 'Rape' Coverage Deserves Notice," Romenesko Letters, The Poynter Institute, Dec. 6, 2010, poynter.org/latest-news /mediawire/109607/letters-aoler-kennedys-assange-rape-coverage-deserves-notice.

25. Jesus Diaz, "WikiLeaks' Julian Assange Is Not Accused of Rape (Updated)," *Gizmodo*, Dec. 3, 2010, gizmodo.com/5705614/wikileaks-julian-assange-is-not-accused -of-rape-updated.

26. Ibid.

27. Kit Eaton, "Anatomy of a Smear: WikiLeaks' Assange Wanted for 'Sex by Surprise,' Not Rape," *Fast Company*, Dec. 3, 2010, fastcompany.com/1707146/anatomy -smear-wikileaks-assange-wanted-sex-surprise-not-rape.

28. Ibid.

29. Johnston, "Letters."

30. Ibid.

31. Kevin Drum, "What Are Julian Assange's Sex Charges All About?" *Mother Jones*, Dec. 7, 2010.

32. Ibid.

33. "Reporting on Sexual Violence Tip Sheet," Dart Center for Journalism and Trauma, July 15, 2011, dartcenter.org/content/reporting-on-sexual-violence#.VChn WytdXIo.

34. Kelly McBride, "How Journalists Can Provide Fair Coverage When Reporting on Rape Charge in Cleveland Case," The Poynter Institute, May 9, 2013, poynter.org /news/mediawire/212688/how-journalists-can-provide-fair-coverage-when-reporting -on-rape-charges-in-cleveland-case.

35. Jessica Valenti, "How to Write About Rape: Rules for Journalists," *Nation*, Oct. 25, 2013.

36. Claudia Garcia-Rojas, *Reporting on Rape and Sexual Violence: A Media Toolkit for Local and National Journalists to Better Media Coverage*, Chicago Task Force on Violence Against Girls & Young Women, 2012.

37. *Reporting on Sexual Violence: A Media Packet for Maine Journalists*, Maine Coalition Against Sexual Assault and the Sexual Assault Crisis and Support Center, n.d.

38. Linnéa, "Sex by Surprise," Feminism and Tea, Dec. 6, 2010, feminismandtea.blog spot.com/2010/12/sex-by-surprise.html.

CHAPTER 9: POP RAPE

1. Lisa Wade, "The Rape Scene in *Observe and Report*," Sociological Images, April 21, 2009 thesocietypages.org/socimages/2009/04/21/the-rape-scene-in-observe-and-report.

2. Amanda Hess, "*Observe and Report*'s Date Rape Apologism," The Sexist, *Washington City Paper*, April 8, 2009, washingtoncitypaper.com/blogs/sexist/2009/04/08/observe-and-reports-date-rape-apologism.

3. Michelle Dean, "Tube Tied: *Mad Men*, I Love You, But Your Fans Are Freaking Me Out," *Bitch*, Aug. 14, 2009.

4. Logan Hill, "Dangerous Curves," *New York Magazine*, Aug. 2, 2009.

5. Carolyn Edgar, "Tyler Perry's Rape Problem," Carolyn Edgar, April 2, 2013, carolyn edgar.com/2013/04/02/tyler-perrys-rape-problem.

6. Nico Lang, "The Soapbox: Tyler Perry Has a Rape Problem in 'Temptation,'" *Frisky*, April 3, 2013, thefrisky.com/2013−04−03/the-soapbox-tyler-perry-has-a-rape-problem -in-temptation.

7. Edgar, "Tyler Perry's Rape Problem."

8. Lindy West, "If Comedy Has No Lady Problem, Why Am I Getting So Many Rape Threats?," *Jezebel*, June 4, 2013, jezebel.com/if-comedy-has-no-lady-problem -why-am-i-getting-so-many-511214385.

9. Lindy West, "How to Make a Rape Joke," *Jezebel*, July 12, 2012, jezebel.com /5925186/how-to-make-a-rape-joke.

10. Ibid.

11. Natalie Finn, "Rick Ross Apologizes for Song's Date-Rape Reference," *E! Online*, April 4, 2013, eonline.com/news/405016/rick-ross-tweets-apology-for-date -rape-lyric-i-don-t-condone-rape.

12. Carrie Battan, "Rick Ross Issues Formal Apology for Controversial "U.E.O.N.O." Verse," *Pitchfork*, April 12, 2013, pitchfork.com/news/50312-rick-ross -issues-formal-apology-for-controversial-ueono-verse.

13. Alan Duke, "CeeLo Green Accused of Giving Woman Ecstasy, but DA Declines Rape Charge," CNN, Oct. 22, 2013, cnn.com/2013/10/21/showbiz/ceelo -green-drug-charge.

14. Colin Stutz, "Following No Contest Plea, CeeLo Green Tweets 'Women Who Have Really Been Raped Remember,'" The Juice, Billboard, Sept. 1, 2014, billboard.com /articles/columns/the-juice/6236564/ceelo-green-tweets-rape-statements-no-contest.

15. Ibid.

16. August Brown, "CeeLo Green Temporarily Deletes Twitter Account After Rape Comments," *Los Angeles Times*, Sept. 2, 2014.

17. August Brown, "Cee-Lo Green Apologizes Again for Rape Comments," *Los Angeles Times*, Sept. 3, 2014.

18. Jethro Nededog, "Insider: CeeLo Green Quit 'The Voice' to Avoid Being Fired (Exclusive)," *Wrap*, Feb. 19, 2014, thewrap.com/nbc-voice-ceelo-green-quits-inside-story.

19. bell hooks, "Seduced by Violence No More," in *Transforming a Rape Culture*,

edited by Emilie Buchwald, Pamela R. Fletcher, and Martha Roth (Minneapolis: Milkweed Editions, 2005), 295–299.

20. Ibid.

21. Jackson Katz, *The Macho Paradox: Why Some Men Hurt Women and How All Men Can Help* (Naperville, IL: Sourcebooks, 2006), Kindle location 3364.

22. Nisha L. Diu, "Interview: Angel Haze, the Rapper Fighting Rape Culture," *Telegraph* (London), Oct. 13, 2013.

23. Ibid.

24. Ibid.

25. Michael P. Jeffries, "How Rap Can Help End Rape Culture," *Atlantic*, Oct. 30, 2012.

26. Lisa Cuklanz and Sujata Moorti, "Television's New Feminism: Prime Time Representations of Women and Victimization," *Critical Studies in Media Communication* 23, no. 4 (Oct. 2006): 302–321.

27. John Mulaney, *John Mulaney: Ice T on "Law & Order: SVU,"* video, Jan. 28, 2012.

28. Ibid.

29. Leeann Kahlor and Dan Morrison, "Television Viewing and Rape Myth Acceptance Among College Women," *Sex Roles* 56, no. 11–12 (2007): 729–739.

30. Margaret Lyons, "Maxing Out on Murder: Good Luck Finding a Decent TV Drama Without Rape or Killing," *Vulture*, April 17, 2013, vulture.com/2013/04/maxing-out-on-murder-shows.html.

31. Jaclyn Friedman, "Rape on TV—More Than Just a Plot Twist," *American Prospect*, Jan. 15, 2014.

32. Ibid.

33. Alyssa Rosenberg, "From Washington to Westeros, How Rape Plays Out on TV," *Washington Post*, April 4, 2014.

34. Kahlor and Morrison, "Television Viewing and Rape Myth Acceptance."

35. Stuart Kemp, "British Film Censor Vows Stricter Approach to Depictions of Rape, Sexual Assault," *Hollywood Reporter*, Dec. 10, 2012.

36. Alan Sepinwall, "Review: 'Game of Thrones'—'Breaker of Chains,'" *HitFix*, April 20, 2014, hitfix.com/whats-alan-watching/review-game-of-thrones-breaker-of-chains-uncle-deadly.

37. Denise Martin, "Breaking Down Jaime and Cersei's Controversial Scene with Last Night's *Game of Thrones* Director," *Vulture*, April 21, 2014, vulture.com/2014/04/game-of-thrones-director-on-the-rape-sex-scene.html.

38. Ibid.

39. Sepinwall, "Review: 'Game of Thrones.'"

40. Margaret Lyons, "Yes, Of Course That Was Rape on Last Night's *Game of Thrones*," *Vulture*, April 21, 2014, vulture.com/2014/04/rape-game-of-thrones-cersei-jaime.html.

41. Rebecca Pahle, "Here's What the Writer and Director of *Game of Thrones*' Controversial Rape Scene (Plus GRRM) Have to Say About It," *Mary Sue*, April 22, 2014, themarysue.com/game-of-thrones-rape-controversy-grrm.

42. Amanda Marcotte, "The Director of Sunday's *Game of Thrones* Doesn't Think That Was Rape," *Slate*, April 21, 2014, slate.com/blogs/xx_factor/2014/04/21/gam e_of_thrones_rape_director_alex_graves_says_the_sex_becomes_consensual.html.

CHAPTER 10: TROLLS, GAMERS, AND THE NEW MISOGYNY

1. Whitney Phillips, "A Brief History of Trolls," *Daily Dot*, May 20, 2013, dailydot .com/opinion/phillips-brief-history-of-trolls.

2. Dylan Matthews, "Your Guide to 4chan, the Site Where Jennifer Lawrence's Hacked Photos Were Leaked," *Vox*, Sept. 2, 2014vox.com/2014/9/2/6096815 /4chan-explainer-questions.

3. Ibid.

4. Whitney Phillips, "What an Academic Who Wrote Her Dissertation on Trolls Thinks of Violentacrez," *Atlantic*, Oct. 15, 2012.

5. Ibid.

6. "Episode 545: If You Don't Have Anything Nice to Say, Say It in All Caps," *This American Life*, NPR, Jan. 23, 2015.

7. Ibid.

8. "Blog Death Threats Spark Debate," *BBC News*, March 27, 2007, news.bbc .co.uk/2/hi/technology/6499095.stm.

9. Greg Sandoval, "The End of Kindness: Weev and the Cult of the Angry Young Man," *Verge*, Sept. 12, 2013, theverge.com/2013/9/12/4693710/the-end -of-kindness-weev-and-the-cult-of-the-angry-young-man.

10. Sandoval, "The End of Kindness."

11. Ibid.

12. Dayna Evans, "J-Law, Kate Upton Nudes Leak: Web Explodes over Hacked Celeb Pics," *Gawker*, Aug. 31, 2014, gawker.com/internet-explodes-over-j-laws -alleged-hacked-nudes-1629093854.

13. According to Reddit's media kit, Feb. 22, 2015.

14. Adrian Chen, "Unmasking Reddit's Violentacrez, The Biggest Troll on the Web," *Gawker*, Oct. 12, 2012, gawker.com/5950981/unmasking-reddits -violentacrez-the-biggest-troll-on-the-web.

15. Ibid.

16. Phillips, "What an Academic."

17. @Sassycrass, "#YourSlipIsShowing: Documenting a Hoax," Storify, June 13, 2014storify.com/sassycrass/yourslipisshowing-documenting-a-hoax.

18. Ryan Broderick, "Activists Are Outing Hundreds of Twitter Users Believed to Be 4chan Trolls Posing as Feminists," *BuzzFeed*, June 17, 2014, buzzfeed.com /ryanhatesthis/your-slip-is-showing-4chan-trolls-operation-lollipop#3egd4rw.

19. David Futrelle, "WTF Is a MGTOW? A Glossary," We Hunted the Mammoth, n.d., wehuntedthemammoth.com/wtf-is-a-mgtow-a-glossary, accessed Oct. 1, 2014.

20. Kate Harding, "No More Mr. Nice Guy," *Salon*, Aug. 7, 2009salon.com/2009 /08/07/nice_guys.

21. Kate Harding, "It's Not All Men. But It's Men," *Dame Magazine*, May 27, 2014, damemagazine.com/2014/05/27/its-not-all-men-its-men.

22. David Futrelle, "Mammoth FAQ," We Hunted the Mammoth, n.d., wehunted themammoth.com/faq, accessed Oct. 1, 2014.

23. Arthur Goldwag, "Leader's Suicide Brings Attention to Men's Rights Movement," *Intelligence Report*, Southern Poverty Law Center (Spring 2012), splcenter.org /get-informed/intelligence-report/browse-all-issues/2012/spring/a-war-on-women.

24. Ibid.

25. Paul Elam, "To the University of Toronto Student's Union," *A Voice for Men*, Dec. 5, 2012, avoiceformen.com/feminism/to-the-university-of-toronto-students-union.

26. David Futrelle, "A Voice for Men's Attempts to Find and Publicize the Personal Information of a Toronto Activist Could Threaten That Young Woman's Safety," We Hunted the Mammoth, Dec. 8, 2012, wehuntedthemammoth.com/2012/12/08 /a-voice-for-mens-attempts-to-find-and-publicize-the-personal-information-of-a-toronto -activist-could-threaten-that-young-womans-safety.

27. Ibid.

28. "'Men's Rights' Group Behind Sexual Assault Posters," *CBC News*, July 11, 2013, cbc.ca/news/canada/edmonton/men-s-rights-group-behind-sexual-assault -posters-1.1353362.

29. Mary E. Williams, "Men's Rights Dopes Strike Again," *Salon*, July 12, 2013, salon.com/2013/07/12/mens_rights_dopes_strike_again.

30. David Futrelle, "The 'Don't Be That Girl' Poster Controversy in Edmonton, and A Voice for Men's History of Rape Apologia," We Hunted the Mammoth, July 12, 2013, wehuntedthemammoth.com/2013/07/12/the-dont-be-that-girl-poster -controversy-in-edmonton-and-a-voice-for-mens-history-of-rape-apologia.

31. David Edwards, "Misogynist Blogger: Make Rape on Private Property Legal so Women Can Have 'Learning Experiences,'" *Raw Story*, Feb. 18, 2015, rawstory.com /rs/2015/02/misogynist-blogger-make-rape-on-private-property-legal-so-women-can -have-learning-experiences.

32. Anita Sarkeesian, "Tropes vs. Women in Video Games," Kickstarter, June 2012, kickstarter.com/projects/566429325/tropes-vs-women-in-video-games?ref=card.

33. Anita Sarkeesian, "Update 4: OMG! 1000 Backers! (and About That Harassment Stuff) Tropes vs. Women in Video Games," Kickstarter, June 7, 2012, kickstarter .com/projects/566429325/tropes-vs-women-in-video-games/posts/242547.

34. Anita Sarkeesian, "Harassment, Misogyny and Silencing on YouTube," Feminist Frequency, June 7, 2012, feministfrequency.com/2012/06/harassment-misogyny -and-silencing-on-youtube.

35. Sarkeesian, "Update 4: OMG! 1000 Backers!"

36. Anita Sarkeesian (@femfreq), "I usually don't share the really scary stuff. But it's important for folks to know how bad it gets [TRIGGER WARNING]," Twitter, Aug. 27, 2014, 2:52 p.m.

37. Stephen Totilo, "Bomb Threat Targeted Anita Sarkeesian, Gaming Awards Last March," *Kotaku*, Sept. 17, 2014, kotaku.com/bomb-threat-targeted -anita-sarkeesian-gaming-awards-la-1636032301.

38. Jordan Owen and Davis Aurini, "The Owen/Aurini Team Is Creating the Sarkeesian Effect," Patreon, 2014, patreon.com/thesarkeesianeffect.

39. Andrew Todd, "Video Games, Misogyny, and Terrorism: A Guide to Assholes," *Badass Digest*, Aug. 26, 2014, badassdigest.com/2014/08/26/video-games -misogyny-and-terrorism-a-guide-to-assholes.

40. Brianna Wu, "I'm Brianna Wu, and I'm Risking My Life Standing Up to Gamergate," *Huffington Post*, Feb. 11, 2015, huffingtonpost.com/bustle/im-brianna-wu-and -im-risking-my-life-standing-up-to-gamergate_b_6661530.html.

41. Ibid.

42. Arthur Chu, "Your Princess Is in Another Castle: Misogyny, Entitlement, and Nerds," *Daily Beast*, May 27, 2014, thedailybeast.com/articles/2014/05/27/your -princess-is-in-another-castle-misogyny-entitlement-and-nerds.html.

43. Todd, "Video Games, Misogyny, and Terrorism."

44. Kurt Vonnegut, Preface to *Wampeters, Foma & Granfalloons* (New York: Dial, 2006), xiii.

45. Jess Zimmerman, "Even People Who Coach Your Team Have to Live in Society," *XoJane*, Nov. 14, 2011, xojane.com/issues/joe-paterno-penn-state-riots.

CHAPTER 11: REASONS FOR HOPE

1. Matt Rocheleau, "Colleges Step up Vigilance of Risks for Students Early in the School Year," *Boston Globe*, Sept. 27, 2014.

2. Ken Gross and Andrea Fine, "After Their Daughter Is Murdered at College, Her Grieving Parents Mount a Crusade for Campus Safety," *People*, Feb. 19, 1990.

3. Lynn B. Mahaffie, "Implementation of Changes to the Clery Act Made by the Violence Against Women Reauthorization Act of 2013 (VAWA)," DCL ID: GEN-14-13, US Department of Education, Office of Postsecondary Education, July 14, 2014.

4. Russlynn Ali, "Dear Colleague Letter from Assistant Secretary for Civil Rights," US Department of Education, Office of Civil Rights, April 4, 2011, www2.ed.gov /about/offices/list/ocr/letters/colleague-201104_pg2.html.

5. Ibid.

6. "ED ACT NOW," Know Your IX, knowyourix.org/i-want-to/take-national-action, accessed October 31, 2014.

7. Ibid.

8. Jaclyn Friedman and Jessica Valenti, editors, *Yes Means Yes!: Visions of Female Sexual Power & a World Without Rape* (New York: Seal, 2008), 7.

9. Jill Filipovic, "Offensive Feminism," in Friedman and Valenti, eds., *Yes Means Yes!*, 20–21.

10. Jake New, "Colleges Across Country Adopting Affirmative Consent Sexual Assault Policies," *Inside Higher Ed*, Oct. 17, 2014.

11. Spencer Kornhaber, "The Case for the Cosby Joke," *Atlantic*, Jan. 12, 2015.

12. Ariel Kaminer, "Accusers and the Accused, Crossing Paths at Columbia University," *New York Times*, Dec. 21, 2014.

Selected Bibliography and Recommended Reading

Adichie, Chimamanda Ngozi. *We Should All Be Feminists*. New York: Vintage, 2014.

Anderson, Irina, and Kathy Doherty. *Accounting for Rape: Psychology, Feminism and Discourse Analysis in the Study of Sexual Violence*. Oxford: Routledge, 2007.

Bancroft, Lundy. *Why Does He Do That?: Inside the Minds of Angry and Controlling Men*. New York: Berkley, 2003.

Benedict, Helen. *Virgin or Vamp: How the Press Covers Sex Crimes*. Oxford: Oxford University Press, 1993.

———. *The Lonely Soldier: The Private War of Women Serving in Iraq*. Boston: Beacon, 2010.

Benedict, Jeff, and Don Yaeger. *Pros and Cons: The Criminals Who Play in the NFL*. Cambridge: Harvard University Press, 2013.

Blank, Hanne. *Virgin: The Untouched History*. New York: Bloomsbury USA, 2007.

Brownmiller, Susan. *Against Our Will: Men, Women, and Rape*. New York: Ballantine, 1993.

Buchwald, Emilie, Pamela Fletcher, and Martha Roth. *Transforming a Rape Culture*. Revised edition. Minneapolis: Milkweed Editions, 2005.

Burns, Sarah. *The Central Park Five: A Chronicle of a City Wilding*. New York: Knopf, 2011.

Cuklanz, Lisa M. *Rape on Prime Time: Television, Masculinity and Sexual Violence*. Philadelphia, University of Pennsylvania Press, 1999.

Ehrlich, Susan. *Representing Rape: Language and Sexual Consent*. Oxford: Routledge, 2003.

Factora-Borchers, Lisa, and Aishah Shahidah Simmons. *Dear Sister: Letters from Survivors of Sexual Violence*. Oakland: AK, 2014.

Freedman, Estelle B. *Redefining Rape: Sexual Violence in the Era of Suffrage and Segregation*. Cambridge, MA: Harvard University Press, 2013.

Friedman, Jaclyn. *What You Really, Really Want: The Smart Girl's Shame-Free Guide to Sex and Safety*. New York: Seal, 2011.

Friedman, Jaclyn, and Jessica Valenti. *Yes Means Yes!: Visions of Female Power and a World Without Rape*. New York: Seal, 2008.

Gay, Roxane. *Bad Feminist: Essays*. New York: Harper Perennial, 2014.

Girschik, Lori B. *Woman-to-Woman Sexual Violence: Does She Call It Rape?* Boston: Northeastern University Press, 2002.

Gould, Jon B. *The Innocence Commission: Preventing Wrongful Convictions and Restoring the Criminal Justice System*. New York: New York University Press, 2007.

hooks, bell. *The Will to Change: Men, Masculinity, and Love*. New York: Atria, 2004.

Katz, Jackson. *The Macho Paradox: Why Some Men Hurt Women and How All Men Can Help*. Naperville, IL: Sourcebooks, 2006.

Kimmel, Michael. *Angry White Men: Masculinity at the End of an Era*. New York: Nation Books, 2013.

———. *Misframing Men: The Politics of Contemporary Masculinities*. New Brunswick, NJ: Rutgers University Press, 2010.

McGuire, Danielle L. *At the Dark End of the Street: Black Women, Rape, and Resistance—A New History of the Civil Rights Movement from Rosa Parks to the Rise of Black Power*. New York: Vintage, 2010.

Morrison, Toni. *Race-ing Justice, En-gendering Power: Essays on Anita Hill, Clarence Thomas and the Construction of Reality*. New York: Pantheon, 1992.

Mukhopadhyay, Samhita. *Outdated: Why Dating Is Ruining Your Love Life*. New York: Seal, 2011.

Mulla, Sameena. *The Violence of Care: Rape Victims, Forensic Nurses and Sexual Assault Intervention*. New York: New York University Press, 2014.

Nathan, Debbie, and Michael Snedeker. *Satan's Silence: Ritual Abuse and the Making of a Modern American Witch Hunt*. New York: Basic Books, 1995.

Raphael, Jody. *Rape Is Rape: How Denial, Distortion, and Victim Blaming Are Fueling a Hidden Acquaintance Rape Crisis*. Chicago: Lawrence Hill Books, 2013.

Russell-Brown, Katheryn. *The Color of Crime: Racial Hoaxes, White Fear, Black Protectionism, Police Harassment, and Other Macroaggressions*. 2nd edition. New York: New York University Press, 2008.

Sanday, Peggy Reeves. *A Woman Scorned: Acquaintance Rape on Trial*. Anchor, 2011.

———. *Fraternity Gang Rape: Sex, Brotherhood, and Privilege on Campus*. New York: New York University Press, 2007.

Scarce, Michael. *Male on Male Rape: The Hidden Toll of Stigma and Shame*. New York: Basic Books, 2001.

Serano, Julia. *Whipping Girl: A Transsexual Woman on Sexism and the Scapegoating of Femininity*. New York: Seal, 2009.

Smith, Andrea. *Conquest: Sexual Violence and American Indian Genocide*. Durham, NC: Duke University Press, 2015.

Solnit, Rebecca. *Men Explain Things to Me*. Chicago: Haymarket Books, 2014.

Tazlitz, Andrew E. *Rape and the Culture of the Courtroom*. New York: New York University Press, 1999.

Todd, Paula. *Extreme Mean: Trolls, Bullies, and Predators Online*. Toronto: Signal, 2014.

Valenti, Jessica. *The Purity Myth: How America's Obsession with Virginity Is Hurting Young Women.* New York: Seal, 2009.

Warshaw, Robin. *I Never Called It Rape: The Ms. Report on Recognizing, Fighting, and Surviving Date and Acquaintance Rape.* New York: Harper Perennial, 1994.

About the Author

Kate Harding is coauthor of *The Book of Jezebel* and *Lessons from the Fat-o-Sphere*. She founded the body-positive feminist blog Shapely Prose in 2007 and has written for Jezebel, Dame, *Bitch*, and numerous publications not ironically named after slang for "woman." A graduate of the University of Toronto and Vermont College of Fine Arts, she lives in Minneapolis with her husband and dogs.

Index